HEROIC POETS,
POETIC HEROES

A volume in the series

MYTH AND POETICS

edited by Gregory Nagy

A list of titles appears at the end of the book.

HEROIC POETS, POETIC HEROES

The Ethnography of Performance in an Arabic Oral Epic Tradition

Dwight Fletcher Reynolds

CORNELL UNIVERSITY PRESS

ITHACA AND LONDON

First published 1995 by Cornell University Press.

Printed in the United States of America

∞ The paper used in this book meets the minimum requirements of the American National Standard for Information Sciences—Permanence of Paper for Printed Library Materials, ANSI Z39.48-1984.

Library of Congress Cataloging-in-Publication Data

Reynolds, Dwight Fletcher, b. 1956

Heroic poets, poetic heroes : the ethnography of performance in an Arabic oral epic tradition / Dwight Fletcher Reynolds.

p. cm. — (Myth and poetics)

Includes bibliographical references (p.) and index.

ISBN 0-8014-3174-3 (cloth : acid-free paper)

1. Ethnology--Egypt—Banī Hilāl. 2. Sīrat Banī Hilāl. 3. Epic poetry, Arabic—Egypt—Banī Hilāl. 4. Folklore—Egypt—Banī Hilāl—Performance. 5. Oral tradition—Egypt—Banī Hilāl. 6. Rites and ceremonies—Egypt—Banī Hilāl. 7. Banī Hilāl (Egypt)—Social life and customs. I. Title. II. Series.

GN648.R49 1995

398′.0962—dc20 94-44173

To Kathryn Lee Gill Reynolds
and Edd Van Ness Stockton

Contents

Illustrations

FIGURES

PHOTOGRAPHS

Foreword

by Gregory Nagy

Heroic Poets, Poetic Heroes: The Ethnography of Performance in an Arabic Oral Epic Tradition, by Dwight Fletcher Reynolds, introduces an important new perspective into the Myth and Poetics series. An intensive study of heroic poetry (the *Sīrat Banī Hilāl* epic) in al-Bakātūsh, the Nile Delta "village of the poets," this book concretely illustrates the centrality of performance in the very process of composition or recomposition in oral traditions. Or, to put it in Saussure's terms, we see how the element of *parole* is key to understanding the *langue* of the poetic process. Reynolds's emphasis on the performative dimension of oral poetics gives the reader a chance to observe how an oral tradition works in its own social framework. The author explains the tradition itself, not just a given text sample of the tradition.

Another highlight of the book is its emphasis on a poetic mentality that assumes a dialogue linking poet and audience with the characters in the story being told. Such a mentality has been investigated in the case of Homeric poetry by classicists such as Joseph Russo and Bennett Simon, but here we see, for the very first time, a detailed demonstration on the basis of a living tradition, and the result is a quantum leap in our understanding of oral epic. Reynolds isolates those tenuous moments of performance when poets and audience members alike expect to find reflections, or interactions, between their reality and the reality of the epic heroes. The poetic tradition of *Sīrat Banī Hilāl* struggles to reconcile and even unite the worlds of poets and heroes, men of words and men of deeds. The heroes may be long dead, but they become ever-present each time the epic performance gets under way.

This book brings another new perspective to the Myth and Poetics series. Unlike most ethnographers of today, Reynolds has taken with him into his fieldwork the questions classicists and other literary critics ask about the very nature of epic as genre. His research in a living oral epic tradition corroborates, and has in fact been strongly influenced by, Richard Martin's work on speech acts in Homer, *The Language of Heroes* (1989), the very first book in this series.

Heroic Poets, Poetic Heroes addresses the performative realities of a living epic tradition. It accounts for the economic forces that shape the dynamics of performance, the individual poet's personal ambition to be popular, and the artistic choices necessitated by the immediacy of interaction with the audience. It demonstrates that epic can represent very different things to audiences of different social and educational backgrounds. Refuting the stereotypical image of a static "folk" poem, supposedly immutable from time immemorial, Reynolds's book reveals an epic tradition open to constant reshaping and reinterpretation, even within its conservative rural setting. In its performative context, epic is revealed as an ongoing interaction of poet, audience, and the heroes that it glorifies.

Preface

Sīrat Banī Hilāl, the epic history of the Banī Hilāl Bedouin tribe, is an astonishingly rich and varied oral tradition. Its roots lie in historic events that took place between the tenth and twelfth centuries C.E. in the Arabian peninsula and North Africa. The exploits and fatal weaknesses of the heroes of the Banī Hilāl tribe have been recounted in Arabic oral tradition for nearly a thousand years, and traces of the tradition are found throughout the Arab world from the Atlantic coast of North Africa to the shores of the Indian Ocean. In different regions and over different historical periods the epic has been performed as a complex tale cycle narrated entirely in prose, as a prose narrative embellished with lengthy poems, as a narrative recited in rhymed verse, and as narrative sung in rhymed verse to the accompaniment of various musical instruments. In some areas, several styles of performance coexist and may be patronized by different social groups. In many regions, verses from the *sīra* also circulate widely as proverbs and riddles. The main characters of the story have become folk archetypes of the courageous warrior, the cunning schemer, the irresistibly beautiful maiden, and the stranger-in-a-strange-land; as such they are often utilized by modern Arab writers and poets as deeply resonant social symbols.

This work treats the *Sīrat Banī Hilāl* tradition as it is found in a single village in northern Egypt, a village known throughout the Nile Delta as the "village of the poets," owing to the large community of hereditary epic-singers resident there. These fourteen households of professional poets all perform in the same basic style: to the accompaniment of the Egyptian two-stringed spike-fiddle, the *rabāb,* they sing the immense tale of the Banī Hilāl heroes in measured, rhymed verse with only occasional intervening prose passages to set the scene or gloss the main action. The most accomplished poets in the village may take well over one hundred hours to sing the entire story. As we shall see, however, there is no such thing as a complete rendition, for there exists a virtually unlimited body of subtales, historical background, and possible descriptive expansions, passed down from master poet to apprentice. These tools and techniques of the trade are many; thus some but never all are deployed in a given performance.

The focus of this book is the intense tripartite relationship that obtains between the poets, their listeners, and the heroes of the Banī Hilāl narrative. In examining the tradition from several different angles, I demonstrate that poets, heroes, and audience members perceive one another, interact with one another, and even rely on one another as social allies (or adversaries) in fascinating and highly significant ways, all of which contribute to the continual re-creation and propagation of the epic tradition. Furthermore, this process is not necessarily restricted to moments that we outsiders would recognize as moments of epic performance, but rather is one that takes place both inside and outside of the epic "text." Though it might at first seem surprising to consider the epic heroes as active participants in this exchange, they are deployed both by poets when singing and by audience members in the ensuing discussions, so that their characters as conceived and constructed by participants invariably leave their mark on the personal relationships and social tensions that are played out during epic performances. Major issues, including ethnic identification, Arabness, religious orientation, traditional codes of behavior, manhood, womanhood, and the hierarchization of social power, are woven into the texture of any modern performance of *Sīrat Banī Hilāl*. The tradition of performing the epic poem in this region is to a great extent kept alive by its role as catalyst for such significant social concerns. While outside researchers approach the epic seeking tradition and cultural continuity, the actual participants in the epic tradition are often present for entirely different reasons.

This book thus offers an ethnographic portrait of a tradition that is definable by its central text, the oral folk epic of the Banī Hilāl, but that is by no means restricted to the boundaries of that text. The Introduction provides a brief historical and geographical survey of the Banī Hilāl epic. Part 1, "The Ethnography of a Poetic Tradition," presents a general ethnographic portrait of the village, followed by a detailed examination of the epic poets' community and their relationship to the larger society in which they live. The implications of this relationship are traced through various traditional contexts for epic singing, the story of the epic itself, and the recurring structures of social interaction observed in epic performances. In Part 2, "Textual and Performance Strategies in the Sahra,"

I examine the epic as a context for social interaction and criticism through the analysis of performance texts from a single milieu, the *sahra,* or private evening gathering. The (living) epic poets and (fictional) epic heroes are seen as figures engaged in an ongoing dialogue with audience members concerning honor, social status, and manhood, represented not only through the narrative of the epic but also in the parallel "ways of speaking" deployed by both poets and heroes.

Three topics that have come to play central roles in contemporary oral epic research are only briefly touched upon in this volume: (1) the process of transmission and composition, that is, the issues of "oral-formulaic composition" and "composition in performance" such as delineated in the work of Milman Parry and Albert Lord; (2) the musical dimensions of the epic performance; and (3) detailed analysis of the poems as literary texts divorced from specific performance events. I have set these issues aside for the moment, to be taken up, I hope, in a companion volume in the near future. The present work, which struggles to bring into sharp focus the types of contextual and interactive processes that shape epic performances, and thus epic texts, has seemed to me a necessary foundation for any satisfactory understanding of renditions of the Banī Hilāl epic from northern Egypt. Whatever its faults, I hope it will be of use to many.

I wish to express my thanks first and foremost to the poets and other residents of the village of al-Bakātūsh who so graciously allowed me to live among them as guest and friend, and who so patiently endured my questions and unbounded curiosity. I sincerely hope they will see this and other works resulting from this project as fitting tributes to the poetic tradition of which they have been patrons and performers for so many years and to their own hospitality. I am grateful to all the poets of al-Bakātūsh and their families, but in particular to the late Shaykhs Ṭāhā Abū Zayd and ʿAbd al-Wahhāb Ghāzī, and also to Shaykhs Biyalī Abū Fahmī and ʿAbd al-Ḥamīd Tawfīq. Special thanks to my research assistants ʿAbd al-Qādir Ṣubḥ and Ḥamdī Jalama, and to my close companions who made certain that I always felt welcome in al-Bakātūsh, among them Ṭulba ʿAbd al-Laṭīf al-Disūqī, Māhir Muḥammad Sulaymān, Ibrāhīm al-Khaṭīb, Aḥmad ʿAbd al-Ḥamīd abū l-ʿAwn, Ḥamdī ʿAbd al-Sattār, and al-Shāfiʿī ʿAbd Allāh. My most deeply felt appreciation, however, goes to Saʿīd ʿAbd al-Qādir Ḥaydar and his family, who acted as my family away from home during my sojourns in al-Bakātūsh and without whose support this project could not have been completed.

Many thanks to Dell Hymes, Roger Allen, and Dan Ben-Amos, for their comments, instruction, support, and guidance.

I also thank those who have assisted me in this research at various points in its development with their suggestions, criticisms, and discussions: Abderrahman Ayoub [ʿAbd al-Raḥmān Ayyūb], ʿAbd al-Raḥmān al-Abnūdī, Pierre Cachia, Giovanni Canova, Micheline Galley, ʿAbd al-Ḥamīd Ḥawwās, Scott Marcus, H. T. Norris, Susan Slyomovics, Abbas El-Tonsi [ʿAbbās al-Tūnisī], and Muḥammad ʿUmrān; George Makdisi and Margaret Mills at the University of Pennsylvania; Joseph Harris, Gregory Nagy, and Jeffrey Wills at Harvard University; and Juliet Fleming, Robin Fleming, Joseph Koerner, Leslie Kurke, and Seth Schwartz at the Harvard Society of Fellows (1986–90). I am grateful also to the late Albert Lord, whose work inspired much of my own enthusiasm for studying oral epic traditions.

If I have received professional guidance from many sources, my prime source of inspiration and enthusiasm has been the members of R.R.A.L.L. (Radical Reassessments of Arabic Language and Literature): Kristen Brustad, Michael Cooperson, Jamal Elias, Nuha Khoury, Joseph Lowry, Nasser Rabbat, Devin Stewart, and Shawkat Toorawa. Their energy and excitement have always been contagious, and the level of creative thinking and intellectual inquiry I have encountered in the many meetings and conferences of this research group remains unmatched by those of any other organization I have known—many thanks.

Funding was provided by the Center for Arabic Studies Abroad I and II (1980–81, 1982–83) and a Fulbright-Hays research grant (1986–87). My appointment to the Harvard Society of Fellows (1986–90) provided the extended period of time necessary to inventory, catalog, and analyze many, many hours of field recordings, which greatly contributed to the quality of the final product. Portions of the section on *mawwāl* have appeared in the essay "The Interplay of Genres: Differentially Marked Discourse in a Northern Egyptian Tradition," in *The Ballad and Oral Literature,* edited by Joseph Harris (Cambridge: Harvard University Press, 1991), reprinted here with permission. The section "Construction of Commercial Images" in Chapter 2 is based on an article published in *Pacific Review of Ethnomusicology* (1989), used with permission of University of California Press. A portion of the Introduction appeared in an article in the journal *Oral Tradition* (1989).

Copies of the tapes cited in this study are on deposit at the Center for the Folk Arts (Markaz al-funūn al-shaʿbiyya), 18 al-Burṣa al-Qadīma Street, Tawfiqiyya, Cairo, Egypt, and in the Milman Parry Collections of Oral Literature, Widener Library C, Harvard University, Cambridge, Massachusetts 02138.

DWIGHT FLETCHER REYNOLDS

Santa Barbara, California

Notes on Transcription and Transliteration

I have used two transliteration systems to represent standard Arabic (SA) and colloquial Egyptian Arabic (EA):

1. Written sources in standard literary Arabic are cited according to the *International Journal of Middle East Studies (IJMES)* transliteration system with the additional underlining of bigraphic symbols that reflect a single phoneme (kh, rather than kh as in *IJMES*, for example, so that the latter is not left undifferentiated from the sequential occurrence of k and h). Standard Arabic forms of some colloquial lexical items have been adopted in the English passages of the text with minimal diacritic markings (thus, throughout the English text, Banī Hilāl, Shaykh, and Abū Zayd rather than Benī Hilāl, shaykh, Abū Zēd or Zeyd, etc.). In addition, a number of the most commonly recurring place-names such as al-Bakātūsh and Kafr al-Shaykh are left without diacritics in the English text. Transliterations have not been used for proper names and terms that have accepted English forms such as Mecca, Islam, and Sufi.

2. In transliterating colloquial Egyptian dialect, I have adopted the basics of the *IJMES* transcription system with the addition of several vowels to accommodate Egyptian colloquial Arabic forms:

a	ā	[ay]	à = alif maqṣūra in SA transliteration
i	ī		
e	ē	[ey]	
o	ō		
u	ū	[aw]	

In addition, certain modifications have been adopted for transliterating Egyptian colloquial Arabic consonants in order to preserve key features that mark code-shifting between colloquial Arabic, "elevated" colloquial, and standard Arabic, a process common in *Sīrat Banī Hilāl* performances. This modified system represents an attempt to provide a broadly phonemic transcription of colloquial texts in a manner that reflects both the occurrence of significant phonological shifts and the commonly understood cognate standard Arabic forms.

ا	ʾ	ط	ṭ
ب	b	ظ	ẓ [TH][1]
ت	t	ع	ʿ
ث	s [th][1]	غ	gh
ج	j/g[4]	ف	f
ح	ḥ	ق	Q/qʾ/q[4]
خ	kh	ك	k
د	d	ل	l
ذ	z [dh][1]	م	m
ر	r	ن	n
ز	z	ه	h
س	s	و	w
ش	sh	ي	y
ص	ṣ	ة	a/at[2]
ض	ḍ	ال-	al-[3]

— -I "helping vowel" (epenthetic)

For Arab scholars who have published in languages other than Arabic, I have, for the most part, both cited their chosen spelling in European languages and provided a transliteration of the original Arabic form.

1. The bracketed standard Arabic allophones are transcribed as such where they occur in the texts.

2. *-at* form in construct state.

3. The definite article has been transcribed in the body of the text (*al-*) as per *IJMES*, without assimilation, except in direct quotations from actual performances: thus al-shams rather than ish-shams in the body of the text, but *al-, il-, el-, and ul-* with assimilation where it occurs, in quotations from performances.

4. The local dialect of al-Bakātūsh, and *Sīrat Banī Hilāl* texts in general in this region, makes use of *j/g* alternation for the phoneme [ج] as well as three forms of the phoneme [ق]: /*q*/, /glottal stop/, and /*g*/, which have been rendered as follows:

Q = /*q*/, voiceless uvular stop, as in standard Arabic *al-Qāhira* 'Cairo'
qʾ = /ʾ/, glottal stop, as in the Cairene pronunciation of *ʾāl lī* 'he said to me'
q = /*g*/, voiced velar stop, as in Upper Egyptian dialect *gallī* 'he said to me'

Since the latter form is by far the most common in texts from this region, this system has the advantage of leaving most occurrences of the phoneme unmarked, while distinguishing only the less common, variant allophones. N.B. In these transcriptions, *q* and *g* represent the same spoken sound, though they reflect two distinct Standard Arabic phonemes.

In addition, numerous forms occur in *Sīrat Banī Hilāl* performances from the region of al-Bakātūsh which appear to reflect case endings similar to those of standard written Arabic; these have been superscripted: *ruḥt-I bilād*^{an} *tirkab il-afyāl* 'I have gone to countries where elephants are ridden'.

HEROIC POETS,
POETIC HEROES

The Tradition

> Then he remembers how he used to like to go out of the house at sunset when people were having their evening meal, and used to lean against the maize fence pondering deep in thought, until he was recalled to his surroundings by the voice of a poet who was sitting at some distance to his left, with his audience round him. Then the poet would begin to recite in a wonderfully sweet tone the doings of Abū Zayd, Khalīfa and Diyāb, and his hearers would remain silent except when ecstasy enlivened them or desire startled them. Then they would demand a repetition and argue and dispute. And so the poet would be silent until they ceased their clamour after a period which might be short or long. Then he would continue his sweet recitation in a monotone.
>
> Ṭāhā Ḥusayn, *al-Ayyām*

This poetic tradition which Egypt's preeminent literary scholar, Ṭāhā Ḥusayn, recalls at the outset of his autobiography is one familiar throughout most of the Arab world—the *sīra*, or epic history, of the Banī Hilāl tribe, which chronicles the tribe's massive migration out of their homeland in the Arabian peninsula, their passage through Egypt, their subsequent conquest of North Africa, and their final defeat one hundred years later. The migration, the conquest, and the defeat are historical events that occurred between the tenth and twelfth centuries C.E. From this skein of actual events, Arabic oral tradition has woven a rich and complex narrative centered on a cluster of heroic characters. Time and again Bedouin warriors and heroines are pitted against the kings and princes of towns and cities. The individual destinies of the main actors are constantly placed in a fragile balance with the fate of the tribe itself as they seek pasturage, safe passage, and a new homeland. With the conquest of North Africa, the Banī Hilāl nomads themselves become rulers of cities, a situation that leads to the internal fragmentation of the tribe, internecine wars, and the tribe's eventual demise.

Across the breadth of the Arab world, narratives about the Banī Hilāl tribe have been set down in written form from the oral tradition since the fourteenth century: from Morocco, on the shores of the Atlantic, to the sultanate of Oman, on the shores of the Indian Ocean, from the Mediterranean in the north, and as far south into Africa as Nigeria, Chad, and the Sudan (see fig. 1).

Sīrat Banī Hilāl is the single most widespread and best-documented narrative tradition of Arabic oral literature. Far more is known about the historical development, the geographical distribution, and the living oral tradition of *Sīrat Banī Hilāl* than the stories that to most Western readers exemplify the Arabic folk tale, the *Thousand and One Nights*. The latter owes its fame and survival not to its position in the Arab world, but to the enormous amount of attention it received in eighteenth-

---

Figure 1. Evidence from the oral tradition

Algeria: M. L. Guin (1884); L. Féraud (1868); V. Largeau (1879); A. Vaissière (1892); A. Bel (1902–03); R. Lartigue (1904); J. Desparmet (1939); Claude H. Breteau and Galley (1973).
Cairo: Edward Lane (1895); Bridget Connelly (1986).
Chad: H. Carbou (1913).
Jordan: Abderrahman Ayoub (1990).
Libya: Abderrahman Ayoub (1979); L. Féraud (1868); H. Stumme (1894); Martin Hartmann (1898).
Mali/Niger: H. T. Norris (1975).
Morocco: M. Ben Rahhal (1889); V. Loubignac (1924–25).
Nigeria: J. R. Patterson (1930).
Northeast Arabia/Kuwait: Bruce Ingham (1982).
Northern Egypt: S. Slyomovics (1987a); D. Reynolds (1989c; 1989d).
Oman: T. M. Johnstone (1980).
Palestine: C. Conder (1883); J. Rosenhouse (1984).
Saudi Arabia: A. Lerrick (1984).
Southern Egypt: Abderrahman al-Abnoudy (1978, 1988); Ṭāhā Ḥusayn (1926–27; Rpt. 1973); R. Critchfield (1978); Giovanni Canova (1977, 1980, 1983); Susan Slyomovics (1986; 1987b).
Sudan: Sayyid Hurreiz (1977); H. MacMichael (1912, 1922).
Syria: G. Canova (1990).
Tunisia: Ibn Khaldūn (14th c.—F. Rosenthal, 1958); A. Guiga (1968); Anita Baker (1978); Abderrahman Ayoub and Micheline Galley (1977); Cl. Breteau, M. Galley, and A. Roth (1978); P. Provotelle (1911).
Yemen: G. Canova (1985); R. J. Serjeant (1951).

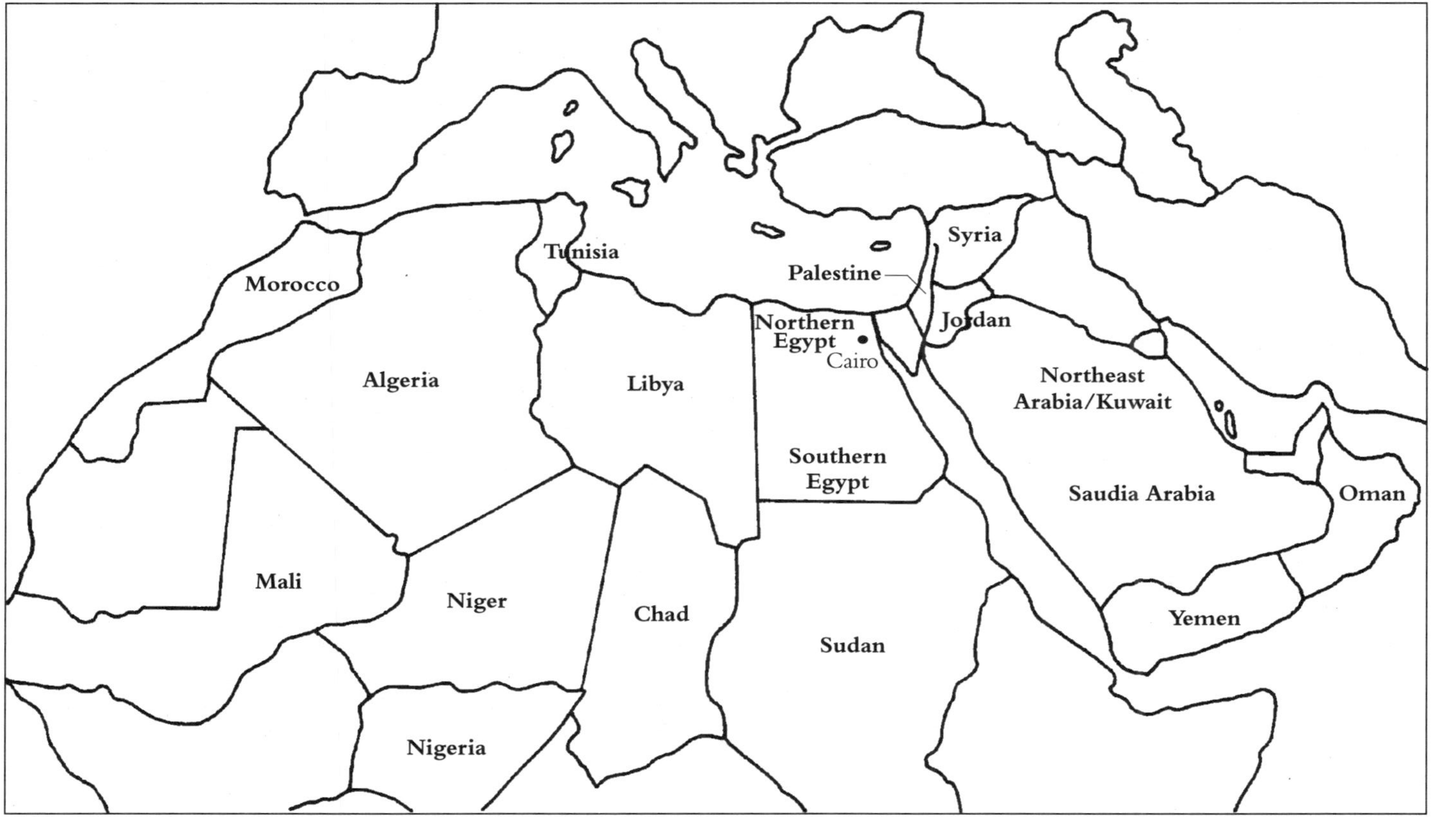
Morocco
Tunisia
Algeria
Libya
Palestine
Syria
Jordan
Northern Egypt
Cairo
Southern Egypt
Northeast Arabia/Kuwait
Saudia Arabia
Oman
Yemen
Mali
Niger
Chad
Sudan
Nigeria

and nineteenth-century Europe.[1] Though *Sīrat Banī Hilāl* is now seldom heard in the urban centers of the Arab world, in rural areas it continues to be performed in prose, in poetry, and in song. The most famous versions are those sung in Egypt by epic singers who perform their versified narrative for nights at a time while accompanying themselves on the *rabāb* 'spike-fiddle', *ṭār* 'large frame-drum', or *kamanja* 'Western violin'.

The folk sīra tradition is familiar to most scholars of Arabic literature, but it has, for the most part, escaped the notice of epic scholars, folklorists, and anthropologists in the West, due primarily to the dearth of translations into European languages, and, in particular, into English. Since the 1970s, however, *Sīrat Banī Hilāl* has sparked new academic interest and even a few translations.

The Question of Genre

Epic as a literary genre has acquired strong associations with high culture, civilization, and nationalism. These cultural and political associa-

1. The collection of tales known in the West as the *Thousand and One Nights* or the *Arabian Nights* bears only a tenuous relation to its Arabic original, which may in fact never have been in oral tradition. The title and famous frame-tale were translated into Arabic, probably as early as the ninth century C.E., from a Middle Persian work that has not come down to us. The multiply-framed stories, which have made the collection famous, are nowhere found in Arabic oral folk tradition and appear to be a device developed solely by redactors and anthologizers within the written tradition.

Antoine Galland, who completed the first "translation" of the Arabic *Alf layla wa-layla*, freehandedly expurgated, retold, and rearranged the tales of his Arabic sources. To these original tales his editor added tales from other sources, and Galland himself filled out nearly one-third of the collection with stories he heard at dinner parties in Paris from a visiting Aleppan Maronite. Later translators padded even this debased collection with ethnographic detail (Edward W. Lane) and Victorian erotica (Richard Burton), or completely falsified insertions (Mardrus). The hundreds of versions and editions of the *Nights* published in Europe remain a monument to the West's fantasies about the Middle East rather than examples of Arabic folk literature.

The extreme popularity of the work in Europe eventually motivated Arabic editions, which appeared in the nineteenth and twentieth centuries. Previous to these reintroduced editions, the popularity of the *Nights* in the Middle East had been limited. Each of the major European translators (Galland, Lane, Burton, Payne, and others) complained of the extreme difficulty of obtaining the few extant manuscripts of the *Nights*, but then triumphantly presented the work to Western readers as a recognized classic of Arabic literature (quite the opposite of its actual status in the Arab world).

For a general if somewhat dated introduction, see E. Littman, "Alf laylah wa-laylah," in *Encyclopedia of Islam*, 2d ed. (Hereafter the *Encyclopedia of Islam* is referred to as *EI*, with EI^1 or EI^2 indicating edition.) Duncan B. MacDonald, "A Bibliographical and Literary Study of the First Appearance of the Arabian Nights in Europe" (1932), provides a detailed account of the compilation of the early European editions. The most important recent academic work on the *Nights* has been Muhsin Mahdi's edition of a fourteenth-century manuscript, *Kitāb alf*

tions have to a great extent muddied the waters in defining the genre (or genres) of European epic poetry and in promoting or discouraging comparisons to similar but distinct genres from other cultures. Quite simply, epic is a literary genre with high status; scholars and researchers of different cultures have had good reason, and clear political agendas, for claiming the existence of an indigenous "national" epic. These high literary overtones, however, often hinder the exploration of actual similarities and divergences.[2]

Sīrat Banī Hilāl has been referred to by Western scholars as epic, saga, romance, tale cycle, legend, and geste.[3] A great deal of the confusion stems from the wide variation in modes of performance across the Arab world, but the gist of the problem arises from the fact that sīra is an indigenous Arabic genre with no exact parallel in European literatures. A sīra is literally a traveling, a journeying, or a path—the nominal form of the verb *sāra* 'to travel, to journey, to move (on)'. It is used to designate a history, a biography, or even a mode of behavior or conduct. The term was first applied within Arabic written literature to the biography of the Prophet Muḥammad, *Sīrat rasūl allāh*, specifically that by Ibn Isḥāq (d. 768 C.E.) in the recension of Ibn Hishām (d. 833 C.E.).[4] Though in the early centuries the term *sīra* had been used with several different meanings, the literary genre of sīra later grew to be more and more closely associated with the idea of biography.

The evolution of the folk genre of sīra (the oral folk epics) is cloudy at best, but it did not parallel the development of the literary genre of the same name. The earliest surviving extracts of the folk *siyar* (pl. of *sīra*) date from the late medieval period, though references to them are found as early as the twelfth century. They most probably have roots in a still earlier oral tradition. These lengthy narratives, told in alternating sequences of prose and poetry, appeared in manuscripts over many

laylah wa-laylah min uṣūlihi al-ʿarabiyyah al-ūlā (The book of the thousand nights and a night from its earliest Arabic sources) (1984), an English translation of which is available as *The Arabian Nights*, trans. Husain Haddawy (1990).

2. These issues are explored in Gilbert M. Cuthbertson, *Political Myth and Epic* (1975); see also Felix Oinas, ed., *Heroic Epic and Saga* (1978), and Arthur T. Hatto, ed., *Traditions of Heroic and Epic Poetry* (1980), among others.

3. See, for example, Susan Slyomovics, *The Merchant of Art: An Egyptian Hilali Oral Epic Poet in Performance* (1987); Cathryn Anita Baker, "The Hilali Saga in the Tunisian South," (1978); Edward Lane, *An Account of the Manners and Customs of the Modern Egyptians*, chaps. 21–23 (1895); J. R. Patterson, trans., *Stories of Abu Zeid the Hilali in Shuwa Arabic* (1930); Abderrahman al-Abnoudy, *La geste hilalienne* (1978).

4. G. Levi Della Vida, "Sīra," *EI*[1]. ʿAbd al-Malik, Ibn Hishām, *The Life of Muhammad: A Translation of Ishāq's "Sīrat Rasūl Allāh"* (1955). For an intriguing analysis of parallels between the life story of the Prophet Muḥammad in relation to the revelation of the Qurʾān, and the life story of an Egyptian epic-singer in relation to the acquisition of the ability to sing epic poetry, see Slyomovics, *Merchant*, 11–13.

centuries, until the nineteenth century. With the arrival of printing, they reappeared in a new form as cheaply printed chapbooks, which are found throughout the Arab world in prodigious numbers. The relationship between the oral and written traditions of the folk *siyar* is complex: some of the *siyar* developed entirely within the oral tradition and were only at a very late date committed to writing, but there is also good reason to suspect that a few of them were literary creations by later authors imitating the oral folk genre for consumption by a popular readership. The *siyar* for which we have manuscript and/or chapbook texts all share key stylistic features, and, at least in their written form, clearly make up a cohesive and identifiable genre: *Sīrat ʿAntar ibn Shaddād*[5] (the sīra of the pre-Islamic black poet-knight, ʿAntara son of Shaddād); *Sīrat al-Ẓāhir Baybars*[6] (the sīra of the thirteenth-century Egyptian ruler and folk hero, al-Ẓāhir Baybars); *Sīrat al-amīr Ḥamza al-Bahlawān*[7] (the sīra of Ḥamza, uncle of the Prophet Muḥammad); *Sīrat Dhāt al-Himma*[8] (the sīra of the heroine Dhāt al-Himma and her wars against the Byzantines); *Sīrat al-malik Sayf ibn Dhī Yazan*[9] (the sīra of the Himyarite king, Sayf ibn dhī Yazan, and his wars against the Abyssinians); *Sīrat al-Zīr Sālim*[10] (the *sīra* of the Bedouin warrior al-Zīr Sālim); and of course, *Sīrat Banī Hilāl*. All except for *Sīrat Banī Hilāl* have now disappeared

5. See Cedric Dover, "The Black Knight" (1954); Peter Heath, "A Critical Review of Modern Scholarship on Sīrat ʿAntar ibn Shaddād and the Popular Sīra" (1984); Martin Hartmann, "The Romance of Antar," *EI*[1]; B. Heller, "The Romance of Antar," *EI*[2]; also idem, *Die Bedeutung des arabischen ʾAntarromans für die vergleichende Litteraturkunde* (1931). For texts in translation see Terrick Hamilton, *Antar: A Bedoueen Romance* (1819); H. T. Norris, *The Adventures of Antar* (1980); L. Marcel Devic, *Les aventures d'Antar, fils de Cheddad* (1878); Gustave Rouger, *Le roman d'Antar* (1923); Diana Richmond, *ʾAntar and ʾAbla, a Bedouin Romance* (1978).

6. See Duncan B. MacDonald, "The Romance of Baibars," *EI*[1]; R. Paret, "Sīrat Baybars," *EI*[2]; Helmut Wangelin, *Das arabische Volksbuch vom König az-Zahir Baibars* (1936). For texts in translation, see the ongoing translations of Georges Bohas and Jean-Patrick Guillaume, *Roman de Baïbars*, vols. 1–5 (1985–).

7. See H. Lammens, "Ḥamza," *EI*[1]; G. M. Meredith-Owens, "Ḥamza b. ʿAbd al-Muṭṭalib," *EI*[2]; S. van Ronkel, *De roman van Amir Hamza* (1895); C. Virolleaud, "Le roman de l'émir Hamza, oncle de Mahomet" (1958–59); and most importantly, Frances Pritchett, *The Romance Tradition in Urdu: Adventures from the Dastan of Amir Hamza* (1991). *Sīrat Ḥamza* has wandered far and wide across the Middle East and South Asia; its origins probably lie in Iran, but versions are found in Arabic, Persian, Turkish, Urdu, Malay, and Sundanese. In most of these regions the story has acquired layers of local features and provides a fine example of assimilation into extant systems of folk aesthetics.

8. Also known as "Dhū ʾl-Himma," "Dalhamma," and "Delhamma." See M. Canard, "Dhū ʾl-Himma or Dhāt al-Himma," *EI*[2]; idem, "Delhemma, épopée arabe des guerres arabo-byzantines" (1935); idem, "Les principaux personnages du roman de chevalrie arabe *Dhāt al-Himma wa-l-Baṭṭāl*" (1961); Udo Steinbach, *Dhat al-Himma: Kuturgeschichtliche Untersuchungen zu einem arabischen Volksroman* (1972).

9. See R. Paret, "Saif b. Dhī Yazan," *EI*[1]; idem, *Sīrat Saif ibn Dhī-Jazan* (1924).

10. G. Canova, "Qiṣṣat al-zīr sālim wa-aṣl al-bahlawān" [in Arabic] (in press); Aḥmad Shams al-Dīn al-Ḥijājī, "al-Zīr sālim bayn al-sīra wa-l-maṣraḥ" (1968).

from oral tradition, though performances from the other siyar were observed as late as the nineteenth century.[11]

The language of the written versions of these prose/verse narratives of battles, adventures, and romance fluctuates between the spoken colloquial and a stilted "classicized" vernacular; nowhere do they reach a level recognized as true *fuṣḥā* (the classical, literary form of Arabic).[12] Oral renditions, sometimes over one hundred hours in length, range from performances narrated entirely in prose to renditions sung entirely in poetry; but they are always performed in colloquial dialect, often in a rhetorically embellished register of the colloquial which includes many words and phrases usually associated with the classical language. As "impure" Arabic, the written texts of the folk siyar were, and often still are, shunned by many Arab and Western scholars; the oral tradition, in local dialects, is usually considered even further beyond the pale.

The folk siyar have thus left a fragmentary but intriguing historical trail behind them through the centuries; they have been both derided as bad literature and occasionally attacked by religious authorities as frivolous works which lead their auditors away from more meritorious study and devotional activities. The following two opinions are typical—the first is couched as moral advice to scribes and copyists, while the second is from an exegetical commentary on a verse from the Qurʾān:

> It is best for [the copyist] not to copy anything from those books which lead [their readers] astray, such as the books of heretics or sectarians. Likewise he should not copy those books in which there is no benefit for God, such as the sīra of ʿAntar and other diverse subjects which waste time and in which there is nothing of religion, and also those books written by practitioners of wantonness, [including] what they have written about the types of sexual intercourse and descriptions of wines and other things which incite forbidden acts.[13]

In reference to Qurʾān 31:5: "When they hear idle talk [*laghw*], they turn away from it," which had usually been interpreted as an injunction against listening to singing, the scholar Ibn ʿAbd Rabbihi (d. 328 A.H./929 C.E.) wrote that the verse referred instead to fictional narratives

11. Lane, *Manners* (1895), 386–419. Also H. T. Norris, "Western Travellers and Arab Storytellers of the Nineteenth Century" (1991).

12. For a critical introduction to the wide-ranging debates on the nature of *fuṣḥā*, see Michael Zwettler, *The Oral Tradition of Classical Arabic Poetry*, chap. 3 (1978). The issues of literacy and diglossia are dealt with further in Chapter 1.

13. Taqī al-Dīn al-Subkī, *Muʿīd al-niʿam* (1908), 186; as cited in Muḥammad Zaghlūl Salām, *al-Adab fī l-ʿaṣr al-mamlūkī* (1971), 121. All translations included in the text are my own unless otherwise noted.

(siyar), not to music and song (which Ibn ʿAbd Rabbihi was at great pains to defend):

> This verse was revealed only about people who were purchasing story books of biographies [siyar] and tales of the ancients, and compared these with the Qurʾān and said that they were better than it.[14]

For both stylistic and religious reasons the folk siyar have thus been excluded from literary canon and research.[15]

Though some aspects of the development of the folk siyar remain uncertain, the texts that have come down to us clearly constitute a distinct genre: found in both oral and written form, the folk siyar are distinguished by their lengthy narratives (chapbook editions sometimes run upward of forty volumes), usually told in alternating sections of prose and poetry (the latter most often the speeches of the main characters), in colloquial or "pseudo-classical" Arabic, focusing on themes of heroism, battle, romance, chivalry, and often including encounters with supernatural beings such as angels, ghouls, and jinn.

Sīrat Banī Hilāl is the last of the folk siyar to survive in oral tradition. Though references and even descriptions of performances of other folk siyar indicate their survival into the early part of the twentieth century, only *Sīrat Banī Hilāl* is observable today as an oral folk epic tradition. *Sīrat Banī Hilāl* is thus the last survivor of an Arabic oral epic tradition which at one time included well over a dozen exemplars. Traces of all of these are found in the written record as brief mentions within other works, or in more complete form as manuscripts or chapbooks. The latter provide a detailed idea of the story line of various of these epics, but unfortunately they give us little of the richness of the oral performance tradition. Careful study of *Sīrat Banī Hilāl* performances, however, may allow us to rekindle some of the performative aspects of kindred examples from the Arabic epic tradition.

History

Several of the folk siyar have as their central character a hero plucked from the pages of history: ʿAntara ibn S̲h̲addād was a poet of the pre-

14. Ibn ʿAbd Rabbihi, *al-ʿIqd al-farīd* (1968), 6:9. Cited in Kristina Nelson, *The Art of Reciting the Quran* (1985), 40. In some sources the term *ak̲h̲bār al-samar* 'narratives from evening entertainments' appears in lieu of *siyar*.

15. For social attitudes toward the colloquial and literary languages, see Ṭāhā Ḥusayn, *Mustaqbal al-t̲h̲aqāfa fī miṣr* (1938), translated as *The Future of Culture in Egypt*, by Sidney Glazer, (1954).

Islamic era; Ḥamza was indeed the uncle of the Prophet Muḥammad; and al-Ẓāhir Baybars ruled Egypt from 1260 to 1277 C.E. Most of these historical figures, however, share little but their names with the corresponding folk heroes and their exploits. *Sīrat Banī Hilāl*, on the other hand, has a more intimate relationship with historical events. Though the main characters appear fictitious, the frame of the sīra is historically correct.[16] The existence of the Banī Hilāl tribal confederation (literally "sons of Hilāl," or even more literally, "sons of the crescent moon") in the Arabian peninsula is documented back to the pre-Islamic period. Throughout the first centuries after the appearance of Islam in seventh century C.E., the Banī Hilāl continued to reside primarily in the Najd region of central Arabia, not participating to any major degree in the rapid centrifugal expansion of many of the other Bedouin tribes during the early Islamic conquests. In the tenth century, however, the Banī Hilāl began to leave Arabia in large numbers. No doubt some waves of this migration were voluntary, but a substantial number of the Banī Hilāl were deported to Upper Egypt by the Fatimid Caliph of Cairo, al-ʿAzīz ibn al-Muʿizz, as punishment for participating in the Qarmatian rebellion and the sacking of the city of Medina.[17] To this day there are populations in Upper Egypt and the Sudan who claim descent from the Banī Hilāl, and some of the most significant modern field recordings of *Sīrat Banī Hilāl* have come from this region.[18]

In the middle of the eleventh century, al-Muʿizz ibn Bādīs, a vassal of the Fatimids then governing the province of Ifrīqiya (modern Tunisia and contiguous territories), shifted his allegiance from the Fatimid Caliphate in Cairo to the Abbasid Caliphate in Baghdad. The Fatimid Caliph, al-Mustanṣir, then supposedly handed over Ifrīqiya to the rapacious Banī Hilāl nomads both to punish his wayward vassal and simply to rid himself of their troublesome presence in Egypt. Whether at the instigation of the caliph or in less organized fashion, the Banī Hilāl traversed the Libyan desert and invaded Tunisia. In 1051–52 they captured the city of Gabès; on November 1, 1057, they sacked Qayrawān and thus completed their conquest. There they ruled for almost exactly one hundred years; during this period, however, the victorious confeder-

16. J. Schleifer notes that the character Dhiyāb was a historical, though minor, figure. See "The Saga of the Banū Hilāl," *EI*², 387.

17. See H. R. Idris, "Hilāl," *EI*²; ʿAbd al-Ḥamīd Yūnus, *al-Hilāliyya fī l-taʾrīkh wa-l-adab al-shaʿabī* (1968); J. Berque, "De nouveau sur les Benī Hilāl?" (1972).

18. See, for example, the various tribes cited as descendants of the Banī Hilāl in H. A. MacMichael, *A History of the Arabs in the Sudan* (1922): *Fūr*, 1:91ff.; *Bani Hilāl* and *Bani Sulaym*, 1:145–51; *Rufāʿa*, 1:239–44; *Bakkāra*, 1:271–76. For the role of the Banī Hilāl legends in regional history, see idem, *The Tribes of Northern and Central Kordofān* (1912), chap. 2; Appendix 3 in the same volume includes summaries of six tales told of Abū Zayd the Hilālī.

ation of tribal groups apparently splintered and fragmented. In their divided state, the eastward-moving Moroccan dynasty, the Almohads (*al-muwaḥḥidūn*), found the Banī Hilāl easy prey. The Banī Hilāl were defeated in two large battles in 1153 and 1160 C.E. Thereafter, small groups from the Banī Hilāl confederation are mentioned sporadically in historical accounts from Morocco and Andalusian Spain for about a century, where they appear as mercenary soldiers; they then disappear entirely. In several regions of North Africa, groups trace their ancestry to this final dispersion of the once mighty Banī Hilāl nomadic tribes.[19]

The Growth of the Poetic Tradition

Our first evidence of *Sīrat Banī Hilāl* as a developing poetic tradition appears two hundred years after the final defeat and dissolution of the Banī Hilāl tribe. The famous fourteenth-century Arab historiographer Ibn Khaldūn, toward the end of his three-volume *Muqaddima* (Introduction), embarks on a spirited defense of vernacular poetry.[20] His viewpoint is unique for his era, for he argues that oral vernacular poetry, which is not composed in *fuṣḥā* (the classical/literary form of Arabic), is not only beautiful but must also be considered true poetry in that it possesses its own rules and constraints (i.e., meter and rhyme). These, he points out, are different from those governing classical poetry, yet since these rules are discernible, oral vernacular poetry must be accepted as true poetry and not derided as doggerel. The poems he cites as examples, as proof of the artistic merit of colloquial verse, are short poems recounting episodes from *Sīrat Banī Hilāl* which he collected from Bedouins living in the deserts of Ifrīqiya. Several of these fragments are parallels of texts recorded in the field in twentieth-century Tunisia and Egypt, six hundred years later.

Little is known of the development of the sīra between the time of the writings of Ibn Khaldūn and the late eighteenth century. At that point, however, the historical record comes alive. Over a period of sixty years, from 1785 to 1845, a series of manuscripts were penned in colloquial Arabic (that they are written in colloquial Arabic marks them as a rare find). The highly colloquial tone and irregular orthography of these texts suggest that they may even have been taken down from oral

19. This demographic dispersion may account for many of the sub-Saharan versions of *Sīrat Banī Hilāl*, such as those found in Nigeria and published by J. R. Patterson (see below).
20. Ibn Khaldūn, *The Muqaddimah* (1967), 3:412–40.

performances, virtual transcriptions of what was heard. Several of the manuscripts, now housed in the Berlin Staatsbibliothek, contain colophons that appear to indicate the names of both scribe and poet. The collection totals more than eight thousand pages of poetry and prose from *Sīrat Banī Hilāl*, and clearly indicates a fertile and vibrant oral tradition.[21] Smaller collections are found in several other European librairies.[22]

Toward the end of this same period, in 1836, the British Arabist Edward W. Lane first published his ethnographic description of Egypt, titled *The Manners and Customs of the Modern Egyptians*, three chapters of which are devoted to the "Public Recitations of Romances."[23] The first, concerning *Sīrat Banī Hilāl*, includes a six-page summary of the opening episodes of the sīra, the birth of the hero Abū Zayd. Lane attests to the great popularity of the folk siyar among Cairenes, and estimates that fifty professional poets in Cairo were engaged exclusively in the performance of *Sīrat Banī Hilāl*, thirty more performed *Sīrat al-Ẓāhir Baybars*, and six performed *Sīrat ʿAntar ibn Shaddād*. He also noted that *Sīrat Dhāt al-Himma* and *Sīrat Sayf ibn dhī Yazan* had apparently been performed up until the period just prior to his own sojourn in Egypt. The performance styles for these siyar in Lane's time showed considerable divergence: only *Sīrat Banī Hilāl* was a musical tradition, sung to the accompaniment of the rabāb 'spike-fiddle', and, although performers of both *Sīrat Banī Hilāl* and *Sīrat al-Ẓāhir Baybars* performed without written texts, reciters of *Sīrat ʿAntar ibn Shaddād* read aloud from books.

Throughout the nineteenth and twentieth centuries, accounts of the *Sīrat Banī Hilāl* tradition have been written by travelers, historians, ethnographers, and even journalists. Most are but brief mentions of performances; a few, however, contain valuable details on performance styles, and some include brief extracts from oral or written texts.[24]

21. The most complete description of these mss. is A. Ayoub's update and correction of the Ahlwardt catalogue, "A propos des manuscrits de la geste des Banū Hilāl conservés à Berlin" (1978).

22. See M. Galley, "Manuscrits et documents relatifs à la geste hilalienne dans les bibliothèques anglaises" (1981), and Svetozár Pantuček, *Das Epos über den Westzug der Banü Hilāl* (1970), 10–12.

23. Lane, *Manners*, chaps. 21–23 (1895).

24. An excellent summary of many of these references is found in C. Breteau, M. Galley, and A. Roth, "Témoinages de la 'longue marche' hilalienne" (1978). This article restricts itself, however, to North Africa and does not give sources from the Arabian peninsula or the Levant. An evocative description of *Sīrat Banī Hilāl* performance in Upper Egypt can be found in Richard Critchfield, *Shahhat, an Egyptian* (1978), 48–57; see, however, the extensive criticisms of this work by Timothy Mitchell, "The Invention and Reinvention of the Egyptian Peasant" (1990).

Modes of Performance

The composite portrait of *Sīrat Banī Hilāl* which grows out of these many scattered accounts is a surprising one, for while key elements of the story line remain constant across geographic and historical separation, the modes of performance and the choice of poetic forms are quite diverse. Some performances are in prose, others are in various types of poetry, still others approach cante-fable with alternating sequences of poetry and prose. Some performances are entirely sung, some entirely spoken, and some move quickly to and from spoken prose, rhymed prose (*sajʿ*), and sung poetry.

Sīrat Banī Hilāl can perhaps be most clearly conceptualized as an enormous narrative, truly epic in length, possessing a set of central plot elements and key characters known by performers who render it in widely diverse genres of oral literature in different geographical regions. In Egypt, for example, there are nonprofessional storytellers who perform the sīra in prose as a cycle of tales, occasionally embellished with short bits of poetry. There are also a handful of public reciters who read aloud from the printed chapbook editions; these, however, are almost completely overshadowed by the professional epic-singers, for whom Egypt is famous, who versify the narrative in sung, improvised poetry in a manner similar to the epic traditions of Yugoslavia studied by Milman Parry and Albert B. Lord.[25] This sung, versified performance style is currently unique to Egypt, though it may have been more widespread in the past.

Within the epic-singing tradition of Egypt the musical styles display an intriguing amount of variety, mirroring in some ways the diversity of verbal forms.[26] A large number of melodies are pressed into service as vehicles for epic singing, occasionally even including modern songs from the popular urban milieu. Some epic poets perform as soloists while others are accompanied by ensembles of up to eight or ten musicians on rabābs and/or violins, reed flutes, and a variety of percussion instruments. Some poets pace their singing with extensive choral refrains sung by other musicians, and some use no refrains at all. *Sīrat Banī Hilāl* is, in short, an oral tradition that thrives on variation in style while maintaining a clear unifying bond in the story itself. And all of these many

25. See Adam Parry, ed., *The Making of Homeric Verse: The Collected Papers of Milman Parry* (1971), and Albert B. Lord, *The Singer of Tales* (1960).

26. ʿAbd al-Ḥamīd Ḥawwās, "Madāris riwāyat al-sīra al-hilāliyya fī Miṣr," and Muḥammad ʿUmrān, "al-Khaṣāʾi al-mūsīqiyya li-riwāyat al-sīra al-hilāliyya fī Miṣr," in Ayoub, *Sīrat Banī Hilāl* (1990), have identified over a dozen differentiable musical styles used in Egypt in the performance of *Sīrat Banī Hilāl*.

"sounds" of the sīra have their own appreciative audiences or they simply would not continue to exist.

However fascinating this panoply of musical styles and poetic forms, in this volume I deal exclusively with the sung, versified renditions found in the Nile Delta region of Egypt, renditions which are performed on the rabāb by hereditary, professional epic-singers. These singers perform as soloists or with one other poet; their renditions are comparable in form, content, process of composition, and performance style to that body of works from around the world which scholars have come to refer to as oral epics or folk epics.

The Story

Within the essentially historical framework of the migrations and conquests of the Banī Hilāl tribe, the sīra has evolved into a series of intricate tales built on tensions among a constellation of central characters. In this it may be differentiated from the other Arabic folk siyar, which all dealt primarily with a single heroic character. *Sīrat Banī Hilāl* may be compared more easily with, say, the King Arthur cycles or the *Iliad*, while the other, now defunct, siyar more closely resemble, in this aspect, *Beowulf*, the *Chanson de Roland*, or *El Cid*. The basic cast of *Sīrat Banī Hilāl* consists of several key male characters playing opposite a single female lead:

Abū Zayd, in Egypt at least, is usually portrayed as the central hero of the sīra.[27] He is the primary hero of the Banī Hilāl tribe; he is not, however, their greatest warrior. Crafty and cunning, "father of ruses" (*abū ḥiyal*), he often prefers, through stratagems and trickery, to avoid battle. This aspect of his character leads to varying interpretations from poet to poet and region to region, for his deceptions frequently skirt the border between honorable and dishonorable conduct. Furthermore, Abū Zayd is black, owing to the extraordinary circumstances of his birth, and is often mistaken by outsiders for a mere slave, which allows him at many points to travel disguised as an epic poet into enemy

27. With increasing numbers of texts now available to researchers, it is growing clearer that one of the main regional differences among local Banī Hilāl traditions is the comparative weight or focus given to the different characters. Libyan texts are reported to focus on the character of Diyāb, son of Ghānim (A. Ayoub, personal communication), North African texts highlight al-Jāzya and/or Diyāb, while Egyptian and Jordanian performances most often place Abū Zayd center stage. Curiously, the Saudi Arabian texts presented by Lerrick, which originate from the region where the *early* part of the epic is to have taken place, focus almost entirely on the *latter* part of the story, that is, on those sections that take place in Egypt and North Africa.

territory. In Egypt it is not uncommon to see an Egyptian audience sitting and listening to an epic poet while he sings about Abū Zayd *disguised* as an epic poet singing to an Egyptian audience sitting round him.

Diyāb (also Dhiyāb), leader of the Zughba (or Zaghāba) clan, is the most powerful warrior of the Banī Hilāl confederation, and it is by his hand that the tribe's ultimate foe, al-Zanātī Khalīfa, is fated to die. However, he is hot-blooded, easily slighted, and very touchy on points of honor—characteristics that often set him in conflict with Abū Zayd. Time and again, after some perceived slight from other members of the tribal council, Diyāb leads his clan out of the confederation, only to return in the final desperate hour of battle to save the Banī Hilāl from total destruction. Though he is rash and often a source of internecine conflict, the tribe must endure his unpredictable behavior, for only he can slay al-Zanātī Khalīfa.

Sultan Ḥasan, the dignified arbitrator, is the mediator of tribal tensions among the Banī Hilāl and the moderating force which often holds the clans together despite the rivalries and conflicts of their leaders. More devout than the other heroes, he is their statesman and chief representative of the tribe in dealings with outsiders.

Al-Zanātī Khalīfa was historically the leader of the Berbers of North Africa, and in North African versions of the sīra he remains so. In Egypt, however, Berbers are virtually unknown, and he is portrayed simply as an Arab chieftain along with all the other central characters. Everywhere, however, he is the principal enemy whom the Banī Hilāl must defeat in order to rule Ifrīqiya. In Egypt, an episode is often sung early in the story of the sīra in which al-Zanātī Khalīfa murders seventy descendants of the Prophet Muḥammad in a mosque while they are at prayer, clearly marking him as a villain beyond redemption. In other regions, poets at times transpose him into a nearly tragic figure struggling against his predestined demise at the hand of Diyāb.

Against these four versions of manhood—brains, brawn, moderation, and evil—stands one idealized vision of womanhood, al-Jāzya, who is, quite simply, the most beautiful and wisest woman in the world. She sits with the shaykhs in the tribal council and shares in their decisions. She at times rides into battle, and several times carries the fate of the entire tribe in her hands when she is married off to various opponents (inevitably smitten with her beauty) in order to gain pasturage and safe passage for the tribe in difficult terrain. She is then left to her own devices to find some means of escape or an honorable deception by which to break off her marriage so that she may rejoin the tribe on their westward journey.

Sīrat Banī Hilāl is often divided into three parts. The first recounts the history of the tribe, the birth of the main heroes, their adventures as youths, and their marriages. Then a severe drought strikes their homeland in the Najd, and the tribal council decides new pasturage must be sought if the tribe is to survive. A scouting party is formed consisting of Abū Zayd and his three nephews.[28]

The second section of *Sīrat Banī Hilāl*, "The Reconnaissance" (al-Riyāda), tells the adventures of these four young heroes as they travel, eventually to Tunisia, seeking a new homeland for their tribe. Disaster strikes three times: the first nephew, Yūnus, is held captive by the princess ʿAzīza after she falls madly in love with him. With Yūnus her prisoner, she attempts to seduce him (a favorite episode in more than one quarter), while he, as did his predecessor, the biblical and Qurʾānic figure of Joseph (Arabic: Yūsuf), stoically resists her charms. The second nephew is killed in battle; the third dies from a snake bite.[29] Abū Zayd returns to the tribe alone, stirring up great anger and suspicion among Diyāb and his men. The situation, however, forces them to cooperate. The Banī Hilāl depart westward toward "Tunīs the Verdant" in search of grazing lands, to rescue Yūnus, and to avenge the murder of the seventy descendants of the prophet killed by al-Zanātī Khalīfa.

The third section of the sīra is "The Westward Journey" (al-Taghrība), an elaborate series of battle cycles and romances which takes the tribe on a not-very-direct route through Iraq, Syria, Cyprus, Jerusalem, Gaza, Egypt, Ethiopia, and Libya before they arrive in Tunisia. There the final battles are fought against the forces of al-Zanātī Khalīfa, and the unavoidable destiny of the tribe is played out. Al-Zanātī Khalīfa, though forewarned by his daughter, Suʿada, who has seen a vision of his death in a dream, rides into battle and is killed by Diyāb. The death of al-Zanātī marks the end of many versions of *Sīrat Banī Hilāl*. At the close of the final battle, most of the great heroes lie dead and the tribe has completed its conquest and realized its search for a homeland.

A fourth section, though, is found in some regions: "The Tôme of

28. The Qarmatian rebellion (*al-qarāmiṭa*), a major factor in the historical migration of the Banī Hilāl tribe, is never mentioned in the epic tradition. In the versions collected by Susan Slyomovics in southern Egypt from the poet ʿAwaḍallāh, the main motivation for the scouting party and later migration of the tribe is evil behavior by the rulers of Ifrīqiya. The drought is apparently not foregrounded, though it is mentioned. See Slyomovics, *Merchant*, 52–53.

29. An alternate and common variant in Egypt is that the second and third nephews, Yaḥyā and Marʿī, are thrown in al-Zanātī Khalīfa's prison, whence they are rescued years later during the conquest of Tūnis. See Abnoudy, *Geste*, 25–26, for the deaths of the nephews as cited earlier, and see below for an account of the imprisonment variant.

Lerrick reports that a similar two-variant oral tradition exists in the Najd region of Saudi Arabia concerning precisely this point in the epic narrative. See Lerrick, "Taghribat," 15.

the Orphans" (Dīwān al-aytām). The Banī Hilāl who were united in victory are divided in the ensuing peace. The rivalries between Diyāb and Abū Zayd sunder the bonds that held the clans together as they argue over the division of land and wealth. Sultan Ḥasan dies, and Diyāb is accused of his murder. Abū Zayd, from the intensity of his weeping and mourning over Sultan Ḥasan's death, goes blind. The final fratricidal battle is fought between Diyāb and his forces and an army of orphans led by al-Jāzya and the blind Abū Zayd. At the battle's end all the heroes are dead; the clans are decimated and are then dispersed as stragglers and refugees over the face of the earth.[30] The Moroccan Almohad dynasty, which historically destroyed the Banī Hilāl confederation, is thus not present in the final scenes of the epic as it exists in the Egyptian oral tradition. Instead, in perhaps an even more moving denouement, the tribe tragically destroys itself.

Given the enormous diversity demonstrated by texts collected in different parts of the Arab world, it is not possible to generalize about smaller structural divisions within the epic. The following description of versions collected in the Nile Delta from the village of al-Bakātūsh, however, illustrates one regional tradition and provides the material and impetus for future comparisons.

The al-Bakātūsh poets divide the Hilālī epic into some thirty episodes, each referred to as a tale (qiṣṣa), and understood to be a narrative unit with a beginning and end which would constitute at least a full evening's performance. Several of these are thought to require at least two nights for a proper performance. In addition, there exists a great deal of marginal material which takes place in between the individual tales; it only emerges when a sequence of more than one episode is being sung, such as at a large harvest celebration or a wedding. The order of the tales is generally agreed upon among the poets, with a certain amount of variation found within some subsections such as the wedding tale cycle, when each of the major heroes goes out and wins one or more maidens as wives, and

30. Abderrahman al-Abnoudy (ʿAbd al-Raḥmān al-Abnūdī) prefers to divide the sīra into four parts: (1) the birth and youth of the heroes; (2) the reconnaissance; (3) the westward journey; and (4) the seven kingdoms (i.e., of the divided Banī Hilāl clans once they have conquered Tunisia). See *Geste*, 22–28. ʿAbd al-Ḥamīd Yūnus has suggested a tripartite division by generation: (1) the generation of the fathers, Rizq, Sarḥān, and Ghānim; (2) the generation of the central heroes, Abū Zayd, Diyāb, and Ḥasan; and (3) the generation of their sons who fight the final fratricidal battles. See *Difāʿ ʿan al-fulklūr* (1973), 185. The chapbooks of the nineteenth and twentieth centuries commonly label the second and third sections "The Reconnaissance" and "The Westward Journey"; they have, however, a number of different titles for the first and final sections of the sīra. In oral tradition, since the episodes are rarely recited "in order," the divisions play little role; they are, however, referred to by poets of the Nile Delta region as (1) "The Birth of Abū Zayd" (Mīlād abū zēd), (2) "The Reconnaissance" (al-Riyāda), and (3) "The Journey" or "The Westward Journey" (al-Riḥla, al-Taghrība).

the first tales of the "Westward Migration" (before the arrival in Tunisia). Curiously enough, although the "Reconnaissance" and the "Westward Migration," the second and third major sections of the epic, both possess well-established names, the first section of the epic does not. I refer to it as "The Births and Marriages":

I. The Births and Marriages
   a. The Birth of Abū Zayd
   b. Mushrif al-ʿUqaylī, the Seventh King
   c. Ḥanḍal al-ʿUqaylī
   d. The Marriage Tales
      —The Maiden Badr al-Naʿām (Full moon of the graceful ones)
      —The Maiden Badr al-Ṣabāḥ (Full moon of the morning)
      —The Maiden Nāʿisat al-Ajfān (Languorous eyes)
      —The Bejeweled Garment of the Daughter of Nuʿmān
      —The Maiden Fullat al-Nadā (Jasmine bud of the dew)
      —The Lady Shāma (Beauty mark) Queen of Yemen
II. The Reconnaissance (al-Riyāda)
   a. The Departure and Journey
   b. ʿAzīza and Yūnus
   c. The Battle in the Garden
   d. The Return of Abū Zayd
III. The Westward Journey (al-Taghrība)
   a. ʿAmir al-Khafājī
   b. Al-Harrās, Malik Qubruṣ (king of Cyprus)
   c. The Passage through Egypt
   d. Manṣūr al-Ḥabashī
   e. The Arrival in Tūnis
   f. Al-Jāzyā at the Wall of Tūnis
   g. The Rescue of the Nephews
   h. The Daughters of the Ashrāf (descendants of the Prophet)
   i. The Maiden Ḍiyāʾ al-ʿuyūn wa-nūrhā (Sparkle and light of all eyes)
   j. The Battles at Tūnis
   k. Death of ʿAmir al-Khafājī
   l. Death of al-Zanātī Khalīfa
   m. The Maiden Ḥusna bint Nāṣir al-Tuwayrdī (Beautiful, daughter of Nāṣir al-Tuwayrdī)

The question then arises whether these tales represent a unified narrative tradition. Is *Sīrat Banī Hilāl*, as it is found in the Nile Delta, a narrative with variations commensurate with those of a single unified oral epic, or is it rather a cycle of tales held together by a loosely organized traditional frame, something that we might better conceive of as "Tales of the Banī Hilāl"? Once again, given the diversity of the regional performance traditions, it seems imperative to establish with care the parameters of each local tradition both as conceived by the performers and audience members, and as indicated by analysis of the texts themselves.

Textual Evidence

At many points in the narratives recorded in al-Bakātūsh, the overarching plot of *Sīrat Banī Hilāl* dictates clear chronological progression. The births of the heroes obviously take place prior to their exploits. The youthful adventures that lead to their respective marriages also clearly precede the drought that forces the tribe from the Arabian peninsula. Then follows the reconnaissance journey of Abū Zayd and his three nephews, followed by Abū Zayd's solitary return to the tribe. Abū Zayd's return subsequently motivates the westward journey of the tribe, the conquest of Tunis, and the death of the major heroes. In terms of large structures, then, it is possible to order the sequence of the tales by the central moves of the epic's plot. However, epics such as the *Iliad* and the *Odyssey* do not unfold according to chronological sequence, and we must be wary of any attempt to impose such an order upon a tradition without evidence substantiating that step.

Within the three large units of the epic—(1) "The Births and Weddings," (2) "The Reconnaissance," and (3) "The Westward Migration"—two subunits possess only sparing internal evidence that might dictate a specific order to the episodes. Based on textual evidence, the wooing and marriage tales, and the stops on the westward journey could be construed as nearly independent stories which could be arranged in several different sequences. Thus, one might perceive the overall plot as dictating a strict chronology of large parts and admitting of certain ambiguities within two of those large units. When examined closely, however, small indications are usually embedded within the rendition of each poet which betray his sense of ordering, though these are not always the same from poet to poet. The tale of Shāma, for example, usually begins with an assembly scene where al-Jāzya, the Hilālī heroine, praises all the warriors for their exploits and for the women they have brought in marriage to the tribe. All of the previous marriage tales are listed. The sole warrior who has not won himself a bride provides the impetus for the tale. Angry at his lack of heroic exploits, he sets out to win Shāma, the queen of Yemen. Shāma, then must be seen as the last of the wedding tales. Likewise, the tale of the *badla* 'a bejeweled suit of clothes' is in essence the second half of the tale of the Maiden of the Languorous Eyes, though it may be sung separately. (The poets usually sing them together as one long episode—five and a half, six, and eleven hours in the three versions I recorded—particularly suitable to a two-night engagement.)

Performance Evidence

Although in living memory no poet of al-Bakātūsh had ever undertaken to sing the epic from "beginning to end," I initiated my fieldwork by requesting a poet to do so (see Chap. 1). Neither the performing poet nor the other poets in the village found this request unreasonable. Indeed, they easily listed which poets would be capable of giving a full rendition and which were not, based on their knowledge of each other's repertory. In all subsequent discussions it became clear that all of the poets conceived of the sīra as a single narrative and could, with little variation, list the order of the episodes. That first recording of the epic resulted in a sparsely sung but linear rendition of *Sīrat Banī Hilāl*. The poet later recalled episodes that he had forgotten, which he then proceeded to perform for me so they could be added to the version he had sung months earlier. While he had forgotten certain episodes during this first series of performances, he supplied a great deal of narrative, linking the episodes with segues or bridges. After recording for several months, I realized I had not heard these sequences performed again, so I asked other poets about these portions of the story. They responded that although as young men they had learned these sections, they were only actually performed when two or more episodes were performed in sequence, a rare event in recent years. In essence, recording all of the individual episodes known to a particular singer would only bring to light a portion of his knowledge of the tradition, for the remaining narrative material exists in the interstices of the episodes, material that emerges only in the sequential performance of more than one episode.

Within the context of the epic-singing community of al-Bakātūsh, the evidence for approaching *Sīrat Banī Hilāl* as a single unit, as a cohesive epic, thus seems fairly conclusive: (1) the poets perceive it to be a single narrative and speak of it as such; (2) the better poets in al-Bakātūsh are capable of singing the epic as a whole, even when they have never before done so; (3) the ordering imposed by different poets, whether in performance or in conversation, is the same, with some minor exceptions in the ordering of the wedding tales and the westward journey tales;

and (4) the texts themselves contain internal evidence indicating a specific and cohesive sequence.

Our conclusion, then, concerning the unity of the epic narrative is somewhat paradoxical. Though *Sīrat Banī Hilāl* is conceptually a single, cohesive narrative for the poets of al-Bakātūsh, it exists only as individual episodes each performed in appropriate contexts. And, as we have seen briefly in reference to narrative "bridges," the traditional episodes do not include the entire epic as the poets know it. Remarkably enough, some of these narrative bridges, which in the al-Bakātūsh repertory are told in laconic prose form, have been found to exist in other regions of the Arab Middle East as full, versified episodes, providing evidence that even the oral tradition with all of its regional variations may prove more cohesive at some levels than researchers have yet imagined.

PART ONE

THE ETHNOGRAPHY OF A POETIC TRADITION

CHAPTER I

The Village

His father and a group of his friends had a particular liking for storytelling. When they had prayed their afternoon prayers, they would gather round one of their cronies who would recite for them tales of ancient raids and the early conquests, tales of ʿAntara and al-Zāhir Baybars, tales of the prophets, the ascetics, and other pious figures, or read to them from books of sermons and from the traditions of the Prophet. . . .

When the sun had set, people would head off to supper, but as soon as they had said their evening prayers they would gather once again to chat for part of the evening. Then the poet would arrive and begin to intone tales of the Hilālī and the Zanātī tribes, and our friend would sit listening during the early part of the night just as he had at the end of the day.

Ṭāhā Ḥusayn, *al-Ayyām*

Al-Bakātūsh strikes the ears of Cairene Egyptians as an improbable name, quite peculiar, a cause even for smiles and laughter. The name, however, is an ancient one, bearing the traces of centuries of linguistic and demographic change. It is attested in Arabic, in various spellings, as far back as the twelfth century, but it is most probably Coptic or even Pharaonic in origin.[1] The inhabitants of al-Bakātūsh, though, have their own explanation for the name, a simple story, part history, part humorous tale, usually recounted tongue-in-cheek to the few visitors who should happen to find the village in their path: "There was once a

1. The Arabic form al-Baqatūsh is found in the *Qawānīn al-dawāwīn* of Ibn al-Mamātī (d. 606 A.H./1209 C.E.) and in *Tuhfat al-irshād min aʿmāl al-gharbiyya*, anonymous ms. in the Al-Azhar Library, No. 6539 Abāza; the form al-Bakatūsh appears in *al-Tuhfa al-sanniyya* by Ibn al-Jīʿān (d. 885 A.H.). The lengthened second vowel is a relatively new spelling. If the name is Coptic in origin it may be derived from a combination of *ba* (def. article) *ke* (other, another), *tosh* (border, limit, nome, frontier, province), in which case, "the village at the other [side of?] the boundary." The Pharaonic possibilities are vaguer, but might include a connection to K D SH the Levantine goddess, in which case, "the village of Kadesh," or more remotely, "the holy village." Cf. J. Cerny, *Coptic Etymological Dictionary* (1976) for Coptic, and Adolph Erman and Hermann Grapow, *Wörterbuch der Aegyptischen Sprache* (1926–63) for Pharaonic. My thanks to Ann Roth and Renée Friedman for assistance on the Coptic and Ancient Egyptian constructions.

foreigner [*khawāja*] named Tūsh who owned all the lands around here. When they came and took away his lands, he wept [*bakā*]. So they called it al-Bakātūsh 'where Tūsh wept.'

When pressed about who came and took the land from Tūsh, some of the younger men of the village might impetuously burst out, "In the time of Gamāl ʿAbd al-Nāṣir [Nasser]," but then quickly realize that the name even in living memory clearly predates the great land reforms of the 1950s. The event is then hurled backward into history, in such street-corner historical discussions, to another point of time of great significance for the Nile Delta peasantry, the time of Muḥammad ʿAlī, who ruled Egypt in the first half of the nineteenth century and who first essayed to modernize Egypt's agricultural system and establish Egypt's independence from the Ottoman Empire.

My presence in the village of al-Bakātūsh derived from its byname, a local blazon known throughout the province of Kafr al-Shaykh and surrounding areas—al-Bakātūsh: Village of the Poets.[2] For the village is home to a community of partially itinerant epic-singers who sing the Arab folk epic *Sīrat Banī Hilāl*. Before introducing the poets and focusing on their position within this village, I examine the village as a community and prepare a canvas upon which I later sketch individual portraits and histories.

The Village

Economic and Commercial Life

Al-Bakātūsh is a large village, with well over ten thousand inhabitants. It is so large that "village" (*qarya*) might at first seem an inappropriate term.[3] The local division of human settlements into categories of hamlet (*ʿizba*), village (*qarya*), town (*bandar*), and city (*madīna*) has a clear logic, however. Al-Bakātūsh might be large, but in the 1980s it did not possess those key features which distinguish town from village: al-Bakātūsh had

2. al-Bakātūsh balad al-shuʿarāʾ.

3. *Balad*, as in the sobriquet *balad al-shuʿara*, can refer to one's home village, town, or even country, while *qarya* refers to a specific size and type of settlement.

Arriving at even an approximate figure for the population of the village and the surrounding hamlets is a precarious undertaking. Residents offered me figures varying from 10,000 for the village itself and 15,000 for the village with tributary hamlets, to 18,000 for the village and 28,000 for the greater community. Even the few "hard and fast" statistics to be found are open to divergent interpretations. There were, for example, just over 850 electricity accounts in al-Bakātūsh in 1986; however, in many cases one account may represent several households where families have run lines to the homes of relatives or married children rather than opening a new account. An electricity account might thus represent a household of eight, or an extended family of more than thirty living in several adjoining homes.

only a weekly market, not a daily market; it had no commercial street or centrally located group of shops, but rather a handful of scattered shops which sold candy, tea, sugar, thread, lamp wicks, soda pop, and other sundries; it had no telephone exchange, no bus or train station, no major mosque. In short, other than the Tuesday market (which rotates from village to village on the remaining days of the week) there is little commercial or business activity aimed at a market broader than the immediate population, and thus few reasons for a stranger to come to al-Bakātūsh.[4]

Al-Bakātūsh is the main village in a region of several square miles, and the "mother village" of eight hamlets, all located at a distance of from one to five kilometers. Al-Bakātūsh is located only a kilometer away from the railway line, and until the 1950s and the construction of paved roads, residents of most of these hamlets had to pass through the village on their way to and from the train stop. Even now that the advent of paved roads, minibuses, and local taxis has diminished the village's role as gateway to the outside world, al-Bakātūsh continues to maintain its dominant position by dint of its larger population and the fact that it is the site of the local elementary and intermediate schools, a small medical clinic, and a government social services office, all of which serve the adjacent settlements as well.

Still a great deal of commercial activity takes place within the confines of the community. The village possesses three small mills which in different seasons grind wheat and corn into flour and also polish rice, although many households still possess a stone handmill for grinding small amounts of grain when the need arises. There are, as well, nearly twenty tailors, an equal number of barbers, several carpentry workshops, three cafés, a post office, and a half dozen or so shops which sell appliances ranging from clocks, lamps, and fans to washers and televisions.

All of these small commercial interests are part-time ventures. Their owners derive only a portion of their income from such trades, and almost all of these services are operated from a room in the family home. Opening hours are irregular, but one can simply call out a greeting from the street and someone in the family will rush to open the "shop" or usher the customer directly into the men's sitting room (*mandara*), where business will be conducted. It is typical for a family to derive income from several different sources simultaneously: a landholding which they may farm themselves or hold jointly with other family members under several different types of agreement, or which they may rent out to

4. Although still referred to by residents as a village, al-Bakātūsh began to acquire some of the trappings of a town (*bandar*) by the early 1990s. Telephone lines had reached the village, and a handful of shops near the center of the village began to emerge as a commercial center.

tenant-farmers in return for a portion of the harvest or a fixed sum; a government salary, for members of the village council, the regional council, local schoolteachers, or one of several different government offices such as the agricultural cooperative; a small business of the type mentioned earlier run part time out of the family home, or a business such as the buying and selling of goods from town in the rotating village markets; certain family members with occupational skills and specialized services, such as Qurʾān reciters who perform at funerals and memorial day ceremonies, or family members who are camel drivers (camels are the major means of transporting harvested crops from the fields into the village). Though the village as a whole is directly dependent on agriculture, only a fraction of the families in the village derive their sole livelihood from the land.

Each of the trades and skills found in the village is rich with traditions and social implications, and though this study deals with only one such craft, that of epic poet, let me offer an additional example here, the village barbers, to demonstrate some of the complexities of a matter as seemingly straightforward as drawing a general socioeconomic portrait of the village.

There were, in 1986–87, between fifteen and twenty barbers in the village, most of whom also had some sort of landholding and/or additional sources of income. Most barbers do not have a full-fledged shop; there are only two in the village, and at these two locations one may find as many as four barbers working in rotation. Other barbers go to their customers' homes or use a room in their own home as a part-time shop. Traditionally barbers are responsible for providing regular haircuts and shaves for the male population; in addition they often perform circumcisions and prepare the bridegroom on the Night of Henna (*laylat al-ḥinnāʾ*), the night before his wedding (see Chap. 2). Payment for regular haircuts and shaves are made by household; all the males of a household, men and boys, are serviced by the same barber throughout the year. The grown men may choose to go to the barber's shop or house, but the barber may also routinely service his customers in their own homes. In return, twice during the year the family pays an agreed upon amount—first of wheat, and then later of corn or rice, in accordance with the seasonal harvests. In the family with whom I lived during my 1986–87 fieldwork, the father and the two young sons paid three *kīla* (one kīla = approximately 15 kilograms = 33 pounds), twice a year. Many village barbers spend one or two days during the week visiting customers out in the hamlets, but they all invariably work in the village on Fridays, when people traditionally desire to look their best for communal prayers.

For circumcisions, the family barber comes to the house to carry out the operation (a function at which they are being supplanted by employees of the local clinic in many cases), for which he receives payment, in accord with the family's economic and social status, of five to fifteen Egyptian pounds (in 1987, 1 pound = approximately $.50 US). But he is also the recipient of *nuqaṭ* or *nuqūṭ* (literally 'drops,' as in drops of water), that is, he receives small payments of 10, 15, 20, and even 50 piasters (100 piastres = 1 pound) from relatives and other guests, who thereby express their participation in the celebration.

The financial and ceremonial culmination of the barber's relationship with a family occurs with the marriage of one of the sons whom he has circumcised as well as groomed and shaved over the years. On the Night of Henna, when bride and bridegroom are respectively washed, dressed, and prepared for the ensuing ceremonies, the barber comes to the groom's house to cut his hair and shave him. Close male friends and relatives are also usually present and participate in washing and dressing the groom. The activities surrounding the bride's preparations are held indoors, hidden from male eyes, but once the groom is fully dressed, he is brought outside with much ado to where the public celebrations will take place and seated on an elevated platform. Throughout the evening he clenches two fistfuls of henna which will dye his palms bright orange (brides are decorated in much more elaborate patterns, according to local custom, but usually on both hands and feet). To one side of the groom, also on the raised platform, sits his barber, who receives nuqūṭ, along with the singer(s) and poet(s), throughout the evening. Depending on the status of the family and the size of the celebration, a barber may earn 20, 50, and even 100 to 200 Egyptian pounds (monthly government salaries range from 45 to 90 pounds) during a wedding.

Though the occupation of barber is surrounded by a rich web of ceremonial and ritual aspects, it is not restricted socially to any specific group of people in al-Bakātūsh, nor does it seem, at least in modern times, to pass primarily from generation to generation of the same family. The majority of the barbers in the village have chosen the trade as one of several alternatives for supplementing their income. Each of the various livelihoods practiced in the community implies a complex body of social relationships with customers, noncustomers, and rival practitioners. Each of the livelihoods is also marked by a rich set of folk occupational stereotypes expressed in proverbs, jokes, and songs.

The heart of the village, however, lies in the agricultural lands which surround it, and the pace of life for nearly everyone is dominated by the agricultural activities of the season. Wheat is planted in November/December and harvested in May/June, and for weeks after the harvest, sheaves of wheat transported by camels arrive in the village to be threshed and winnowed. The number of sheaves is so great they seem to inundate the village. Clover is planted beginning in January, cropped forty days later, and then as many as three more times before it is left to go to seed. Along with shepherding the grazing of the household's animals, many young villagers perform the daily chore of cutting clover for fodder. Fava beans, planted in the fall and winter, are harvested in the spring. Cotton is planted by the end of March, though water shortages may delay this until April, and then picked by hand in August. In between planting and picking, however, during the month of June, cotton is once again the focus of village life, especially for the children of the village, for as soon as the school year has ended, they go out into the fields to help fight the cotton worm, the most damaging of the indigenous agricultural pests. Each day for a month they go out to examine the plants leaf by leaf, removing the worms and placing them carefully in a small cloth sack each child wears around his or her neck. Also in June the rice is planted, then harvested in October, and once again the streets and alleys of the village are filled with sheaves waiting to be threshed and winnowed. Corn (maize) is planted throughout the spring and summer according to the availablity of land, but the largest amounts are planted in May/June and then harvested three months later in late August or early September. Additional vegetables such as onions, eggplant, tomatoes, cucumbers, squash, and various greens are planted in small plots and consumed locally rather than grown as cash crops.

The great turning point in the modern history of the village was the advent of the government land reforms of the 1950s under the presidency of Gamāl ʿAbd al-Nāṣir (Nasser). The royal family's holdings, as well as many of the large landholdings (*iqṭāʿ*, pl. *iqṭāʿāt*) of the upper classes, were broken up and redistributed among peasant families. These lands were at first awarded outright or sold to peasant families; later a system of perpetual leasing was established. The lands of al-Bakātūsh are currently equally divided between private (800 *faddāns*) and government-leased lands (800 *faddāns*) (a *faddān* is slightly larger than an acre). The neighboring village of al-Minshalīn, as a counterexample, had all of its lands redistributed during the early reforms; it encompasses 1,531 faddāns of private land and no government-leased lands.

Social Structures

The village is divided into large extended families of varying wealth and power. Membership in one of these families is a decisive criterion in one's social status in al-Bakātūsh. Last names represent a smaller genealogical division, that is, one's last name usually reflects membership in an immediate family of siblings, cousins, and their respective nuclear families. The extended family organization is a much larger unit usually including hundreds of members. The extended family of the *ʿumda* (village mayor or headman) constitutes over one-fourth the population of the village; less than a half dozen other extended families account for another half of the population, while the remaining familes are all significantly smaller in number and social status. Though there is little doubt as to the current prestige and material power of the large families, several of the smaller families maintain a contestatory tradition of prestige through their claims of belonging to one of the "original" families of the village, or from houses that were great and powerful at some point in the past. These competing claims focus on the concept of *aṣl* 'origin' and the derived adjective *aṣīl* 'original, noble, of good lineage.' As we shall see, local epic-poets easily deploy and manipulate these contestatory views of social power in the village to stir up or rebuke an audience or audience member.

Education and Literacy

Al-Bakātūsh's first public school was established in the late 1950s; an intermediate school was added several years later. Egyptian law currently makes elementary and intermediate education compulsory, though enforcement is at times spotty. The Egyptian secondary system offers several different types of postintermediate education, including academic institutions that are preparatory schools for the universities, technical schools, and vocational schools. Depending on the institution, the students from al-Bakātūsh who attend postintermediate schools may travel from ten to eighty kilometers round-trip on a daily basis. Just over forty students from the village were attending university in 1986–87.

In general, literacy rates vary with age groups and gender. Males over forty-five who are literate tend to be from the wealthiest and most powerful families in the village; the illiteracy rate among older men is otherwise quite high. None of the poets of al-Bakātūsh are literate. For males under forty-five, the literacy rate climbs dramatically, especially as one moves downward into the thirty-and-under age group. Most males, literate or not, have had some exposure to the *kuttāb* 'Qurʾānic school', where they memorize passages from the Qurʾān and are given a rudimentary religious education, which may or may not involve an introduction to the alphabet.[5] A handful of men in the village have

5. For a romanticized but detailed description, see Muḥammad ʿAbd al-Jawwād, *Fī kuttāb al-qarya* (In the village school) (1939).

pursued higher studies in religion at urban schools, including al-Azhar University in Cairo, Egypt's preeminent religious institution, and are, as a result, recognized in the village as authorities on religious subjects.

I have no reliable data on literacy among females, but rates are most certainly significantly lower among women of all ages and probably approach 100 percent in the higher age groups.

Literacy in the Arab world is not the direct equivalent of literacy in other areas of the world, however, for the diglossic (two-tongued) nature of Arabic culture forces the student who wishes to learn to read and write to learn a new form of the language along with the writing system.[6] One restricted domain of discourse in Arab culture is conducted in various forms of the written language, *fuṣḥā*, referred to in Western scholarly literature variously as classical Arabic, modern standard Arabic, standard written Arabic, and literary Arabic, while all remaining domains of discourse are conducted in various forms of colloquial Arabic, commonly differentiated regionally into dialects (Egyptian colloquial Arabic, Palestinian colloquial Arabic, etc.) and, by scholars and researchers, even further into various sociolects such as educated-Cairene colloquial. (Standard written Arabic and Egyptian colloquial Arabic are henceforth abbreviated as SA and EA respectively.)[7]

Standard written Arabic, as the literary language of the Arab world, is essentially the language of nearly all written communication as well as of formal speech acts such as religious and political addresses, and television news broadcasts. SA is a second language for all those who

6. The term "diglossia" was originally coined in French (*la diglossie*) by William Marçais to describe the language situation in Arab North Africa, in a series of three articles which appeared in *L'Enseignement Public* (1930–31). Charles Ferguson later adopted the term to describe language situations in the Arab world, modern Greece, Haiti, and German-speaking Switzerland, in a seminal article, "Diglossia" (1959). The term has generated an entire literature of criticism as well as two-level, three-level, five-level, and even eight-level models for describing the interaction of the many forms of written/oral, formal/informal, and standard/regional varieties of Arabic.

Although the original concept of diglossia was certainly a step forward in understanding the sociolinguistic diversity of the Arab world, the subsequent focus on distinct codes, such as written and spoken, has recently come under a great deal of critical scrutiny and at this point may serve more to obfuscate than to clarify the complexity of language use in Arabic-speaking communities.

7. A valid case can be made that in some areas of the Arab world, the colloquial dialects have achieved some currency as written languages (particularly in Egypt and Lebanon), and that standard written Arabic is not, in fact, particularly standardized across time or geographical distribution, nor does it exist only as a written code (though it clearly derives its existence and perpetuation through use of the written code). In the present work, however, the distinction between SA and EA is used almost entirely to mark differing transliteration systems between spoken Nile Delta–region colloquial Egyptian dialect and standard written forms which are more widely known and recognized, without implying any definite characteristics (social or formal) to either as a language. The term "classical" is applied only to modify texts from the early centuries of Islamic civilization (c. seventh to thirteenth centuries C.E.).

use it: there are no native speakers of standard Arabic. The colloquial dialects are the medium of all other types of spoken communication as well as of a limited amount of written communication such as scripts for plays, a small number of published collections of colloquial poetry, and (in Egypt at least) personal correspondance. Every Arab, no matter how educated or how accomplished he or she may be in the use of fuṣḥā, speaks a colloquial dialect as mother tongue.

For the speaker of any given colloquial dialect, there exists a large body of lexical items in standard written Arabic which are immediately recognizable from cognate colloquial forms. This body of cognate materials is, for nearly all speakers, further enhanced by some basic contact with the literary language, and with classical texts, through religious schooling and ritual, as well as, in recent times, through the mass media. The stylistic and grammatical differences, however, along with the extensive body of vocabulary not cognate with colloquial forms or usages, render much communication in standard written Arabic almost incomprehensible for speakers of colloquial Arabic unschooled in the literary language.

Technological Change

In the mid-1970s electricity arrived in al-Bakātūsh, setting off the most rapid sequence of technological and social changes the village had yet undergone. The traditional configurations of socializing and visiting were transformed by the availability of electric lighting, and the arrival of televisions irrevocably altered earlier patterns of evening pastimes and entertainments. At the time of my fieldwork in 1986–87, virtually every extended household in the village possessed a television. Two television channels are received from Cairo, one broadcasting Arabic programs and the other for the most part broadcasting foreign programs with Arabic subtitles. The latter is viewed only by a small audience in the village since few are literate enough to read the rapid subtitling in standard written Arabic. Electricity is available only a few hours each day, however, and the timing of the commencement and termination of electric current can be capricious, so all households continue to possess and maintain traditional forms of lighting such as kerosene lamps and candles.

In 1979, another current of social transformation began: two young men from al-Bakātūsh traveled to Iraq to labor as guest workers. The next year perhaps two dozen followed, and the year after that over one hundred. In 1987, several hundred young men in the village were working abroad, primarily in Iraq and Saudi Arabia, and the first groups had returned to settle again in the village. Their return has physically, economically, and socially reshaped the village. These young men returned with large amounts of capital, capital with no predetermined relationship to the previous distribution of wealth among the powerful versus weaker families of the village.

Virtually every returning worker began establishing his new status in the village by knocking down the family home of locally produced sun-baked brick and rebuilding with commercially baked "red brick."[8] The new home includes an apartment or apartments in which the returning son (and perhaps his younger brothers) can wed and raise families. Between my initial fieldwork in 1983 and my return in late 1986, a major portion of the village had been rebuilt in red brick.

This rebuilding is rapidly reshaping social norms, for the new houses are built on models quite different from the traditional mud-brick homes. Social spaces, the divisions into public and private, male and female, the relationship between head-of-household fathers and their sons who now control the largest quantity of economic resources within the family, are all in the process of redefinition.[9]

Religious Life

Religious life in the village takes place along a rich spectrum of competing interpretations and orientations. One end of this spectrum is occupied by the five Sufi mystical brotherhoods which are active in al-Bakātūsh. At the other end is found a small, but visible, group of educated young men who embrace the new reinterpretations of Islam which are so poorly termed in the Western media "fundamentalism," a term for which there exists no single Arabic word or direct equivalent.[10]

8. Sun-baked brick is produced in the village itself and resembles adobe (the word "adobe" derives from the Arabic word for brick, *al-ṭūb*. Building with "raw brick" (ṭūb nayy), as it is called, does not require outside labor. Red brick is the brick familiar to Europeans and North Americans and requires that bricklayers and builders from town be hired. In early 1987, one thousand red bricks cost £120 Egyptian (approx. $60 US); the price thereafter increased rapidly throughout that year.

9. See Dwight Reynolds, "Feathered Brides and Bridled Fertility: Architecture, Ritual, and Change in a Northern Egyptian Village" (1994).

10. In Arabic one may refer to various religious groups by their individual names: the Muslim Brotherhood (*ikhwān al-muslimīn*), or Ḥamās in the Gaza Strip, or the Salafiyya movement; or one can use the blanket term "the Islamic groups" (*al-jamāʿāt al-islāmiyya*) which would include a number of groups whom scarcely anyone could characterize as "fundamentalist." There is no term for those groups, and only those groups, which Westerners refer to and study as "fundamentalist." The term always has been and remains a borrowed analogy from Christianity, which inaccurately characterizes the diversity of the phenomena it is used to describe in the Islamic world. The closest term to the English is a neologism which has apppeared in some Arabic newspapers over the past two or three years, *uṣūlīyūn*, from the Arabic word for "origin," *aṣl*.

Somewhere between the two, a majoritarian/urban model derived from central institutions such as the al-Azhar Islamic University also exists in various forms. Though these different currents can be identified and perhaps even labeled ("folk-Sufi," "mainstream-urban," "politico-revisionist"), they exist separately for only a small percentage of the population. For most of the inhabitants of al-Bakātūsh, aspects of one trend interact freely with aspects of another, and there is little attempt to delineate or define. I return to the religious background(s) of the village when I address the question of audiences and the social significance of the epic, for *Sīrat Banī Hilāl* is marked in several ways in terms of religious and social alliances.

The Context of Verbal Art

One further aspect of the general culture of the village is worthy of note here, for it is one not immediately apparent to outsiders. Oral communication in al-Bakātūsh takes place in an environment that recognizes and praises skilled use of verbal art, and that is densely populated by references and allusions to exterior "texts." The citation of classical Arabic texts is among the most commonly deployed public signals indicating education and its accompanying status. Conversation and discussions are punctuated by allusions to or actual citations of Qurʾānic verses, sayings of the Prophet Muhammad (*ḥadīth*), habits and actions of the Prophet (*sunna*), and sometimes classical poetry, as well as colloquial proverbs, song lyrics, and poetry. This practice of alluding to outside "texts" is equally true among literate and illiterate social strata, the main difference lying in the deployment of memorized classical Arabic poetry and a more rigorous concern for authenticity in citations (particularly in reference to religious sources) among the literate, and a more extensive use of colloquial proverbs and song lyrics among more traditional groups. In short, oral communication takes place here in a highly "intertextual" environment.

My research focused on performances of the *Sīrat Banī Hilāl* epic and those genres of poetry, song, and narrative commonly performed in conjunction with the epic. Though I noted as often as possible the communicative life of other forms of verbal art, I was usually prevented from recording these directly. The study of *Sīrat Banī Hilāl* opens onto but one of many realms of verbal art in the village.

The attention and care paid to the aesthetic forms of daily interaction become most obvious to an outsider in the patterns of greetings and salutations. Throughout the Arab world there exist eloquent and elegant greetings for a multitude of occasions. "Morning of Goodness," "Morning of Light," "Morning of Jasmine," "Morning of Roses," and so on are sequences learned by all foreign students of Arabic at some point in their studies.[11] But the application of such greetings to living situations is governed by a set of rules nearly as elegant as the greetings themselves. For example, in al-Bakātūsh I was often instructed concerning the rules of who should initiate a greeting sequence: He who is riding greets him who is walking; he who is walking greets him who is sitting; he who enters greets those already present; a smaller group greets a larger group; a stranger greets the "son of the village" (i.e., local inhabitant).

The rationale is simple: one initiates greetings with "Peace be upon you" (al-salām[u] ʿalaykum), to which the response should be, "And upon you be peace—welcome!" (wa-ʿalaykum al-salām, tafaḍḍal). "Welcome" here indicates an invitation to eat, drink, sit, or rest, in which the speaker essentially assumes the role of host. The stranger must greet first so that he may be transformed into a guest, and each of the listed priorities exist so that whoever is more likely to be near home, or have resources for hospitality most readily available, must be given the opportunity both to respond to the initial greeting and offer hospitality. This behavior is seen to conform to the Qurʾānic injunction to return a greeting with its like or with a better one; the offer of hospitality fulfills this latter function.[12] The rider, the walker, the entering person, the small group, and the stranger are all presumed to be at a disadvantage in offering hospitality.

Finally, the most obvious yet perhaps most significant factor conditioning my personal impressions and experiences in al-Bakātūsh is that I lived in a world that was almost entirely male. Though I knew the women and girls of a handful of households where I was a frequent guest, I moved in only one-half of the society of al-Bakātūsh. Furthermore, the

11. See Charles A. Ferguson, "Root-Echo Responses in Syrian Arabic Politeness Formulas," in *Linguistic Studies in Memory of Richard Slade Harrell* (1967), and idem, "The Structure and Use of Politeness Formulas" (1976).

12. Such greetings are considered a religious obligation, based on the following Qurʾānic verses:

> And when those who believe in Our revelations come unto thee, say: Peace be upon you! (6:54)

> When ye are greeted with a greeting greet ye with [one] better than it or return it. Lo! Allah taketh count of all things. (4:86)

> But when ye enter houses, salute one another with a greeting from Allah, blessed and sweet. (24:61)

Quotations from Muhammad M. Pickthall, *The Meaning of the Glorious Qur'an: Text and Explanatory Translation* (1977).

specific focus of this research, epic singing in private evening gatherings, occurs in an entirely male world. As a result, all that I presume to report and record here reflects primarily male, and to a great extent public, social patterns and interpretations.

Fieldwork

I first visited the village of al-Bakātūsh in 1983 during my second year-long period of study in Egypt. Under the tutelage of several of Egypt's finest folklore researchers, ʿAbd al-Ḥamīd Ḥawwās, Muḥammad ʿUmrān, and ʿAbd al-Raḥmān al-Abnūdī, I had begun to survey the Nile Delta region, concentrating on locating singers and *Sīrat Banī Hilāl* poets. The methodology (if it may be called such) was primitive. I simply took buses and local taxis from village to village. At each stop I would locate, then sit in, the local café until I had struck up a conversation, which usually occurred with startling rapidity and great ease since my height (6'5") and my accent immediately made me an object of curiosity. The "folk arts" (*al-funūn al-sha*ʿ*biyya*) have become, through the intervention of the mass media and various government programs, a recognized entity even outside of urban centers and constitute an easily comprehensible object of study. I had no difficulty ascertaining what types of singers were available where, who were the most popular performers at local weddings, and a broad spectrum of general information about commercial "folk" stars and other topics. At the same time, I interviewed cassette-tape store owners about their inventories and what types of music were most popular; often these shop owners were extremely helpful in locating local performers.

As I began working in the area contiguous to the province of Kafr al-Shaykh, I began to hear repeated references to al-Bakātūsh—Village of the Poets. At one point I simply cut short other work to travel directly to al-Bakātūsh. My first visit was quite simple and matter-of-fact: I experienced no anthropological angst of arrival for I had been in dozens of villages similar in nearly every way to al-Bakātūsh, and I had as yet little idea that I would later come to spend many months there. I simply asked someone whether there were indeed epic poets living in the village; he responded affirmatively and offered to guide me to the home of whichever poet I desired. We chatted briefly about which poets were good; I was soon ushered into someone's home for tea and a poet was sent for. Within a few minutes I had met Shaykh Biyalī Abū Fahmī and over a second cup of tea had arranged to record a half-hour sample from the epic. After nightfall I left to return to the nearby city of Disūq, where I was staying in a hotel, having determined that there were a dozen or more poets in the village: al-Bakātūsh was indeed the village of the poets. On my second visit I met Saʿīd ʿAbd al-Qādir Ḥaydar and his family, who lodged me and ever after took on the role of my patrons and protectors in the village. Without their continued support and friendship, none of my later research could have taken place.

I traveled many times from Cairo to al-Bakātūsh in that spring of 1983 and quickly met most of the other poets in the village. I taped brief samples of their singing and conducted very basic interviews about their repertories—how they had learned to sing the epic and other such topics. My formal academic background, up to this point, had been restricted to Arabic language and literature studies, and these haphazard attempts represented my first folkloristic fieldwork. I had been informally introduced to folklore research and fieldwork methodologies by a group of friends and colleagues in the United States—ʿAbd al-Raḥmān Ayyūb, Susan Slyomovics, and Bridget Connelly—and was also being guided by the Egyptian folklorists mentioned earlier.

It soon became apparent that the village of al-Bakātūsh was a rich and fascinating fieldwork site. The community of epic poets there turned out to be the largest single community of epic poets in Egypt, and no one had previously conducted research there. More important from my point of view was the fact that none of these poets had been swept up in the studio production of commercial cassette tapes of the epic, which was occurring in nearby towns. In addition to the community of epic poets, al-Bakātūsh proved to possess a rich heritage of folk arts and traditions rapidly disappearing in many other areas. In 1983, before even commencing my graduate studies, I resolved to do my doctoral fieldwork in this village. Though I explained this decision to friends in the village, I doubt anyone gave credence to a young American's flight of fantasy.

I did return to live in the village for ten months in 1986–87 and returned again in 1988 for a brief visit. During the intervening three years I had studied toward a doctoral degree in folklore and folklife at the University of Pennsylvania and had encountered a completely new set of issues and concerns. I returned to ask very different questions and to pursue very different goals than I had during my first visits.

I was welcomed with the extreme generosity and open hospitality for which the Egyptian countryside is rightly famous, but arranging a living (and livable) situation for an extended period of time did not prove easy. There is no extra or vacant housing available in an Egyptian village; residency patterns and population pressures have in most areas rendered housing quite scarce and problematic. New housing is built only when needed—at the marriage of a son, for example. With the help of my "patron family," however, a solution was finally arranged. "Solution" is surely the term, for I was indeed a "problem." As a young and unmarried man, I could only be housed in a situation that provided the proper distance between myself and any unmarried girls. Also, though one could probably have rented a whole house if one paid a high enough price, owing to restrictions in grant monies and by choice I lived in al-Bakātūsh on a monthly budget of £100 Egyptian (which equals $50 US, or double a typical monthly government salary), not including the money I paid to poets at those performances for which I was primary patron.

A place was found for me in the home of Aḥmad Bakhātī, whose family acted not only as my landlords but as my closest contacts after my patron family, that of Saʿīd ʿAbd al-Qādir Ḥaydar. I lived in what would otherwise have been the Bakhātī mandara, or men's sitting room, to which function it reverted upon the arrival of any guests, and ate all of my meals with the family throughout my stay. Previous to my arrival, they had rented the room for a year to a schoolteacher who had taught at the local elementary school before being transferred, so the family had had some experience dealing with an outsider. Also, since Aḥmad Bakhātī is a policeman in the provincial capital of Kafr al-Shaykh, it was hoped his position would alleviate some of the suspicions that would inevitably follow upon my arrival in the village.

As a guest in the village, as a foreigner, and perhaps particularly as an American, I was the beneficiary of rich and enthusiastic hospitality. I was showered with invitations to eat with different households, and I was included in the activities of many different male social groups, ranging from evening gatherings of village elders to the spontaneous escapades of the younger men. It is extremely important, however, to balance this portrait of village hospitality and the access I was permitted to village life with the undercurrent of unease that also accompanied my presence.

I never encountered difficulties with people who actually knew me and with whom I socialized regularly. For many people in the area, however, I was merely a figure who passed by, often carrying notebook or camera, about whom they heard anecdotes and rumors many times removed from their source. The suspicions that accompanied my presence and my work did not surprise me. In fact, the tightness of social alliances and the bitterness of rivalries in the village were so strong, the monitoring of people's whereabouts, purchases, and diet so intense, that I could hardly feel I was being accorded special treatment.

Each time I left the three-room house where I lived with the Bakhātī family, the mother of the household would invariably check to make sure that anything I was carrying was well concealed and out of sight. On one occasion when I had purchased material at the weekly market for a new *galabiyya* (the nightshirt-like apparel worn by men) and was on my way to the tailor's, she seized the clear plastic bag in which I was carrying the cloth, took out the cloth, wrapped it in newspaper, and returned it to the bag. She chided me for giving people something to talk about. I protested that everyone already knew I had bought cloth at the market (at least a half dozen people had offered opinions as to color and quality), and in a few days everyone would see the new galabiyya. No change—avoid the evil eye and don't give people a chance to talk; wrap it up!

Another example: one late afternoon I was sitting with friends on their *maṣṭaba*, the brick bench attached to the front of the house where much of the neighborhood's socializing takes place. As usual, our conversation was sometimes quiet, held just between the three of us, and sometimes loud, including small groups on similar maṣṭabas in both directions down the alley. A man passed us, greeted us, then turned down a small alleyway. Conversation stopped. Everyone in the alley was perturbed and people began to whisper: "Allah! Allah! what is this?" Finally the commotion grew to a high pitch and a man opposite us stood up, walked to the corner and took a long look down the alleyway. He returned and announced to the whole alley, "He's borrowing a sickle from so-and-so." Everyone relaxed and conversations began to flow again. The problem? This man had no known reason for being down that alleyway: he had no relatives there, and there were no shops, no tailor, no other plausible reason for his presence. In the late afternoon, most men are still out in their fields, so the presence of a man wandering about the village was a source of consternation. Once his purpose was made public, the vigilant eyes of the neighborhood could relax.

For the first few months of my stay, every few weeks was marked by some encounter that seemed to belie the hospitality and friendliness I encountered face to face. The first month it was the issue of maps: So as not to get lost on my late afternoon walks through the fields and neighboring villages, I had drawn in my notebook a map of the major paths that link the dozen nearest settlements to al-Bakātūsh. Once while I was out, a guest started rifling through my notes and translations and found the map (written in Arabic). By the time I had returned from my walk the village was awash in rumors about the "American spy."[13] In

13. It must be remembered that Egypt has been at war four times in the past forty years with a nation that derives its existence from American support. I was treated hospitably and generously even by families who had lost sons to American bullets wielded by American-financed soldiers.

the second month I began taking pictures, usually at the behest of the people I was photographing. Someone, however, thought I was photographing too much, for the news soon reached the district police station, where I was invited to make an appearance. A few weeks later a Muslim-Christian riot broke out in the town next to us, and the village felt a resurgence of tension about my presence. A month later, while I was walking through the village, a man pulled me into his doorway and whispered to me, "I want you to know that I don't believe the things they are saying about you. If you need help, you can come to me." I was shaken by the encounter, and it took several days of discreet questioning to find out what the problem was. This time word was being spread that I had come to convert the young men of the village to Christianity, to lure them away from Islam.

Each of these incidents, and a dozen or so smaller ones, were handled the same way. My friends in the village (and I, on their instructions) would loudly and at every opportunity, such as in the cafés, at evening gatherings, and in private conversations, explain what I was doing and why. It was a constant public relations campaign.

Suddenly, after five months, the difficulties ceased. At the time I assumed the village had finally grown used to my presence, that some critical threshold had been reached; I was after all really interested in poetry and folk music. In the late summer I contracted hepatitis and had to move to Cairo for several weeks while I recuperated. Delegations arrived from the village every few days to check on my health and to bring news. When I returned to the village there was no trace of tension. People told me again and again how sorry they were that I had taken ill while in their village.

After my year of research, when my final departure drew close, I again moved to Cairo for a couple weeks. During the last visit I received from friends from al-Bakātūsh, we stayed up nearly till dawn talking and reminiscing. Before we fell asleep my closest friend and staunchest defender in the village asked if I knew a certain man. I recognized the family name and said so, but did not know the man in question. Everyone laughed and asked me, "Are you sure?" They then described him to me and mentioned that he was one of the village guards. I could just barely conjure up the man's face. They laughed some more and finally explained.

Months earlier, someone had seen me coming home late at night from some gathering or another and apparently coming out of an alleyway where they could not imagine my having any legitimate business. They reported it to the village "mayor" (*ʿumda*) with the result that this man from the village guard had been assigned to follow me around the village for the ensuing months. When I went into a house, he would sit at a nearby café; when I left, he would follow. Just at the point when I had imagined my relations with the village to be relaxing and everyone's suspicions to have been allayed, I had in fact been placed under full-time surveillance. My friends were tickled that even after months I had not noticed. I, however, felt as if someone had kicked a chair out from under me. My feelings of having crossed immense cultural distances and achieved some personal understanding were being put in question. That sense of ambiguity was to linger for a long time.

I was lucky enough to have another opportunity to visit al-Bakātūsh a year later in 1988. There were no small incidents this time to mar what was, on the surface at least, essentially a reunion of friends. Letters and photographs that I had sent, articles and photos of al-Bakātūsh that had been published as a result of my work, had strengthened the friendships that had begun the previous year. All this bolstered the romantic interpretation of fieldwork as human contact and the search for understanding. Recollection of that one moment of discovery, however, always throws into doubt all I think I understood and all I encountered. It is, I believe, a productive state of doubt.

Remuneration

At the outset of my 1986–87 stay in al-Bakātūsh, I was forced to make a number of decisions that had significant ramifications for my subsequent research. These decisions included how I was to remunerate poets for performances, interviews, and later, lessons; how I would begin to record the sīra, what types of performances I would accept as "authentic"; and how I would then transcribe and translate the texts I recorded. Each of these issues required compromises between ideal methodologies and the realities presented to me in the field.

Since there were fourteen poets in the al-Bakātūsh community when I began my work, all of whom were accorded different status by audiences and the poets themselves, I avoided a potential quagmire of negotiations and rivalries by seeking agreement from the poets upon a single rate of payment for all. Eventually we arrived at the figure of £2.50 Egyptian (approx. $1.25 US) per hour of recording. I, along with the poets, at first did not disclose to other villagers the amount the poets were being paid for their work with me. However, rumors began to circulate quickly in the village that they were receiving as much as £10 an hour (approx. $5.00 US), and the voices criticizing the poets for exploiting me grew so vehement that the poets were forced to request that I announce publicly in a number of different contexts the fees they were receiving. Still, a few of the villagers found even £2.50 to be extravagant and warned that the poets would pad their singing with "empty talk" to earn more money. I, on the other hand, stressed that the poets were being paid this sum not only for actual performance time but for all the hours they spent with me in interviews, answering my endless questions and discussing points of transcription and translation. The poets did indeed offer hundreds of hours of their time toward "the thesis" (*al-risāla*), for which they refused remuneration. Eventually the majority of the villagers declared the deal a fair one.

Clearly a single rate of payment carried the danger of encouraging lengthy performances. Several factors negated much of this influence, however. First, I paid this fee only for recording which was conducted specifically for my research at evening gatherings which I hosted, and of which I was thus the primary patron. In all other contexts I paid poets only as other audience members did, that is, in small gifts of ten or twenty piastres and in cigarettes offered during breaks in the performance. This meant I had a body of comparative material with which to judge those performances I had personally solicited. Also, all solicited recordings (outside of my lessons) were conducted with audiences just as in other evening gatherings, or *sahra*s, which provided a further obstacle (the audience's patience) to unnatural lengthening of the texts. Finally, the poets of al-Bakātūsh with whom I worked closely were all concerned that the performances I take back to America be good ones. I was instructed several times by poets that I should not use a particular section because it had not been sung well, and received offers to record a second time passages with which the poet was not satisfied. (Needless to say, these unsatisfactory segments often proved far more informative for my research purposes than the "good" performances.)

Recording Conditions

I chose to record under two different sets of circumstances. First, particularly during the early part of my fieldwork, I solicited and recorded performances held in the Ba<u>kh</u>ātī home where I lived. Here I could request specific portions of the epic, and although an audience was always present, it was understood that I might ask to have a section sung over again or otherwise alter the course of the performance (though in fact I rarely did so). Second, I recorded in a variety of other contexts where performances were being held independent of my presence in the village. I also attended performances that I did not record, in an effort to judge the effect of the tape recorder. I concluded that although performances I solicited were in a number of ways different from "natural" performances, I could detect no major differences between the natural performances I recorded and those I did not. Quite simply, the poet was concerned with the response of his patron and audience in these situations, and had little time to worry about the presence of the tape recorder.

The most important step I took in soliciting performances was to request, at the outset of my fieldwork, a complete performance of the epic in sequential order from Shaykh Biyalī Abū Fahmī. Though he had never before done so, Shaykh Biyalī readily agreed to make the attempt, which resulted in a thirty-two-hour version of the epic recorded over eleven nights. During my stay, however, we discovered a number of sections which were part of his repertory but had not been included in this first chain of performances. The missing sections brought the total to about thirty-seven hours.[14] When I compared this complete performance to his performances in other contexts, I realized I had received a clear, but starkly unembellished version. The episodes I listened to in other contexts were on the average a third longer than my recordings. Far from having lengthened the stories, Shaykh Biyalī, under the constraint of singing the stories "from beginning to end," had truncated them. After this first recording of Shaykh Biyalī's beginning-to-end version, I recorded other poets, only occasionally requesting specific episodes.

Apprenticeship as Methodology

The recording of performances and variants, and the interviewing of performers and audience members are all standard folkloristic research methods, to the extent that we can speak of a standard methodology in our field. I chose al-Bakātūsh as a research site, however, in hopes of combining standard research procedures with a technique that is common in ethnomusicology, and to some extent in anthropology, but which appears only infrequently in folkloristic fieldwork: I hoped to apprentice myself to a master poet to acquire a more detailed understanding of the poets' conceptualizations of their craft, the process of tranmission, and the process of composition in performance. This is not a case of the researcher utilizing himself or herself as informant, but rather of placing himself or herself in a recognized social relationship for the transmission of knowledge about a craft or skill. As we all know from

14. Each of the missing sections were tales I recorded first from other poets. When Shaykh Biyalī heard I had recorded them elsewhere, he immediately insisted on singing them himself, with apologies for having left them out of his original version.

personal experience, to explain a process to an outsider is a very different thing from showing the outsider how to actually do that process. Teaching allows a performer or artist to remain within the medium and the tradition he or she knows. It also provides a laboratory for experimentation, purposeful or inadvertant, on the part of the field researcher.[15]

I was concerned that the selection of a master poet and the initiation of a student relationship would prove difficult and, furthermore, might limit my access thereafter to other poets and performances. The process began, however, with little effort on my part.

When I had been in the village about three months, at the end of an evening performance, everyone went home except for two poets, Shaykh ʿAbd al-Wahhāb and Shaykh ʿAbd al-Ḥamīd, and ʿAbd al-Ḥamīd's son, Ragab. These conversations, late at night, when I was the only nonpoet present, were some of the most rewarding moments of my fieldwork. I kept the tea and cigarettes flowing and was regaled in turn with tales of great poets and performances of the past. Shaykh ʿAbd al-Wahhāb, however, always made a great deal of the fact that he never drank tea, only coffee. So I brought out the kerosene stove, and he instructed Rajab and me in the fine art of coffee-making.

While Ragab and I struggled to get the coffee just right, a conversation began between the two elder poets about what type of wood one should use in the making of a rabāb—ebony or ash. They then moved on to whether or not it was good to have mother-of-pearl inlay on the instrument. They then spoke of rabābs that had been played by famous poets of the past. I was rapidly drifting out of the conversation, for it was three o'clock in the morning, but a new tack in the conversation brought me back to a full state of wakefulness. Rajab turned and said to me: "You know, when you get back to America you could perform this poetry on the lute [*ʿūd*]." (The fact that I could play Arab lute was always a thing of great interest, for it is an urban instrument and nobody in the village played or owned one.)

I responded, "But what I'd really like to do is learn to sing it on the rabāb."

For a moment they just stared at me. Then Shaykh ʿAbd al-Wahhāb chuckled, "I'll get you a rabāb and put you to work here beside me" [anā hashūf lak rabāb wi-ashaghghalak hinā jambī].

"By God I'd love to!" [wallāhi yārēt!] I replied.

Then Ragab chimed in, "Why didn't you tell us you wanted to do this. We'll get you a rabāb and you can go sit with Uncle ʿAbd al-

15. For extensive discussion of apprenticeship as methodology, see Michael W. Coy, ed., *Apprenticeship: From Theory to Method and Back Again* (1989); also Mantle Hood, *The Ethnomusicologist* (1971).

Wahhāb an hour every day and he'll show you how to place your fingers."

It would be nice, I suppose, to be able to say one had had deep and theoretically earth-shattering statements flash through one's mind at the key turning points in one's fieldwork. Instead I could only think of Mickey Rooney turning to Judy Garland, saying, "I've got an idea. Let's put on a show! We'll use old MacGregor's barn for a stage and . . . and . . ."

In two minutes my apprenticeship had been secured, though we talked on excitedly about it for another half hour before everyone went home to bed. What I had feared would be the most difficult transition of my fieldwork had taken place with no effort or planning on my part. Not only was my apprenticeship launched with full approval of the poets' community, but there was never any question of my loyalty to my poet-teacher, even though I recorded and worked with many other poets.

Language

Perhaps the most difficult aspect of fieldwork for a researcher to assess, yet one of the most crucial, is his or her own linguistic competency. And one of the most rarely discussed aspects of folkloristic and anthropological fieldwork, at least when it reaches published (i.e., public) form, is the process by which primary textual data move from collection to transcription, to translation, and finally to publication, and what role the "author" does or does not play in that process.

My training in Arabic language and literature as an undergraduate at UCLA had been supplemented by two year-long periods of study in Egypt before I undertook the fieldwork that constitutes the core of this work. As a result, my comprehension of and ability to communicate in the Cairene dialect of Egyptian colloquial Arabic was fairly fluent by the time I arrived in al-Bakātūsh in 1986 for an extended stay. The local rural dialect posed a number of problems, however; some were rooted in actual dialectal differences, some in my lack of knowledge about the material realia of daily life in rural areas, and some in my general lack of social and personal knowledge about this particular community.

The dialectal differences proved minimal and, after I had become accustomed to some of the basic sound changes, posed few problems. Friends in al-Bakātūsh quickly seized on the project of teaching me the vocabulary of everyday life, and of teaching me to speak less *faṣīḥ* 'classically'. Time and again I was asked to recite strings of new words I had been taught, such as the parts of the waterwheel and its fittings (*sāqiya*: *madār, nāf, hudya, ṭāra, tirs, g͟humā, bak͟hnaqa, qunnāfa*), or types of water vessels (*qulla, ballāṣ, zīr, safīḥa*), or types of bread (*bakkōna, miraḥraḥ, qarqūsha, shāmī*, etc.); in this way I was rapidly equipped to deal with most topics of daily conversation.

Lingering problems in spoken communication comprehension had much more to do with local knowledge of history, genealogies, and social relations, which often eluded me. The simplest example is found in the practice, in conversation, of referring to men by their given names, or as "father of X" with reference to their son's name, by one or more nicknames, or as "son of X" with reference to their father's name. An even more confusing variation is found in the practice of referring to a man as "father of X," where X is his father's name, not his son's.[16] At times the significance of entire narratives, where I easily understood the sequence of events, completely escaped me because I did not know that Muḥammad, Abū ʿAlī 'Father of ʿAlī', and al-Gamal 'the Camel' were all the same person. Most problems at this level of comprehension could, however, be rectified in later discussions with friends

More disconcerting were my long-term problems in understanding female speech. Women and girls regularly utilize demonstrably different sentence contours than males do, as well as using certain differences in pronunciation and choices in vocabulary. A single, easily identified example is their dropping of word-final consonants, accompanied by lengthening of the preceding vowel in certain environments. Since one type of utterance I most frequently overheard was that of adults calling their children, differentiating male versus female vocatives proved to be a simple, verifiable example: female *yā muḥammā* versus male *yā muḥammad*. The pattern of dropping word-final consonants carries across a number of different environments and for me at least, particularly in rapid conversation, required a period of adjustment. Obviously my difficulties learning to understand female speech arose directly from the limited opportunities to actively carry on conversations that involved female speakers. A female researcher would not have encountered this problem to the same degree or at least not for any significant period of time.

In addition, the language of *Sīrat Banī Hilāl* performances constitutes a subdialect of its own, distinct from both standard Arabic and colloquial Arabic at nearly at levels. It possesses a distinctive lexicon, which includes a rich terminology for weapons, armor, types of horses and camels, a

16. This latter occurs most often when a man has not yet fathered a son or has had a son die; the assumption is that he will, as is customary, name his son after his own father, thus "Y, father of X" refers not so much to Y's father (X), but to an as yet unborn son to be named X. The female pattern is parallel, "mother of X," though I do not know of any case of a woman being called by the name of an unborn son or daughter.

vocabulary concerning the practice of geomancy (a method of reading the future involving lines drawn on the ground or the reading of the position of tossed bones, shells, or other items), and a plethora of terms for desert landscape features and other topics rarely brought up in daily communication. At the phonological level, phonemes that have differing pronunciations in colloquial Arabic and standard Arabic (such as SA /*th*/ versus EA /*s*/, and SA /*dh*/ versus EA /*z*/) as well as phonemes that have differing colloquial dialect pronunciations in the region (such as SA /*q*/ versus EA /'/ or /*g*/, and SA /*j*/ versus EA /*j*/ or /*g*/) often alternate between the various possible pronunciations during performances. Such alternation is at times deployed to heighten poetic or comic characterizational impulses by the poets (such as occurs in the portrayal of foreign versus Arab characters, slaves versus nobles, female characters, religious figures, etc.)[17] and at times appears to play only a clarifactory role (as when a line is repeated in performance rendered in a different dialect pronunciation). The language of the sīra even possesses a few syntactic features of its own, such as the negation of the simple past tense with *lam* when governed by *yārēt* or *yā layta*. (See, for example, *yārētuh lam ḍarab*, for, "If only he had not struck!" where the particle *lam* does not exist in spoken colloquial Egyptian Arabic at all, and yet in standard Arabic cannot be used to negate a past tense such as *ḍarab*.)

Although these features have usually been addressed by Western and Arab scholars alike as failed attempts on the part of poets to "classicize" their poetry (a linguistic incarnation of the "gesunkenes Kulturgut" argument), a much sounder approach would be to recognize this hybridization as a natural register of colloquial Arabic, which might be termed "artistic" or "elevated" colloquial, and to study its features and functions within Arab society. This "artistic colloquial" might also be approached, given its intriguing blend of dialectal and classical features, as a true poetic koiné similar to the language of the Homeric poems.

Transcription and Translation

I was fortunate during my 1986–87 fieldwork to be both befriended and assisted by two enthusiastic and highly competent "sons of the village," without whom my work would have been far more difficult. Shaykh ʿAbd al-Qādir Ṣubḥ and Ustā*dh* Ḥamdī Jalama undertook the task of writing out preliminary, longhand transcriptions of over one

17. I have elsewhere touched on the sociolinguistic portrayal of women in *Sīrat Banī Hilāl* performances. See Dwight Reynolds, "The Interplay of Genres in Oral Epic Performance: Differentially Marked Discourse in a Northern Egyptian Tradition," in *The Ballad and Oral Tradition* (1991).

hundred and fifty hours of *Sirat Banī Hilāl* performance. Both men are college-educated; they not only assisted with the work of transcription but they also proved to be interested and interesting discussants for my on-going work and ideas.

Much ado is often made of the difficulty of writing colloquial Arabic in Arabic script, for in many cases the script cannot portray the sounds of the colloquial without so altering the standard form as to make the words nearly unrecognizable. And yet, based on only a handful of examples supplied by myself and the reading of a few collections of colloquial poetry I brought with me to the village, these two young men immediately commenced writing out complete colloquial transcriptions from audio recordings—a fact that should give us pause when assessing the supposed difficulties of learning to write colloquial Arabic. In addition, I transcribed approximately one-fifth of the materials independently, but soon found it easier to revise, where necessary, the transcriptions ʿAbd al-Qādir Ṣubḥ and Ḥamdī Jalama produced. The final result was that at the time of my departure from al-Bakātūsh, all of my field recordings had been transcribed once, and a good portion of them had been independently transcribed a second time.

The work of translation was, at one and the same time, a more solitary and a more communal pursuit. It was a communal venture at heart, I think, and by this I refer to the thousands of questions I directed to poets, friends, and members of my host families concerning the meaning of specific words and phrases. By the end of my fieldwork, however, I had rough translations for only one-tenth of the performances I had recorded. A portion of these were later reviewed by researchers and friends in Cairo. Still the responsibility for poor, clumsy, and even incorrect translations rests firmly with me. The fragments of the *Sīrat Banī Hilāl* epic which appear in this work have passed through the helping hands and minds of many people. Though great care has been exerted to reproduce them meticulously and accurately, I hope they will be experienced in their new and highly constraining written form as artistic and carefully crafted voices.

CHAPTER 2

Poets Inside and Outside the Epic

> Then the sun set, and the full moon sat cross-legged on his throne, the air became pure and sweet, time grew serene, the pinnacle of happiness and joy was reached, the lights of the quarter glowed, and the circle of dancers at the big tree by the waterfall in the center of the village grew crowded. The sounds of the great wedding exploded from beneath the feet of the dancers, from between the palms of those clapping, from the throats of the singers, from the drums and the tambourines, from the roofs of the houses, from among the openings of the huts, from the enclosures and the courtyards, from the lanes and the stables. Tonight every graybeard is in love, every youth yearns, every woman is womanly, and every man is Abū Zayd al-Hilālī.
>
> al-Ṭayyib Ṣāliḥ, *Ḍawʾ al-bayt*

The poets of al-Bakātūsh and their families exist in the village as neither complete insiders nor complete outsiders—not truly strangers, yet not truly friends of the villagers. Both villagers and poets are quick to note that they are separate groups coexisting, though villagers are perhaps quicker to point this out than poets. The mere existence of such an extensive group of poets, a community of fourteen households and nearly eighty members, set within the larger community of al-Bakātūsh, poses a riddle. This group is the largest community of epic poets known in Egypt, in fact, in the entire Arab Middle East; in the rest of the Nile Delta region, all the other related communities of poets are composed of groups of two, three, or at most four households. Economically it makes little sense for performers of the same tradition to group together, providing stiff competition in a diminishing market. Several preliminary questions then must be posed concerning the community of poets in al-Bakātūsh: Who are these poets historically and ethnically? How did such a large community come to exist? How does the community of poets interact with the village at large?

Beyond detailing these basic ethnographic concerns, I pose a further set of questions, for my focus is the *Sīrat Banī Hilāl* tradition within a specific social context: How do the sociological realities and interactions of these two communities affect the performance tradition? In what ways does this tradition reflect, provoke, counteract, or provide space for the negotiation of its cultural circumstances (for along with the differentiation of a socially distinct group within a society, as performers of a specific artistic tradition, follows an imposed complex of roles, economic relationships, concepts of identity, and perceptions of power)? The artistic tradition I am examining takes shape within an intricate environment of social ties and tensions. Yet studies of artistic traditions often provide ethnographic information about social context primarily as a backdrop to textual analyses, which draw few, if any, conclusions regarding the dynamic relationship between the two domains. Rather than leave this social background undifferentiated, with the semblance of univalency, in the following two chapters I draw specific correlations between social realities outside and inside the "text" of the epic.

Origins, Ethnicity, Identity

Poets as Gypsies

The identity and historical origins of the epic poets of the Nile Delta involve complex, sensitive, and often highly ambiguous issues. The villagers refer to the poets simply as *s̲h̲uʿara,*[1] lit. 'poets', sometimes as *ʿarab* 'Arabs', and far more rarely as *g̲h̲ajar* 'Gypsies', as the latter term possesses strong pejorative connotations. The poets use the first two terms but consciously avoid the latter. In utilizing these terms, villagers and poets map different perceived relationships between the two communities and thereby codify different sets of attributed characteristics. In a society where names and naming directly reflect origins and identity, the repertory of terms for defining and referring to subgroups is highly significant.

The poets and the members of their families refer to themselves in public as shuʿara and as ʿarab, as do the villagers, but in private the poets call themselves ḥalab (sometimes *ḥalaba* or *wilād ḥalab*), a term whose literal derivation means "Aleppans," that is, people from the northern

1. The villagers make a clear distinction between the classical Arabic word *s̲h̲uʿarāʾ* (accent on the final syllable, with long /*ā*/ and final glottal stop) and the vernacular *s̲h̲uʿara* (accent on the first syllable, short final /*a*/ with no glottal stop). For example, several times I was asked, "Of course you have *s̲h̲uʿarāʾ* in America, but do you have *s̲h̲uʿara*?" The questionner meant approximately, "Of course you have literary poets in America, but do you have epic-singing/Gypsy/rabāb poets?"

Syrian city of Aleppo. The term *ḥalab* in al-Bakātūsh is an in-group term and occurs only in very specific contexts. Though some villagers know the term, they do not refer to the poets of al-Bakātūsh as ḥalab, nor have I ever heard a member of the poet community mention the term in front of non-ḥalab other than myself. This label, along with other means of identification discussed below, is perceived by the poets as a powerful marker delimiting the boundary between their community and that of the village at large.

Shared Terms
Poets (s͟huʿara)
Arabs (ʿarab)

Villagers (in private)	*Poets (in private)*
Gypsies (g͟hajar)	Ḥalab (ḥalab)

The term Ḥalab is a bit of a puzzle, for the poets have maintained no traditional explanation tracing their history to the city of Aleppo, nor do they have any traditional explanation of this geographic nomenclature.[2] Possibly the Ḥalab did indeed come to Egypt via the city of Aleppo, but it is unlikely they were originally from there. Their migration to Egypt in any case took place several centuries ago.

In general the Ḥalab are recognized as one of several groups in Egypt which share the status of ghajar, or Gypsies, along with the Jamāsa, the Nawar, the Tatar, the Ghawāzī, the Maṣlūb (or Maslūb), and others.

2. Other researchers over the past hundred and fifty years have also found the Ḥalab to possess no etiological account of their name, or at least none they were willing to share with outsiders. See, for example, F. R. S. Newbold, "The Gypsies of Egypt" (1856), 291.

It has been suggested that the term *ḥalab* may derive from the verb *ḥalaba* 'to milk' and may be the remnant of a pastoral or nomadic origin. There appears to be no historical evidence for either the "Aleppan" or the "milkers" argument other than the posited etymologies themselves; in addition, none of the Gypsy groups of the Arab Middle East are closely associated with either herding or husbandry, but rather tend to be bound to such low-status, often itinerant, professions as tinkering, blacksmithing, dancing, and so forth. The noun *ḥalba* in colloquial Egyptian Arabic (see Martin Hinds and El-Said Badawi, *A Dictionary of Egyptian Arabic* [1986]) denotes a ring or arena in which an artists performs; thus the term *wilād ḥalab* might be a derogatory name meaning approximately "sons of the circle" in reference to the circle of viewers who gather around street performers. (My thanks to Nabil Azzam for this possible derivation.) Finally, the verb *ḥaliba* in classical Arabic meant "to be dark or black" most often in reference to hair (see Edward Lane, *Arabic-English Lexicon* [1984]) and the adjectival form *ḥulub* could denote either "black" or "intelligent" (see A. Kazimirski, *Dictionnaire Arabe-Français* [1860]). The term may have become attached to these itinerant musicians due to both their dark skin coloring and their reputation for cunning. Given the lack of other evidence, this latter possibility strikes me as the most plausible.

The divisions between the groups are none too clear and often vary from informant to informant (along with information about the traditional occupations of each group) and clearly vary from region to region. A further complication springs up among informants and in sociological research where the term *ghajar* is sometimes used not only to denote Gypsies in general but also a specific group, separate from the others listed above.[3] In most areas of Egypt the Ḥalab are best known as blacksmiths rather than as poets. The poets of al-Bakātūsh acknowledge this, but claim that certain branches of the Ḥalab have always been epic singers. The two groups, blacksmiths and poets, have little to do with one another in the Nile Delta region at least. They are not found in the same communities, they do not commonly intermarry, and I was unable to uncover any less formal social ties. Still, the possibility of a historical link between these two groups is highly suggestive, for the connection between blacksmiths and bards has been noted and studied in several other parts of the world.[4]

Within the Arab world there are indications of the marginal and lowly status of itinerant blacksmiths, and even a handful of clues, for the most part still unexplored, about their relationship to poets of various sorts. In the Darfūr region of Sudan, for example, a region where *Sīrat Banī Hilāl* is known and recited, H. A. MacMichael notes that "Iron-workers, as usual throughout Darfūr, are held in detestation, but both the Zaghāwa and the Berti [tribes] harbour small colonies of servile iron-workers from the west."[5] The blacksmiths, he goes on to explain, do not inter-

3. The most recent attempt to clarify the relationships between various "gypsy" groups in Egypt is by Nabil Subhi Hanna [Nabīl Ṣubḥī Ḥannā], *Ghajar of Sett Guiranha: A Study of a Gypsy Community in Egypt* (1982), and his more extensive *al-Binā᾽ al-ijtimā῾ī wa-l-thaqāfa fī mujtama῾ al-ghajar* (Social structure and culture in Ghajar society) (1983). Hanna prefers to classify these groups into three main categories: Ghajar, Ḥalab, and Nawar (*al-Binā᾽*, 105–10), with numerous secondary names applied regionally or to specific subgroups: Hajāla, Ṭawāyifa, Shahāniyya, Tatar, Ṣu῾āyda, Qarādatiyya, and Tahwājiyya, as well as a distinct division of pseudo-Ghajar groups, such as the Ghawāzī, Mashā῾ila, Ramādiyya and Samā῾ina or Samā῾iniyya (pp. 110–28).

Hanna also includes, however, a caveat that there is a great deal of mixing between the groups (p. 105) and openly admits that his tripartite division is unclear to both the Egyptians and the Ghajar themselves (p. 115). Although Hanna at points mentions musicians and singers among the Ghajar, he at no point identifies them with epic singers of the *Sīrat Banī Hilāl* tradition. Slyomovics, in her recent work on a *Sīrat Banī Hilāl* reciter in southern Egypt, after a discussion of Gypsy identity and social role in Egypt, leaves the question of her informant's background unresolved (see Slyomovics, *Merchant*, 13–18). It is beyond the scope of this study to attempt any general survey of these groups, but the bibliography surveys the most readily available materials on the Ghajar of Egypt.

4. See, for example, Patrick R. MacNaughton, *The Mande Blacksmith* (1988); also idem, "Nyamakalaw: The Mande Bards and Blacksmiths" (1987).

5. MacMichael, *A History* 1: 65, also p. 89.

marry with the rest of the population and constitute a virtual hereditary caste. Curiously, it is not their association with iron that appears to incite the contempt of the Zaghāwa, but their use of fire in metalworking.[6]

A possible link between blacksmiths and epic poets can be found in the name used for itinerant metalworkers in the Arabian peninsula variously referred to as the Ṣleyb, Ṣlubbah, or Ṣolubba, and a clan of epic singers in southern Egypt, known as the Maṣlūb, documented by Slyomovics.[7] Alison Lerrick writes that the solitary Banī Hilāl epic reciter shc encountered in the Arabian peninsula from the Ṣlubbah tribe had a unique performance style:

> I mention this particular transmitter because, of all the sources used in establishing the corpus, this transmitter was the only one who might be qualified as a "performer." (Note that the Slubbah are an "inferior" tribe, which in the past lived from hunting game and performed menial tasks such as smithing and leather-working.) It may therefore be of significance that only a member of the Slubbah "performed" the poems. Although this transmitter did not know an inordinate number of the poems I was looking for, his delivery was most striking. Unlike the other transmitters, he delivered the poems slowly, pausing at intervals for emphasis and making wide gestures with his arms to illustrate the poems. For example, he would mime the raising of a spear or make other expressive gestures with his hands and fingers. He thus resembled, to a certain extent, a professional minstrel.[8]

The similarity of the names of the Arabian Ṣlubbah and the southern Egyptian Maṣlūb, both possibly derived from the root *Ṣ L B*, and the similar itinerant, outcast status of the groups suggests the possibility of historical links.[9] Neither group, however, is represented in the Nile Delta region studied here. Furthermore, nowhere in Egypt is a direct connection made between metalworking and epic-singing groups such as has been studied in West Africa, nor is there a commonly held belief system that links the powers of these two crafts.

6. Ibid., 89; also n. 2, same page.

7. Charles M. Doughty, *Travels in Arabia Deserta* (1936), 1: 323–28. Note references to rock carvings of Abū Zayd and his wife, ʿAliya, in 1: 348–50, and to the grave-heap of Abū Zayd's mother, 1: 479. Slyomovics, *Merchant*, 14; Michael Meeker, *Literature and Violence in North Arabia* (1979), 21–22; Robert Montagne, *La civilisation du désert* (1947), 67–69. Note photograph, p. 128, of a Ṣleyb poet playing the rabāb.

8. Lerrick, "Taghribat," 12.

9. An argument against any historical links between the two groups has been raised by Giovanni Canova: though the term *maṣlūb* is usually pronounced with velarized /ṣ/, its plural, masālīb is usually not, making it seem more likely that the Egyptian group derives its name from a separate, distinct root /s l b/.

Arrival in al-Bakātūsh

According to information given to me by the poets about the history of their families, the family of Shaykh ʿAbd al-Wahhāb G͟hāzī[10] was the first family of poets to settle in al-Bakātūsh.

Shaykh ʿAbd al-Wahhāb G͟hāzī was born in al-Bakātūsh in 1919; his father, Shaykh G͟hāzī, was also a native of al-Bakātūsh, born sometime in the mid-1890s. His grandfather, however, was born in al-Buḥayra Province, west of the Nile. Though no one knows how long the family had been living in al-Bakātūsh before the birth of Shaykh ʿAbd al-Wahhāb's father, he was not the eldest child, so it is possible the family had been in the village for several years. Thus the family's arrival seems to have occurred sometime during the decade prior to 1890.

The family of Shaykh Ṭāhā Abū Zayd arrived in the same generation, though the dating of births here is slightly less precise. Shaykh Ṭāhā was by his own account "around seventy" in 1987; his father had been born in al-Bakātūsh, but his grandfather came originally from the eastern province of al-S͟harqiyya before settling in al-Bakātūsh. Neither family has preserved any explanation for their settling in al-Bakātūsh other than their ancestors found it to be a village of "good people" (*nās kwayyisīn*). Both villagers and poets recount that the poets' families had attempted to settle in several locations in the region, but until their arrival in al-Bakātūsh, they had only been permitted to stay for short periods of time. All evidence points to a significant shift among the poets over the past seventy-five years from a highly itinerant to a more settled lifestyle.

From these two original groups, the arrivals of all the other poets can be traced to familial and marital ties: Shaykh ʿAntar ʿAbd al-ʿāṭī was born in the province of al-Buḥayra, but when he was eleven years old, his father divorced his mother. He, his mother, and his two sisters then came to live with maternal relatives in al-Bakātūsh. He grew up supporting this female household, eventually marrying off his two sisters to poets of the al-Bakātūsh community; then he himself married the daughter of an al-Bakātūsh poet.

In a similar way, Shaykh Muḥammad Aḥmad's father was invited to come and live in al-Bakātūsh after the death of his own father (Muḥammad's grandfather). The invitation came from his paternal relative,

10. It is common practice to refer to men by their given name, then the name of their father, sometimes adding even their grandfather's name, and finally their "family name," this latter being to some extent a convention instituted in the twentieth century. Thus Shaykh ʿAbd al-Wahhāb G͟hāzī is ʿAbd al-Wahhāb, son of G͟hāzī. The term *shaykh*, from which English "sheik," is an honorific of address and reference; I have used an anglicized form closer to the original s͟hayk͟h, though without the diacritics. For the family names of the poets, see below.

Shaykh G̲h̲āzī (father of Shaykh ʿAbd al-Wahhāb). When Shaykh Muḥammad Aḥmad's father died, leaving his son still a teenager and unmarried, the young Shaykh Muḥammad was taken in by Shaykh ʿAbd al-Wahhāb's family and later married to one of Shaykh ʿAbd al-Wahhāb's daughters.

Another poet, Shaykh ʿAbd al-Ḥamīd Tawfīq, grew up in a family that traveled great distances. His grandfather was born in the eastern province of al-S̲h̲arqiyya and eventually settled in al-Bakātūsh. The father, Shaykh Tawfīq, continued to travel with his young family until his death, at which point his son, ʿAbd al-Ḥamīd Tawfıq (born in the province of al-Minya, south of Cairo), came to live with his grandfather in al-Bakātūsh, from whom he learned to sing Sīrat Banī Hilāl and with whom he traveled as a young apprentice.

Of the fourteen households of poets in al-Bakātūsh, all but two have come to the village from the province of al-Buḥayra, west of the Nile. Shaykh Ṭāhā's family came directly from the eastern province of al-S̲h̲arqiyya, and Shaykh ʿAbd al-Ḥamīd's family came from al-S̲h̲arqiyya via the southern provinces.

Similar accounts of marriages, untimely deaths, and divorces account for the arrival of the other family units. (See fig. 2 for a schematized presentation of the male lines of descent in the poet community.)

The growth of the al-Bakātūsh community of poets seems to have been a natural accrual of familial and marital ties. Just as there is a history of family units moving into al-Bakātūsh, however, there is also a history of individuals leaving the community by marriage (usually, though not always, women), as well as whole family units leaving to settle in new locations. Two such departures occurred in recent years when families left al-Bakātūsh and moved north to the village of Sadd al-K̲h̲amīs in the markaz 'district' of Sīdī Sālim, where previously there had been no poets residing; the move, therefore, was seen as auspicious.

In addition, during the second period of my research, 1986–87, a further departure took place, one that resulted in tragedy. The family of Shaykh Muḥammad Aḥmad bought a house in a hamlet about one hour east of al-Bakātūsh, sold their home in al-Bakātūsh, and moved. Two weeks later, while riding his donkey on the side of the road, Shaykh Muḥammad Aḥmad was struck and killed by a passing taxi; he was survived by his wife and four young children. The young widow and her children chose stay in their new home and not to return to al-Bakātūsh.

Departures from the al-Bakātūsh community have been motivated almost entirely by economic pressures. The existence of more than two or three poets in the same location places a greater economic burden on

Figure 2. Poet families of al-Bakātūsh

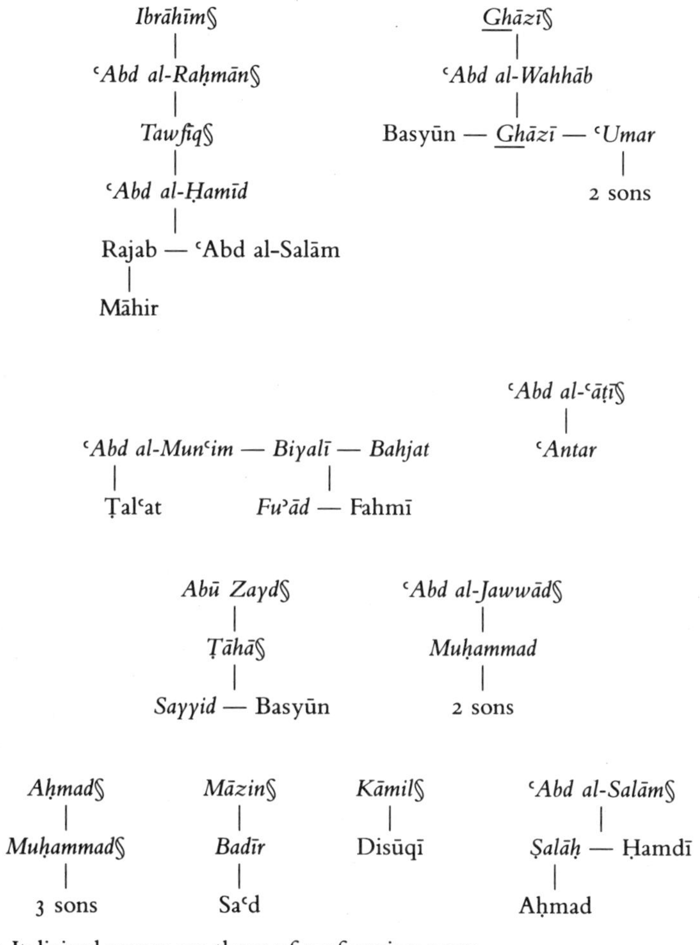

Notes: Italicized names are those of performing poets
§ = deceased poets

all concerned. With such a high concentration, poets must travel farther, acquire secondary sources of income, and eventually even separate. All of these conditions are found in al-Bakātūsh. Female members of the poet community have probably always contributed a significant portion to the household income; in recent years, however, income earned by wives and daughters, as well as by younger men in the community who are working at outside jobs, has surpassed the income brought in by the poet heads of households. Poets who have left al-Bakātūsh with their families have all moved to outlying areas such as Sīdī Sālim, or to areas in the province of al-Buḥayra which are considered more rural, further removed from urban influences, and consequently where a greater audience for *Sīrat Banī Hilāl* is still to be found. These poets spoke openly about both the economic advantages to be gained in more rural areas and the social disadvantages they experienced in not having a community of their own with whom to socialize in their new locations.

For the poets and their families, relations within their community are determined by many overlapping layers of familial and marital ties. Everyone is related, usually by blood and marriage, and all are related to at least eleven other smaller communities of poets in the Nile Delta as well as more loosely related to other communities in urban areas and farther south in Upper Egypt.[11] Despite the strong ties that bind them to other poets' communities, the poets all stress their roots in al-Bakātūsh.

Interaction with the Village at Large

Poets as Outsiders: "Looking In"

The phrases "they are not from among us" (*humum mish minenā*) and "they are not originally from here" (*humum mish aṣlan min hinā*) followed me about like an endless litany for the first few months of my stay in al-Bakātūsh. Only when the villagers were entirely convinced that I fully understood this distinction did they cease to remind me of this invisible boundary. Such is the sense of the poets as outsiders and newcomers in al-Bakātūsh that young men of the village in their twenties often told me that the poets had arrived, or had been brought in, sometime immediately preceding the young men's births or when they had been very young children. Invariably they were startled when older men would explain that some of the poets' families had been in the village for several generations.

Time and again I encountered a sequence of questions which occurred whenever anyone asked publicly about the origins of the poets. The interlocutor would ask, "Where are you [pl.] originally from?" The poet would respond, often somewhat gruffly, "From al-Bakātūsh." Then the

11. The communities recognized by the al-Bakātūsh poets include families in Basyūn (Gharbiyya), Sadd al-Khamīs/Sīdī Sālim (Kafr al-Shaykh), Faraskūr (Damyāṭ), Zāwiyat Abū Shūsha/Dilinjāt (Buḥayra), Nakhlat al-Baḥariyya/Abū Ḥummus (Buḥayra), Kūm Ḥamāda/Dilinjāt (Buḥayra), Zāwiyat Qarawān/Shibīn (Gharbiyya), Kafr Ibrāsh/Mashtūl al-Sūq (Sharqiyya), as well as the (unrelated) family of Sayyid Ḥawwās in Sandabast/Ziftā (Gharbiyya) and several nonperforming households in the greater Cairo area and in the southern province of al-Minya.

question would be recast as "Where were you [sing.] born?" And many villagers, particularly the young, would be surprised to learn that not only were poets in their late sixties and early seventies such as Shaykh Ṭāhā Abū Zayd and Shaykh ʿAbd al-Wahhāb born in al-Bakātūsh, but that their fathers before them had been as well. Often this information stopped the line of questioning, but occasionally someone would persist to the grandfather's generation and receive what they had expected all along, the name of a different region or province.

Many accounts of the arrival of the poets in al-Bakātūsh were proffered me by villagers, all of which probably contain some nuggets of historical truth. One typical version is recounted here:

> Dwight: Does anyone know anything about their origins?
>
> Shamlī: A long time ago there was a a big open area near Disūq . . . and the ghajar [Gypsies] came and started living there, *badū* [Bedouin] from the desert, in tents.[12] Eventually one poet and his wife came to al-Minshalīn [village near al-Bakātūsh], but they would not let them live there; they came to al-Bakātūsh and settled. And then they brought relatives and married off their children and their number grew. They used to live in tents at the edges of the village, when the area you [to me] live in wasn't built on at all.
>
> Dwight: When it was still the fish pond?
>
> Shamlī: Right. God was generous to them, and they started building small huts; then that one bought a little land for a house, and now they all live in houses.
>
> (Shamlī Ḥarfūsh, 5/9/87)

The poets did in fact first live in tents at the edge of the village. Where they first began to build houses is now known as "the poets' alley" (*ḥāret al-shuʿara*), although not all the residents of the alley are poets. It is still only a few yards removed from the open fields. Seven of the fourteen households are in this alleyway, five others are in adjoining alleys, and two (Shaykh ʿAbd al-Wahhāb Ghāzī and Shaykh Biyalī Abū Fahmī, the two most popular performers) have relocated to other areas of al-Bakātūsh. (See fig. 3 for a map of the village and the locations of the poets' houses.)

Though nearly two-thirds of the houses in al-Bakātūsh have been rebuilt in red brick over the past decade as a result of money earned by family members working abroad, all of the houses in the poets' alley are mud brick, and in 1988 all but one of the poets' households still

12. This conflation of poets/Gypsies/Bedouin is quite common. See discussion below of the term *ʿarab* in this chapter.

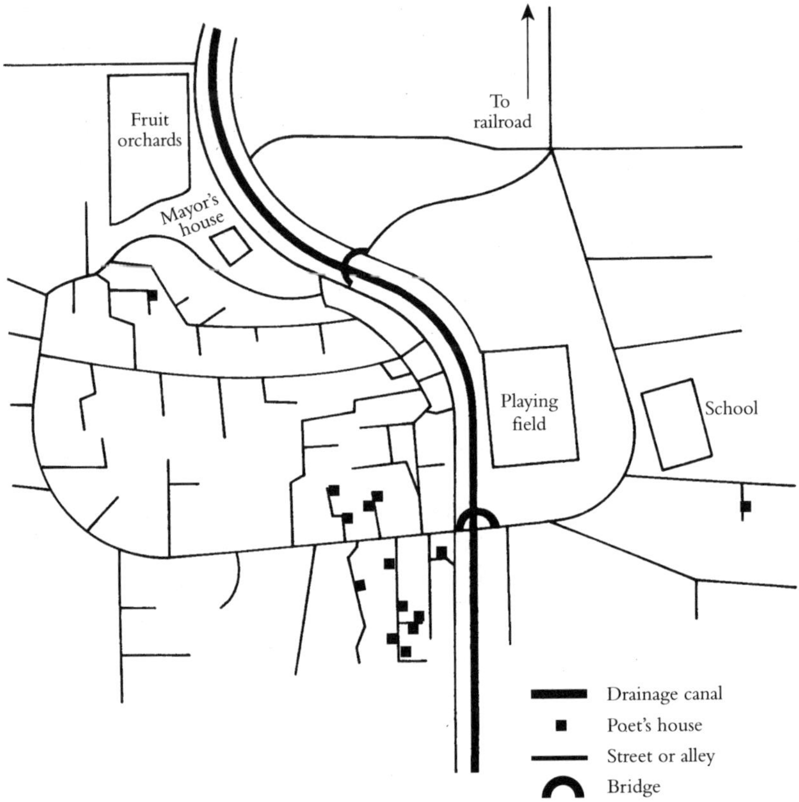

Figure 3. Residence patterns in al-Bakātūsh

lived in mud-brick homes. Furthermore, none of the poets own agricultural land of any sort, though they do own the plots their houses stand on. The poet community taken as a whole constitutes the lowest economic stratum of the village.

Other than the poets' lack of landownership, the mark of separation between the two commmunities most often cited by villagers and poets is the fact that the two groups do not intermarry. Villagers marry other villagers, and poets marry from other poets' families. As one Ḥalabī woman put it: "We don't marry peasants [*fellāḥīn*] and they don't marry us. The Ḥalab marry each other. We have our own customs—we don't marry except with each other. That way no one can say 'You're the daughter of a such-and-such' [*bint kāzā wa-kāzā*]" (wife of Shaykh ʿAbd al-Ḥamīd, 6/3/87).

Despite this often-repeated stricture against mixed marriages, two have taken place in al-Bakātūsh in living memory. One was successful: it has lasted many years and represents the only poet household living in a red-brick house; the two sons have work abroad, and the father no longer performs *Sīrat Banī Hilāl*. Though this man was very forthcoming in interviews and clearly at one point in his life possessed an extensive repertory (he was often cited by the oldest men in the village as one of the top three poets of al-Bakātūsh), he refused to perform or be recorded throughout my stay. The other marriage lasted only a few years and then ended in divorce.

A further, and curious, indication of the separation of the two communities involves the issue of family names. As we saw in Chapter 1, the social power structure of al-Bakātūsh is built on the interaction of large clans of interrelated families. These clans are perceived as "powerful" versus "weak," and "original" versus "newcomers." Within the clans a secondary level of identification of families corresponds to some extent to the use in the West of family names. It is this name which appears on one's personal identification carnet, the official papers that must be carried by all Egyptians which state their name, address, occupation, and military service (if any). The name on the identification carnet is only rarely that of the larger clan, or extended family, to which one belongs. Thus to identify a person in conversation in al-Bakātūsh, or to distinguish between persons who have the same given name, one says So-and-so al-Najjār, or al-Shūra, or Ḥaydar, or Jalama, that is, using "family names." To understand the implications of this information, however, one must often also be aware that these are members of the extended families, or clans, of Ḥarfūsh, Janāḥ, Kurdī, or Sirḥān.[13]

To the villagers of al-Bakātūsh, the poets have no family or clan names. They are known and referred to only as Shaykh—— —— *al-shāʿir* (lit. the Poet), using their given name and then father's name before the title "the Poet." This title is applied to all members of the poets' families, whether or not they are poets in the usual sense of the term. Young men who have never played rabāb and never sung, who are in the army, or work as builders, apprentice carpenters, or traders, are still So-and-so "the Poet." This is the only means the larger community has for identifying them. It is also the only means the government has for

13. These forms are those used when citing a specific name; in reference to the extended families, collective noun formations are used so that, for example, one refers to the Ḥarfūsh extended family as the Ḥarafsha, the Sirḥān family as the Saraḥna. Some short extended-family names, such as Janāḥ, do not take this collective nominal form and remain unchanged.

For an examination of differing levels of household and family organization, and their respective roles in village power structures, see Jacques Berque, "Sur la structure sociale de quelques villages égyptiens" (1955).

identifying them. The word *al-shāʿir* appears as their "name" on the poets' identity cards and even the passports of the few who possess them.

Most villagers simply denied that poets possess family or clan names. In fact, many expressed surprise that I knew the first names of all the poets individually, and would even laugh and ask for a physical description to see if they could place the poet of whom I was speaking (and this in a community where great pride is taken in being able to identify all members by name and ancestry). To identify any villager, they would ask for the father's name and family name. For them, the poets' families did not participate in the larger, on-going genealogy of the village; they were not locatable on the intricate map of blood, conjugal, and marital ties in which all other residents of the village were presumed part.

One intense encounter in the early part of my fieldwork proved this common notion that poets do not possess family names wrong and led to a rapid change in my status vis-à-vis the poet community. I was spending an evening with a group of young men from the poets' families, none of whom themselves were performing poets, and we began to discuss disagreements that had occurred recently between the fathers of several of the young men present. The tensions were easy to understand: here were men in their late teens and early twenties who as yet had little independence from their fathers, and when disagreements arose, these often affected their close friendships within this small community. One young man made an offhand remark: "It's just the old story of the X's versus the Y's again" (using collective noun forms usually reserved for extended-family names). I immediately asked what he meant, and, after hesitating a moment, he explained which of the fourteen households belonged to which of three extended clans. This new information in fact explained a great deal about who performed with whom when there were big jobs such as weddings which require two poets, and about internal relations within the poets' community. I was not, however, aware of how sensitive this information would prove to be.

Later in the week I began to record from a poet with whom I had not previously worked. The sahra/recording session was to be at the home of my host family, Aḥmad Ba<u>kh</u>ātī. After the poet arrived and had settled in the mandara, the men's sitting room, we were immediately served a pot of tea and began to talk. One other villager joined us (most people would not actually enter until they heard the music begin). I asked a number of my usual questions about repertory, family history, and so forth, and then, in an attempt to verify the information I had received about family names, I asked the poet, "So, are you from the clan of X or Y?"

The poet looked quite shocked, and his face immediately displayed his displeasure. He leaned over to me and, with a sharp glance at the villager, who, thank heavens, seemed to be occupied with his own thoughts, whispered angrily, "Where did you learn those names?" I covered my blunder as best I could, but other guests began to arrive and we had to rise to greet them. I was given no opportunity to undo my faux pas during the evening.

The following afternoon I went to visit a poet whom I had already recorded. I recounted the incident quite openly, holding back only the circumstances in which I had originally learned these names. This poet assessed the situation as grave and stated that if the poet I had spoken with chose to tell other poets in the village about it, my position in the community could become quite strained. He and his wife grilled me about who had mentioned these names to me. I put them off, but they basically made up their own minds about who it must have been. I explained many times over that I was not there to divulge secrets, but had indeed been unaware that these names were not commonly used. I had thought they were used like everyone else's names. The poet's wife argued on my behalf: "He understands now [*huwwa wākhud bāluh dilwaqt*], and there was no real harm done."

A plan was laid out. My friend was to go visit the other poet and explain the situation. In an hour I was to drop by the other poet's house "by chance" for tea. This I did. When I arrived it was clear that all was settled. We talked the situation over, and, though the hour was early, dinner was brought out and served. There was clearly no possibility of refusing this invitation, though I had already accepted a dinner invitation elsewhere, for it was my first invitation to eat a meal in a poet's home; it was only one of many times I was forced by circumstances to eat a meal twice over to meet the demands of village etiquette. As we drank tea after the meal, my friend stated once again for everyone's benefit, "He didn't know it was any different from other names in the village." Our host looked at me and smiled, "But now he knows." I never learned anything more about the subject. One happy result, however, was that within days I had received invitations to eat at nearly all of the poets' homes. One barrier had been set up, but another had been removed.

The inhabitants of al-Bakātūsh hold various attitudes about the regional nickname for their village—the Village of the Poets (*balad al-shuʿara*). On the one hand, the nickname represents part of the village's fame and status in the region; on the other, this aspect is often referred to sarcastically and even used directly to insult the inhabitants. A significant emblem of this ambiguity occurs whenever reference is made to al-

Bakātūsh in conversation, for it is likely to be accompanied by a hand gesture intimately associated with the village: holding the left arm straight down, the right arm saws across it horizontally in imitation of a poet holding and playing a rabāb (the right arm figures as the bow, the left as the instrument). Reactions to this gesture range from overt anger and demands for an apology to good-humored laughter and half-hearted attempts to ignore it.

The following short incidents outline some of the tensions and contradictory feelings the villagers associate with the presence of the poets, after which I examine how the poets view their relationship to the larger community:

In a long interview conducted with an inhabitant of al-Bakātūsh who works as an elementary school teacher, the conversation wove back and forth between aesthetic evaluations of different poets and performances, and the embarrassment and confusion he felt as a young man going to school in town, where everyone teased him about the reputation of the village. He recounted that one day he walked into his high school classroom to find that someone had written his name in chalk on the board and under it the words "Village of the Poets." The teacher entered soon afterward and, not noticing the writing, began to teach class. The epithet remained on the board all during the first part of class till the teacher finally turned to write something on the board and, of course, erased it.

This man, now in his early forties, described how painful that jibe had been and how even now he grows angry thinking about it. With some clear consternation about my possible reaction, he went on to explain how he and his classmates, when they found a poet performing on the train, for example, would rough the poet up and force him off the train at the next stop, wherever that might be. Apologetically he noted that he now thinks of this with shame, but not with as much shame, he added, as he used to feel at school when other students would shout "Village of the Poets" after him on the way to and from school.[14]

During my stay in the village in 1986–87, one of the poets traveled to Saudi Arabia on pilgrimage, after years of painstaking saving. Two younger villagers who openly sympathized with the new revivalist interpretations of Islam remarked to me that this pilgrimage would surely not be accepted by God. Among the reasons they cited were that (1) poets lived off vagrancy (*tasawwul*); (2) their livelihood was really only a form of begging; (3) acquiring enough money for the pilgrimage through begging must be considered wrong or forbidden (ḥarām); and

14. The name of this informant has been omitted at his own request.

(4) the epic itself is un-Islamic ignorance, for it represents frivolity and licentiousness (*lahw*).

They believed that "there is something of the *ḥarām* [wrong, forbidden] in this [pilgrimage], because that is money he got from begging. One shouldn't go around wearing old, torn clothes and then go off on pilgrimage—and then he'll come back and continue begging. One should go on pilgrimage with money one has earned from *working*! That is why his *ʿumra*[15] won't be accepted [*maqbūla*] [i.e., by God]" (5/10/87).

I conducted no systematic survey of villagers' attitudes toward the poets as I attempted to do about their attitudes toward the epic (see Chap. 3). Though discussion of the epic embarrassed no one, discussion of the poets and their role in village society was clearly more sensitive, if only because the poets themselves, whom I most closely befriended and wished to portray sympathetically, would have suffered embarrassment at any continuous or obviously systematic investigation of their presence and history. Though I had many discussions with people about the relations between the poet and nonpoet communities, these were usually the result of opportunities I exploited in daily conversations, not preplanned schedules of questions.

Some basic patterns, however, are readily apparent: tolerance, or the lack of it, toward the presence of the poets in the village modulates in tandem with people's attitudes toward the epic itself. Groups who still patronize the epic, though they may not consider the poets their social equals, openly defend their presence in the village. This defense is usually couched in religious or aphoristic sentiments dealing with the equality of men before God, the idea that we shall all encounter the same final judgment, or that God created men in different ranks (a reference to two verses from the Qurʾān usually taken to refer to social and economic differences between classes).[16] In addition, villagers who are positively disposed toward the poets often state simply that the poets are poor (*g͟halbānīn*) and should therefore be treated with sympathy.

Groups who disdain the epic are equally likely to object to the presence of the poets in the village on social or moral grounds. Slyomovics, conducting work in Upper Egypt, encountered a society where the epic

15. *ʿUmra* is pilgrimage effected at any time other than the annual month of pilgrimage; it is usually considered to count as only one-half of a full pilgrimage.

16. "He it is who hath placed you as viceroys of the earth and hath exalted some of you in rank above others, that He may try you by [the test of] that which He hath given you. Lo! Thy Lord is swift in prosecution, and lo! He is Forgiving, Merciful" (Qurʾān 6:165).

"We have apportioned among them their livelihood in the life of the world, and raised some of them above others in rank that some of them may take labour from others; and the mercy of thy Lord is better than (the wealth) that they amass" (Qurʾān 43:32).

Both quotes from Pickthall, *Glorious Qurʾan*.

itself was apparently still nearly universally respected, yet even then the person of the poet was not respected.[17] In al-Bakātūsh the situation is far more complex, with diverse educational and age groups expressing widely differing opinions about both the epic and its performers.

In the context of the tight social bonds of village life, the poets and their families exist in a slightly dislocated world. Although visiting, drinking tea, and sharing meals are major pastimes in village social life, I encountered villagers in poets' homes less than a dozen times—and I *never* encountered a poet on a social visit in a villager's home. There is no apparent social division in public places; in cafés, in the groups seated on the bridge at dusk, and at public celebrations, no overt separation occurs. But privately, the poets' community socializes in its own restricted circles.

The definiteness of these social boundaries was forcefully brought home to me at the very end of my stay with the death of the poet Shaykh Muḥammad Aḥmad. At the death of a villager, every household must send a male member to visit the family during the first week following the death. These mourning visitors are received in the men's guest room, or outside if the weather permits, where benches are set up for this purpose. The visitors are offered something to drink and cigarettes by relatives of the deceased. The proper duration of the visit is held to be in proportion to the closeness of one's relationship to the deceased. Every household must send a representative; failure to do so constitutes a breach of etiquette which signals enmity. When such a breach occurs, the incident is cause for lengthy discussion by adult members of the community.

During the period of mourning after the death of Shaykh Muḥammad Aḥmad the Poet, no villagers were in attendance other than those who accompanied me on my visits. Rather than spilling out into public space, filling the open areas, the threshing floors, and the alleyways themselves, the funeral of the poet occupied a single, small room in the home of another poet.

To sum up then, the poets' community exists in many ways as a marginalized and peripheralized social group. Though not precisely a distinct ethnic group, the members are perceived by other villagers as possessing origins and identities different from their own. The poets are marked and perceived by villagers as accepted outsiders, but still outsiders. They are separated by residential patterns, lack of land ownership, and special economic status. The poets are excluded from the marriage ties, patterns of social exchange and obligation, and access to

17. Slyomovics, *Merchant*, 13–18.

power which are normal to other villagers. Their social roles are defined by their status as outsiders.

Villagers as Outsiders: "Looking Out"

Publicly, the poets stress their roots in al-Bakātūsh; in the privacy of their homes, however, they discuss relations with the community at large in different terms—terms of opposition and differentiation. Villagers are referred to as *fellāḥīn* (SA *fallāḥūn*), that is, farmers or peasants, or, in poets' slang, as the *ʿas̲h̲īr*. The first term is normally a term of pride in rural areas. It derives from a verb meaning "to till, cultivate, and farm." The derived form, *fellāḥ,* renders the doer of the action, that is, the farmer. Another derived form, *falāḥ*, gives an abstraction signifying success, prosperity, well-being. This second nominal form occurs in the daily call to prayers and is thus very much an active derivation of this root.[18] In political discourse, the term *fellāḥ* is coded to refer to "real Egyptians," people who own and farm the land, the backbone of Egypt, Egypt's greatest resource. In an urban milieu the term may be used derogatorily to indicate lack of education, provincialism, naiveté, even stubbornness. In the village setting, however, even those who are educated, who hold government posts, and who represent the elite of village society do not often use the term pejoratively, for it strikes too close to home.

The second term for villagers, *ʿas̲h̲īr*, derives from the concept of companionship and time spent living in proximity to someone. *ʿIs̲h̲ra* is what one develops with neighbors who are not related by blood or marriage; it is the friendship and loyalty that arises from propinquity. The term *ʿas̲h̲īr* is rare in Egyptian colloquial Arabic, however, for one does not say that so-and-so is my ʿas̲h̲īr,[19] though if one asks how and why two people are friends, the response might well be simply: ʿis̲h̲ra.[20]

In private discussions among the poets these terms take on new meanings, for they codify those characteristics that in the poets' perceptions

18. That these two ideas, "farmer" and "prosperity," are commonly linked is clear from a recurring children's joke that plays on the mixing up of the two words and has the muezzin calling "ḥayy ʿalā l-ṣalā, ḥayy ʿalā l-ṣalā, ḥayy ʿalā l-fellāḥ" (instead of *falāḥ),* "Come to Prayer! Come to Prayer! Come to the Farmer!" rather than "Come to Success!"

19. This form, for example, does not appear in either Socrates Spiro, *Arabic-English Dictionary of the Colloquial Arabic of Egypt* (1980), or in Hinds and Badawi, *A Dictionary of Egyptian Arabic.*

20. A similar concept lies in the phrase *ʿēsh wi-malḥ* (lit. bread and salt), i.e., "we have broken bread together"—a "companion" in the literal sense of the word. For an extensive discussion of these terms, also in an Egyptian context, see Lila Abu-Lughod, *Veiled Sentiments* (1986), chap. 2, particularly pp. 63–65.

are not shared between the two communities. They contrast the terms *fellāḥ* and *ʿashīr* with the terms *ʿarab* 'Arabs' and *shāʿir* 'poet'.[21] To themselves they relegate the qualities of eloquence and cleverness, and the status of bearers of, and participants in, ancient Arab customs and traditions. They represent an "Arabness" that predates and is purer than that of cultivators and tillers of the soil.

The evenings I spent in the homes of the poets were often filled with displays of verbal art; folktales, proverbs, riddles, and improvisatory poetry were the most common genres. After a particularly well-told tale, one poet's son leaned over to me and said, "You'd never hear anything like that in a fellāḥ's home; all he has to talk about is his water buffalo and his clover harvest!" This comment sums up quite well the tone with which tales and poetry were performed: this is what separates and defines us. Though never bitter or vindictive in their criticism, the poets constantly contrasted the eloquence of their conversation with the mundane realities of the fellāḥ's world. My own ability to recite poetry by heart, to play lute (ʿūd) and rabāb, and to sing were often cited by the poets as evidence that I was somehow closer to them than to the fellāḥīn, though I had many times recounted that my maternal grandfather and grandmother grew up on a farm and a sheep ranch respectively.

It is in this capacity as preservers of eloquence and beautiful expression (*faṣāḥa wa-balāgha*) that the poets referred to themselves as *shuʿara*. Another of their roles is symbolized by use of the term *ʿarab*. In this capacity, the poets view themselves as true Arabs, maintaining customs and traditions that either never existed among the fellāḥīn or have now died out.

In Egypt, several specific groups are referred to as Arabs. The desert Bedouin are called Arabs, as are persons from the Arabian peninsula. Egyptians usually refer to themselves as Arabs only in the context of Pan-Arab nationalism and in terms of international politics, a reference to the Nasserite ideal of a single Arab nation encompassing all Arabic speakers. Finally, however, "Arab" is also a term used in referring to marginal social groups within Egypt and functions as a systematic indicator of the Other within Egyptian society. Thus, the poets of al-Bakātūsh are addressed and referred to in the village as Arabs because they are Gypsies. The heroes of the epic are also referred to as Arabs, for they are Bedouin heroes. The poets, however, inside and outside their performances stress that they are Arabs just like the heroes of whom they sing. In reality, no known historical link exists between the Bedouin and the epic poets. The epic heroes are Arabs because they were Bedouin;

21. Despite the simple metathetical relation between the opposing terms *ʿashīr* and *shāʿir* (*ʿ/Sh/R* and *Sh/ʿ/R*), I never heard the two used as puns in wordplay or in poetry.

the epic poets are Arabs because polite consensus allows speakers to substitute "Arab" for "Gypsy." The only time I heard this appellation challenged, by a young man who stated that the poets were not Arabs like the desert Arabs, an older man cut him off by jumping into the larger, political frame and declaring, "We're all Arabs, aren't we?"

The Term "Arab" in Egyptian Usage

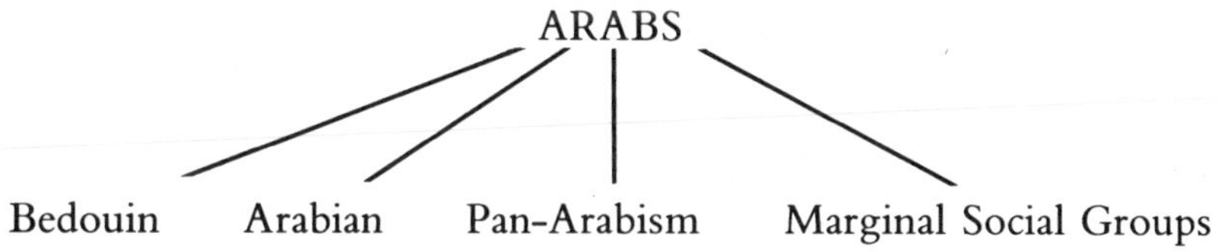

Thus:

Bedouins = Arabs *and* Poets = Arabs

One of the most popular types of folktales told in evening gatherings in the poets' homes clearly portrays the poets' sense of differentiation from the villagers and of their own distinct identity. Tales of this type further substantiate the asserted ties with desert Arabs.

One tale opens with a king and his *wazīr* 'vizier' deciding to disguise themselves and go out into the world to see and understand the condition of the people.[22] They wander in the desert and encounter a Bedouin encampment. The husband, the shaykh of the Arabs, is not present, but his wife greets them and invites them in: "Greetings, O Princes!" (ahlan yā umarāʾ). Later she greets them again: "You have honored us, O Captives!" (sharraftūnā yā usarāʾ). Still later she calls out: "O welcome, O Poets!" (yā marḥab yā shuʿarāʾ).

When the shaykh of the Arabs returns, the king and the wazīr tell him angrily, if somewhat perplexedly, that his wife greeted them once with due respect but then twice insulted them. The shaykh asks what his wife said and they tell him. He responds that her greetings were all

22. This motif is one of the most common in Middle Eastern folk literatures. Not only does it occur many times in collections such as the *Alf layla wa-layla* (The thousand and one nights), but is also attributed to innumerable rulers in historical chronicles and probably has some basis in fact. In al-Bakātūsh, stories are also told of Jamāl ʿAbd al-Nāṣir (Nasser) coming to nearby villages and staying several days, often doing many good deeds such as helping widows. Despite the fact that Nasser's photograph was displayed everywhere, in these anecdotes the villagers never realize their guest's identity until after he leaves. At least three quite different narratives of this genre concerning Nasser are currently in circulation in al-Bakātūsh.

respectful. They ask how can it be respectful to address guests first as princes, then as captives, and finally as poets. The shaykh responds: "As our guests, are you not our captives? If we spread out rugs on the left, will you not come and sit on the left, and if we spread out rugs on the right will you not come sit on the right (i.e., you will do as we say). And after you leave us, if we have been generous will you not 'poetize' to your neighbors of our generosity, and if we are stingy, will you not 'poetize' to your neighbors of our stinginess?"

The king and wazīr agree and are mollified. They then continue on their way and meet an old man, a fisherman, walking with a cane. They greet him and he returns their greeting but then adds: "What was two has become three; what was far has become near."

The king and wazīr are so puzzled by his response that they offer the old man ten pounds for an explanation: "I was young and have become old, I used to walk on two legs and now walk on three, and the city I used to be able to see from far away, I can now only see when near."[23]

A number of these tales share a characteristic demonstrated in the tale summarized above. After the main encounter with the Bedouin (*ʿarab*) which forms the bulk of the story, the narrative moves on to a secondary, and briefer, encounter with a non-Bedouin. In some tales this move clearly demonstrates the difference between the ʿarab and other groups, for where the former were generous, the latter prove stingy and mean, where the Bedouin seems to have insulted his guests, his words turn out to be both proper and wise, and in the second encounter the king often encounters men whose words appear to be compliments but are meant as sarcasms or insults. In the tale presented above and several others, the secondary move appears not to be presented as a direct contrast, but rather as a commentary. Another tale moves in slightly different fashion.

There was once an Arab who lived in a tent in the desert. One day a king and his wazīr decided to go out to see the state of the world. They wore green upon green. They arrived at the tent and the king clapped his hands. The woman saw that they were guests and immediately prepared room for them to sit. They drank tea, and the Arab slaughtered a she-camel for them and fed them (still not knowing who they were). As the king left, he slipped sixty dinars into a handkerchief and left it beneath one of the cushions. The woman found it and called to her husband to run after the guests because one of them had accidentally left his money there. He ran after them and caught up with them.

23. Texts of stories in this chapter are paraphrased from handwritten notes of various performances; none are from audio-recorded or directly transcribed versions.

But the king said no, that was money for the meal they ate. The Arab refused it. So the king, in order to do something for the Arab, explained that he was a king and invited the Arab to come visit in the city.

There the Arab stayed as a guest in the palace and went with the king to mosque. He saw the king after prayers asking God, *yā rabb* (O Lord!) with his palms outstretched, as if asking for wealth. When the Arab returned to his tent in the desert, he decided to do the same thing. But when he said "Yā rabb," a wind lifted his tent from over his head and blew it away. When he and his wife set up the tent in the spot where the tent had landed, they found a treasure.

Time passed and the Arab built a beautiful palace and garden. The king decided to visit the generous Arab who had befriended them. To their surprise they found he now had a palace and garden. The wazīr began to suggest to the king that they kill the Arab to gain his money. At first the king was quite opposed, but "Much speech affects the mind" (kathr al-kalām yuʾaththir fī l-dimāgh), and he was eventually convinced to pretend to have dreamed a dream and to ask the Arab to interpret it. The wazīr suggested that the king tell the Arab that in his dream he heard three times the sound "how" (*hawhaw* is the Egyptian Colloquial Arabic verb for a dog's barking), the idea being that the Arab would say it was only the barking of a dog, which the king would take as an insult and use as a pretext for killing him.

Instead, the Arab responded that this dream is one seen only by the mighty and high-born and presented his explanation in a poem:

awwal haw rāziq iṭ-ṭīr fī j-jaw
tānī haw rāziq il-ʿibād taw bi-taw
tālit haw nadmān fī ʿār is-saw
wi-bnī fī milkak wi-ghēr milkak law

The poem is built on reinterpreting the sound *haw* as the masculine singular pronoun *huwa* 'he', particularly in the specialized form *hū* used during the Sufi *dhikr* ritual (extended recitation of the name of God). Thus the first two verses refer to God as Sustainer of the birds and the beasts, and to God as Sustainer of all true worshipers, while the third and fourth verses refer to Man, who should eschew evil and should not covet the wealth of others, and here, of course, specifically to the wicked wazīr.

The first *haw* is He who gives sustenance to the birds of the air;
The second *haw* is He who gives sustenance to His worshipers
immediately and always;

The third *haw* is he that (should) repent of evil-doing,
And of coveting your wealth, even if it be the wealth of
others.

After hearing these words, the king drew his sword and killed the wazīr, and instated the Arab as his new wazīr. Once again the honesty and virtue of the word-wielding Arab triumphed through his display of poetic prowess. The vast majority of these tales concern cleverness, propriety, eloquence, and virtue. In each tale the Bedouin (that is, the ʿarab, for the term "Bedouin" [*badū*] occurs only rarely in the epic or these folktales) are those most skilled in courtoisie and etiquette. Just as the king and other characters within the tales learn to appreciate these special qualitites of the "Arabs," so the families of the poets are inculcated with an appreciation of their own identifying characteristics during these domestic performances. The connection between epic poets and the ʿarab is, furthermore, often made entirely overt when these tales are told in the presence of children, for it is not uncommon for adults to comment afterward to the children that their fathers/uncles/grandfathers are just as eloquent as the characters of the story. These are in fact tales that set in direct confrontation the idealized self-image of the Poet against the outer world's derogatory portrayal of his craft and community.

As members of the category "Arabs," the poets also conceive of themselves as having a special relationship with other groups designated as Arabs. The Nile Delta poets particularly feel this way toward a group known as the *ʿarab al-g͟hināma* or the 'herding Arabs.' These are not desert Bedouin, at least not in modern times, in the full sense of the term, but rather tribal groups who spend most of the year in the eastern province of al-Sharqiyya where they own land and maintain permanent residences. Following the seasons, they drive their herds across the delta into the province of Kafr al-Shaykh and other areas, where they graze their animals on the stubble left in the fields after the harvests. At this time the open areas between al-Bakātūsh and the provincial capital, Kafr al-Shaykh, are thickly dotted with black tents and grazing herds.[24] Weddings among the "herding Arabs" are celebrated with epic performances and with *ḍarb al-kaff* (lit. the striking of the palms), that is, traditional Bedouin-style dancing accompanied by a line of men singing and clapping.[25] Since ḍarb al-kaff is the preferred evening activity and

24. An account of the ethnic makeup of the population of Sharqiyya Province in the mid-twentieth century can be found in ʿAbbās M. ʿAmmar, *The People of the Sharqiyah: Their Racial History, Serology, Physical Characters, Demography and Conditions of Life* (1944), 1: 1–43.

25. The distinctive clapping style of this activity gives it its name. The left palm is held face up, fingers pointing away from the body; the right hand then claps downward and outward onto the left hand in a thrusting movement so that both swing out and away from the body.

often lasts all night long, epic performances must take place during the day. The al-Bakātūsh poets state incontrovertibly that the "herding Arabs" are the only group for whom they are willing to sing during the daytime, "while the sun is in the sky." The ʿarab al-ghināma are also known as supporters of the Zaghāba clan in the epic (the clan of Diyāb rather than the clan of Abū Zayd), and the poets tell many anecdotes about angry audience members from the "herding Arabs" causing trouble owing to a perceived slight against "their" hero, Diyāb.[26]

Among the domestic customs which the poets believe mark them as true Arabs is the absolute obligation of serving two rounds of drink, whether this be tea, coffee, hibiscus infusion, fenugreek infusion, cinnamon infusion, or other fare, to any male who enters the house as a guest. Though offering drinks and refreshments to guests is common in many contexts in Egypt, the poets hold to this more rigidly than other villagers and cite the serving of two rather than only one round as a distinguishing characteristic. One poet in the village constantly drank coffee rather than the usual tea. In private he cited this to me and to his children and grandchildren as an Arab custom; in public he stated that he drank coffee for health reasons, that his stomach could not handle tea.

In the poets' community, younger children and even young adults will, when greeting an older male (particularly a relative), bend down and kiss the back of his hand. Though this custom was apparently widespread in Egyptian society until the early twentieth century, villagers who accompanied me on visits to the poets' homes expressed shock and surprise at this behavior, and on several occasions wrested their hands away before the greeting was completed.

Another custom perceived by the poets as essentially Arab is that men and women socialize and talk much more easily within the poets' community than in the larger community, and children are more easily included in adult conversation. I rapidly grew to know almost all of the female members of the poets' community, while even after several years of contact I have met the womenfolk of only a handful of nonpoet households in the village. Again, this behavior is attributed to pure Arab tradition, in opposition to the traditions of the villagers. The villagers, however, maintain a diametrically opposed interpretation: these customs mark the typical "Gypsy" lack of manners and propriety and are in no way associated with Arab (Bedouin) heritage. The behavior of the

26. In this sense, audiences who support Diyāb against Abū Zayd are well known for precisely the same qualities as their hero: temperamentalness and hypersensitivity in all matters touching upon honor and reputation.

women, in particular, is attributed to the general looseness and flirtatiousness of Gypsy women.

Many of the features from which villagers construct the negative "Gypsy-poet" image are thus redeployed within the poets' community as part of their subversive counterimage. For villagers, the poets' lack of land marks their lack of origin, but for the poets this feature marks their affinity to the true Arabs, the Bedouin; living by words rather than by physical labor makes poets (in villagers' eyes) resemble beggars, but for poets, this is the mark of their Arab eloquence (*faṣāḥa*); their unusual domestic customs render the poets and their families suspect to the villagers, but these same customs constitute signs of enduring identity for the poets. The same characteristics are again and again given two opposing interpretations, interpretations that never come into direct conflict due to the social distance between the two groups—except at the moment of epic performance.

The Poet and the Poem

External Links

The concept of the poet as eloquent, gracious, well mannered, clever, and truly Arab is an in-group ideal to which the poets cannot stake claim publicly; after all, these characteristics are claimed in contrast to the villagers' supposed lack of them. They constitute a private, subversive source of pride and identity. In public, the poets have but one source from which they may derive a sense of respectability vis-à-vis the villagers—the epic itself, the artistic tradition they perform which is in demand by the society around them. The poets stress their identification with the epic in various ways, and they do so with some success, for the villagers indeed associate the poets with a number of internal aspects of the epic. As noted earlier, an initial association is based on the idea that both poets and epic heroes are "Arabs." Though the claim may be denied by some, the fact remains that poets and epic heroes are linked by accepted social nomenclature.

A second element that links the poet to the epic, and specifically to the epic heroes, is that many heroes within the epic are portrayed as rabāb-poets, and it is certainly no surprise that epic poets *within* the epic are universally eloquent, generous, and courteous (see below, "Reflections within the Epic"). In fact, a constant commentary is constructed about relations between poets and the larger world when epic heroes within the poem disguise themselves as poets and are badly treated by the characters they meet. In the end, of course, those characters learn that the form of the humble poet conceals not only a master of history and of eloquence, but a brave and chivalrous hero.

Time and again throughout the epic, the epic-hero-cum-poet sings within the epic. At the moment of performance these sections provide a unique mirroring of "narrated" and "narrative" event: a modern epic poet playing rabāb in front of an Egyptian audience sings of one of the epic heroes disguised as an epic poet playing the rabāb singing in front of an Egyptian audience.[27]

Further mirroring occurs at times because the poets of the Nile Delta are often named for heroes in the epic. Thus we may have a living poet Abū Zayd singing in the voice of the epic character Abū Zayd, or a living poet Badīr singing in the voice of the epic character Badīr. Two poets and several children in the al-Bakātūsh community bear the names of heroes from the epic, as do several other poets throughout the Delta. Daughters may be named for female characters or linked directly to the poets' metier through the girl's name Rabāb. One poet, Shaykh Biyalī, achieves even an iconic identification with the epic through his locally celebrated walrus mustache (see photographs in Chap. 3) which parallels the famous mustache of the epic hero Diyāb. In performance, whenever the hero is said to have "twisted his mustache and laughed" (barram s̲hawāribuh wi-ḍiḥik), Shaykh Biyalī also does so in a gesture that invariably elicits laughter and even cheers.

One final connection can be made from the fact that the poets, as do many Gypsy groups, possess a secret language, which they call *raṭāna*, attested to by foreign researchers over the past 150 years.[28] The heroes

27. For explorations of the relationship between narrated events and narrative events see Richard Bauman, *Story, Performance, and Event: Contextual Studies of Oral Narrative* (1986). See also Natalie Moyle, "The Image of the Āşık in Turkish Halk Hikāyeleri" (1986).

28. My exploration of this aspect of the community was cut off abruptly when an elder poet found out that the younger men were teaching me words from this argot. I did learn enough, however, to posit a few general statements about its nature. Several classes of words can be quickly identified: (1) Arabic words, or Arabic-derived words: such as *ʿas̲hīr* cited earlier, or *karasa* 'to sit' (derived from Ar. *kursī* 'chair'; this is also apparently in use in Upper Egypt though with slightly different implications). (2) Onomatopoetic words: such as *taftūfa* 'cigarette' (some of these items are also found in the slangs of other social groups). And (3) completely non-Arabic vocabulary items: such as *lamgūn* 'boy' (see Newbold *lambūn*), *kahān* 'food', or *konta* 'village, people, atmosphere, or surroundings'. This final category appears to constitute the largest body of lexical items.

I did not, however, encounter many words with standard prefix-suffix combinations such as Ḥannā describes (see Ḥannā, *al-Bināʾ*, 155–74). Standard verbal, substantive, adjectival, and adverbial categories are represented, though Arabic pronouns are used even when the remainder of the utterance is in raṭāna.

Perhaps the most curious aspect of this argot is that of all of the Gypsy groups of Egypt, the Ḥalab argot alone appears unrelated to European Romany. Everett Rowson, in an as yet unpublished study of Cairene urban argots, has found that the ḥalab argot is in use among lower-class musicians in Cairo.

of the epic also possess a secret language (their local Ḥijāzī dialect) which plays a key role in several episodes. For the poets of al-Bakātūsh, the existence and use of raṭāna constitutes another body of secret knowledge, along with their geographical origins, family names, and their verbal art.

To return momentarily then to the appellations used in al-Bakātūsh to refer to poets:

Shared Terms	
Poets (shuᶜara)	
Arabs (ᶜarab)	
Villagers (in private)	*Poets (in private)*
Gypsies (ghajar)	Ḥalab (ḥalab)

We see now that the shared terms are those that function as publicly acknowledged links between the poets and their poetry, that is, their public source of respectability. The term *ghajar* is used in contrast to express the villagers' feeling of social superiority and their ambiguity toward the presence of the poets, while the term *ḥalab*, unknown and unused among most villagers, can be read as emblematic of the poet community's efforts to maintain a restricted body of knowledge, power through secrecy, with which to offset the pejorative images held up by the larger society.

Reflections within the Epic

The external links forged between poets and the epic tradition through use of the term "Arab," the names they share with epic heroes, their domestic customs, and their use of a secret language are all found in reflected form within the epic poem. An examination of recorded texts from live performances reveals key moments at which the relationship between the poet inside and outside the poem is held up for scrutiny and then commented upon by performing poets.

The storyline of the episode titled "The Maiden of the Languorous Eyes" (Nāᶜisat al-ajfān), for example, is motivated entirely by a poet's performance, and during the subsequent events of the tale, the hero Abū Zayd travels several times disguised as a poet. His resulting heroic adventures and exploits unfold against the background of this disguise-identity of a rabāb-poet:[29]

29. Many other sections, such as "The Tale of Ḥanḍal [SA Ḥanẓal]" and the tales of "The Reconnaissance," contain similar passages.

At the beginning of the episode, the famed poet Jamīl 'Beautiful', son of Rāshid 'the Rightly Guided', and his three companions arrive at the Hilālī camp. He is presented to Sultan Ḥasan who asks the Poet Jamīl to sing for the men gathered in his pavilion. The poet begins with praise for the Prophet Muḥammad, and then praises the heroes of the Banī Hilāl tribe for their bravery and generosity. The Poet Jamīl sings for a number of nights and then announces his impending departure. The Banī Hilāl assemble gifts for the poet and his companions; some give one camel, some give two, and some give ten. Sultan Ḥasan reckons the worth of the Arabs' gifts and then adds their equal, doubling the poet's payment. But Ḥasan grows proud (*yiftakhar*) upon seeing the wealth offered by his tribe and asks the poet if any of the kings and warriors who have hosted him have ever given him such a large gift. The poet evades the question the first time by thanking Sultan Ḥasan profusely and wishing God's blessings upon him. Sultan Ḥasan persists, however, and asks again. Finally, the poet grows angry and rebukes his patron, adding that in truth, Ḥasan's gifts are the least he has received among the Arabs. He picks up his rabāb and sings a long ode telling the tale of his life, a veritable oral autobiography, recounting how he became a poet, and describing all the kings and heroes for whom he has sung and, in particular, what their gifts to him were. His ode closes with the following phrases:[30]

Text 2.1

I have wandered the lands of Sind, and Hind (=India), and Yemen,
I have gone to lands where elephants are ridden,

But I have not encountered fiercer than al-Zanātī (of Tunisia) with his zeal,
nor more generous than (King) Zayd al-ʿAjāj among men.

And there are none more noble than this one and that one but our Prophet,
the Hashemite; for the weak (before God) He pleads."

Ḥasan is angered by this and accuses the poet of falsehood, but the poet retorts that King Zayd bestowed upon him a necklace whose jewels are as large as a dove's eggs the like of which has never been seen, which he then draws from his blouse as proof. Sultan Ḥasan relents and asks

30. Complete transliterations for all numbered texts are found in the Appendix.

the Poet Jamīl to sing to him on the rabāb the praises of this King Zayd. The poet sings praises of his past patron and in so doing mentions that King Zayd has no son, but only a daughter, the Maiden of the Languorous Eyes. She has been taught horsemanship and rides into battle, she has been taught the sciences and the recitation of the Qurʾān, and she is without doubt the most beautiful woman alive. These words once again anger Ḥasan, for his sister, the heroine of the Banī Hilāl tribe, al-Jāzya, is renowned for her beauty, wisdom, and horsemanship. He threatens to hang the poet. Abū Zayd (who has not been present until this point) hears of this travesty and reaches a compromise with Ḥasan. He will personally travel to the kingdom of Zayd al-ʿAjāj to test the king's generosity and to discern if the daughter is as beautiful as she has been described. This willingness to suffer the hardships of the journey provokes laughter in most performances, for those listeners who know the tradition well sense that once again Abū Zayd's weakness for the ladies has got the best of him, and he intends nothing short of wooing and winning this maiden, whereupon follows the main story of "The Maiden of the Languorous Eyes."

A critical point about this scene is that the tale itself constructs a dialogue about the relationship between poet and patron which forms both the beginning and the ending of the tale. The Poet Jamīl's autobiographical ode, inserted into this dialogue, begins with an account of his youth in Yemen and how he studied Qurʾān, the religious sciences, prosody, and grammar, but then forsook all these pursuits once he "tested" (*jarrab*) his voice on the rabāb and found it "full" (*malyān*). The art of poetry (and its power) is set in direct contrast to the worthy, but more common arts of a traditional religious education.

Jamīl then departed, according to his song, with three of his relatives and traveled the world for forty years. His travels in fact foreshadow the coming reconnaissance trip of Abū Zayd and his three nephews (al-Riyāda, part 2 of *Sīrat Banī Hilāl*), as well as the westward migration of the Banī Hilāl tribe as a whole (*al-Taghrība*, part 3). Jamīl's lifestory recounts in miniature the journey that is told in more detail during the reconnaissance and in greatly expanded form during the tribe's migration. All of the future adversaries and allies of the tribe are listed and attributed with varying degrees of hospitality, sagacity, and generosity.[31] Of all these princes, chiefs, and kings, the only patron who proved

31. An interesting point in this summary of the lands and rulers that the tribe will later encounter is that Jamīl's ode as it is sung in al-Bakātūsh contains the names of cities and rulers that do not appear in the Bakātūsh repertory as full episodes, but are full episodes in some of the eighteenth- and nineteenth-century manuscripts housed in the Berlin Staatsbibliothek; see Ayoub, "A propos."

stingy was al-Zanātī Khalīfa; on the other hand, he proved to be the fiercest warrior the poet ever encountered in his travels.

As Jamīl reproaches Ḥasan in song and lectures him on the proper behavior of patrons, it becomes difficult indeed to separate the voices of the poet inside and outside the epic; *we* now sit in Ḥasan's place as patrons of thc epic. Differentiation of voice and addressee becomes even more difficult in the performing poet's explanatory prose asides to the audience, which comment directly on poets, patrons, and performances, as in this prose excursus from a performance of this scene by Shaykh Biyalī Abū Fahmī (2/14/87). At several points the Arabic allows for either a present- or past-tense reading, both of which are indicated:

Text 2.2

Narrative:

So (Ḥasan) said to him, "O Poet Jamīl."

He said to him, "Yes, O Father of ʿAlī [=Ḥasan]."

He said to him, "You have journeyed among many people, the great ones among the noble Arabs—has anyone bestowed gifts upon you and treated you as generously as have I and my Arabs?"

Excursus:

Now the poet was [is] of great politesse[32]. The poet was [is] of great politesse, for every poet who picks up the rabāb is of great politesse. Why? Because he sits with good people [*nās ṭayyibīn*]. Because a poet never possesses bad manners. He travels with his rabāb. I do not laud poets merely because I am a poet! [laughter from audience]—it is because the histories [*riwāyāt*] tell us so! The poet was [is] of great politesse. Were he not of great politesse, he would never pick up the rabāb and sit with good people. How could he be a poet of kings and Arabs and be impolite? He was [is] of great politesse. And the audience [al-qaʿda], as well, when they listen[ed] to a poet, they were [are], as well, the pinnacle of respectfulness.

Narrative:

So Ḥasan looked at him like this, and said to him, "O Poet Jamīl."

He said to him, "Yes."

He said to him, "You have journeyed among many people, the great ones among the noble Arabs—has anyone bestowed gifts upon you and treated you as generously as I and my Arabs have?"

The Poet Jamīl looked at him.

We said that the poet was of great politesse, that is, polite.

32. The Arabic term *adūb* is an intensive form formed from the word *adab* 'politeness', hence my paraphrase, "of great politesse." Later in the text the poet glosses the meaning with the more common word, *muʾaddab*, which I have translated simply as "polite."

> He said to him, "O Father of ʿAlī, you are like the river Nile, and the nobles among whom we have traveled are like Nile rivers. And the river, in it is regular water [*miyāh*] and pure water [*zulāl*], but one [part of the] river cannot be preferred over the next [part]."
>
> If only he had cut short his talk and fallen silent, that Ḥasan . . . the poet had given him a beautiful answer with good judgment.

But with Ḥasan's insistence, as we have seen, the poet must finally drop his courteous evasions and tell the truth, which brings about the rest of the tale. Sultan Ḥasan is a character normally marked by his evenhandedness in dispensing justice, his skill as an arbitrator, his authority, honor, and religious devotion. Yet as patron, he falls easily into the trap of overestimating his own generosity, of underestimating the worth of the poet, and of denigrating the poet's social status and position. Though this tale is basically one of the tales of courtship and marriage (there are a half dozen such episodes in which each of the great heroes ventures forth and wins himself a bride), the frame of this episode places the relationship between poet and patron at issue; though Abū Zayd eventually returns with a new bride, he also returns to castigate Sultan Ḥasan and exonerate the Poet Jamīl.

Of course not all performances of this scene contain such explicit commentaries by the performing poet; they are scarcely needed at this point, for the narrative itself overtly juxtaposes good and bad patrons, and the poet is eventually proven to be a man of honor and veracity.

A little later in the same story, Abū Zayd travels disguised as an epic poet to visit King Zayd al-ʿAjāj. On his way he meets and joins a caravan of merchants, who welcome the new member of their group and ask that he entertain them. They drink heavily and fall asleep while Abū Zayd is singing. Suddenly they are attacked by a lion larger than a bull; the merchants flee, yelling, "Run, poet, run for your life!" Abū Zayd, however, draws his sword, kills the lion, slits open its belly, and eats its liver. The merchants and their brave "poet" continue on their route. They soon come to the land of Marwān al-ʿUqaylī, cousin to the seven kings of the ʿUqayla tribe whom Abū Zayd killed earlier in the epic. Marwān has been warned by a geomancer that Abū Zayd the Hilālī will cross his kingdom and so blocks the road. He demands that the merchants identify Abū Zayd, but they explain that their only traveling companion is nothing but a rabāb-poet. Marwān guesses that the poet is Abū Zayd and attacks him. Abū Zayd seizes a horse, rides against Marwān, and eventually kills him. The merchants are now terrified of Abū Zayd and apologize for their earlier disrespectful behavior, for which Abū Zayd graciously forgives them. The "poet" is revealed to be a hero, and those who felt themselves his social superiors are recast as characters indebted to the hero for their very safety and well-being. It takes little imagination to see that the constant narrative equation of hero and poet implies the reverse as well: as heroes are also poets, so poets are also somehow heroes. *Sīrat Banī Hilāl*, at this level, is a continuous discourse of heroic poets and poetic heroes.

The opening scene of "The Maiden of the Langourous Eyes" thus sets up a commentary on the relationship between poet and patron through the characters of the Poet Jamīl and Sultan Ḥasan the Hilālī. This commentary lies not only within the narrative, but is regularly exteriorized by performing epic poets in their prose asides to the audience. In the subsequent events of the tale, when Abū Zayd travels with the merchants disguised as a poet, the action of the narrative projects a reciprocal correlation between poet and hero, representative of a larger equation of poets and heroes that is maintained not only in the epic narrative, but also in the exterior world of village social life.

Poet, Patron, and Sexual Taboo

Another episode of the epic provides an even more complex negotiation of relationships between the figures of poet, hero, and patron within a frame of honor, shame, and sexual taboo. This scene also normally meets with a great deal of response from male audience members; they laugh, shout comments, and even make overtly sexual remarks and jokes.

In the "Tale of Ḥanḍal the ᶜUqaylī," King Ḥanḍal treacherously attacks the camp of the Banī Hilāl at night while it is defended only by the elder heroes of the tribe (the younger heroes are in Mecca fighting a war against Ḥarqalī, son of Dayshān). Ḥanḍal kills off one by one, in battle, the generation of the fathers, pillages the camp, and seizes eighty maidens of the Banī Hilāl tribe as captives. The maidens are held in the ᶜUqaylī camp, where they are forced to wear camel-hair shirts, are beaten morning and night, made to carry waterskins during the day, and forced to dance in Ḥanḍal's pavilion in the evening as entertainment for his men. When the young heroes return from Mecca, they find they are now the leaders of the tribe, the camps of the Banī Hilāl have been decimated, and, worst of all, the honor of the tribe is at stake, for the maidens of the tribe are captives in Ḥanḍal's court. This episode is thus a major turning point in the epic, as the narrative focus passes from the initial generation of heroes to their children, who will occupy center stage until the final episodes of the epic.

Rather than declare war immediately, which Ḥanḍal surely expects,

Abū Zayd decides to travel to Ḥanḍal's realm, disguised once again as a poet, to discover the whereabouts of the Hilālī maidens and to reconnoiter. As he nears Ḥanḍal's pavilion he sees the maidens carrying waterskins, signals his identity to them, and speaks to them in their secret tongue. Abū Zayd then enters the pavilion, presents himself, and is received as a wandering poet. Ḥanḍal asks the visiting poet if he is adept at describing women and proposes that the poet describe the captive maidens in verse. He orders the maidens brought before him and commands them to dance. Upon seeing the maidens, Abū Zayd begins to weep, and Ḥanḍal asks him why. Abū Zayd responds that he weeps at Ḥanḍal's dim-wittedness: how can he ask a poet to describe maidens dressed in camel-hair shirts? Ḥanḍal orders the maidens bathed and dressed in the finest of silks. They reenter the pavilion, and Abū Zayd sings their description:[33]

Text 2.3

"You have, O Ḥanḍal, eighty maidens, 1
Each maiden more resplendent than the moon in (the month of)
Shaʿbān.

"O their heads are the dainty heads of doves, 2
And their hair flows down their shirts.

"Their arms are like silvery swords 3
In the hand of a warrior descending to the field.

"Their cheeks are rose petals, exalted be He who fashioned them! 4
The fashioning of the Master, the One, the Glorious!

"If they walked on the sea the very fish would chirp; 5
If a shaykh saw them his saintliness would fly.
If a learned man saw them he would forget the Qurʾān;

"If the cloth-vendor saw them (May he be recompensed!) 6
He would reckon fine wool as plain calico!

33. The compactness of Arabic script often means that what is expressed easily in two hemistichs across a single printed line in Arabic may necessitate two or more lines in English translation. Also, poets occasionally miss a rhyme and sing three, or even four, hemistichs before "closing" the verse with the appropriate end-rhyme. In general, each line of English here represents one hemistich (one half-verse) in the Arabic.

"We are sitting here in the pavilion of prosperity, O King Ḥanḍal; 7
May God assist you! A well-built pavilion,
a well-built pavilion, O your Excellency the Sultan,
(with) marvelous furnishings!

"In it are water-pitchers of crystal, beautiful to the thirsty one; 8
(And) faucets of silver (from which) a river of pure water flows.

"We are sitting in your pavilion, 9
May God improve your state, Ḥanḍal, O Sultan."

King Ḥanḍal looked at Abū Zayd and said to him, 10
"Welcome, O Poet of the Arabs.

"You will have from us silver, you will have from us gold, 11
You will have from us horses, along with camels.

"The land is your land, O Poet of the Arabs, 12
The land is your land and the country is your country.
And we are for you, sir, servants and slaves."

Spoken:
Abū Zayd said, "Many thanks, O King Ḥanḍal, 13
(but) why do you give me silver, why do you give me gold?

Sung:
"Let my gift be one of these maidens of heavenly features, 14
To serve your grandfather the poet an elderly, worn-out man."

Ḥanḍal answered Abū Zayd and said to him: 15
"Take Rayya, Daughter of Abū Zayd, O Poet of the Arabs."

Spoken aside to audience:
(We said that Abū Zayd had married Butayma, the sister of Diyāb, after he married ʿAlya the Zaḫlaniyya who had been with him since long ago, and he had with her three boys and a girl: Ṣabra, and Mukhaymar, and ʿAkrama, and Rayya.)

Sung:
"Please take Rayya, Daughter of Abū Zayd, from me as a gift, 16
And may she live with you, O Prince, throughout time.

"Please take Rayya, Daughter of Abū Zayd, from me as a gift, 17
And may she live with you, by God, O Prince, throughout time.

"Heavens! When you take Rayya, O Poet of the Arabs, 18
Your gray hair and your years will disappear!
You will be once again a youth like long ago!"

Abū Zayd gave a signal to Rayya, 19
She came forward.

Spoken:
Ḥanḍal went over and grabbed Rayya by her arms, 20
And said, "Take her for yourself, O Poet of the Arabs!

Sung:
"And may she live with you, O Prince, in peace. 21
And may she live with you, by God, O Prince, in peace."
[Music]

Rayya, daughter of Abū Zayd, came forward and clinched the
trick: 22
She said to him, "Shut up, O Coward! It never was and will not
be!
O Ḥanḍal, O Treacherous One!

"I am the daughter of Abū Zayd, Shaykh of the Arabs, 23
The daughter of the Shaykh of the Arabs, Abū Zayd!
You'd give me to a rabāb-poet who wanders among the Arabs?

"I am the daughter of Abū Zayd, Shaykh of the Arabs, 24
Possessor of heroism (lit. father of heroism) from long ago.

"When my father Abū Zayd the Hilālī learns of this, 25
He'll cause your blood on the ground in floods [to flow]!"

Abū Zayd initiates this poem by describing the Hilālī maidens in a "blazon," a list of bodily parts each of which is described by simile or metaphor.[34] He then suggests that their beauty is so great that all natural boundaries of propriety would vanish at their sight—a foreshadowing of the unnatural and improper suggestions which follow. He concludes, after having also briefly described the king's pavilion, by wishing God's blessings on his patron, Ḥanḍal the ʿUqaylī.

34. See Nancy Vickers, "The Blazon of Sweet Beauty's Best: Shakespeare's Lucrece," in *Shakespeare and the Question of Theory*, ed. Patrica Parker and Geoffrey Hartman (1985); and idem, "This Heraldry in Lucrece's Face," in *The Female Body in Western Culture: Contemporary Perspectives*, ed. Susan Suleiman (1986).

Ḥanḍal is well pleased and offers the poet rich gifts: silver and gold, horses and camels. Abū Zayd, however, puts forward the slightly scandalous suggestion that he instead be awarded one of the maidens of the Banī Hilāl as a gift. Ḥanḍal then unwittingly proposes the unthinkable in offering Rayya to her own father, and then, in not very elliptical terms, further suggests their sexual union. Rayya immediately rejects the proposed coupling, not on the basis that the poet is her father (which she presumably cannot reveal), but on the basis that she is the daughter of a hero and therefore cannot be given to a mere poet.

Abū Zayd appears in this narrative, as in many episodes of the epic, as an ambiguous, bifaceted figure who unites both poet and hero in a single character. In this scene, however, the "real" Abū Zayd (i.e., the epic hero publicly recognized as Abū Zayd) is absent, and this basic duality is represented in two characters: the poet element of his persona is present in the form of the disguised Abū Zayd, while his daughter, Rayya, lays public claim to his heroic aspect.

Abū Zayd in disguise here is reduced to playing only "the poet" and not the unified hero/poet. This idea is supported by the subsequent events of the tale in which the poet's true identity is discovered, but rather than emerging immediately as the hero Abū Zayd as is his wont, he is promptly tossed into Ḥanḍal's prison. That is, he is *not* unveiled as a poet and revealed as a hero (as when Abū Zayd in the "The Maiden of the Languorous Eyes" leaps up to fight the lion, or seizes a horse and rides into battle against Marwān the ʿUqaylī), but rather is unveiled as a poet and proves curiously unable to demonstrate heroism; he is instead led impotently off to a prison cell.

Rayya, as Abū Zayd's daughter, lays genetic claim to Abū Zayd's heroic aspect by citing her father as "possessor of heroism," quite literally in the Arabic, "father of heroism" (*abū baṭūla*). Thus she genealogically designates herself as the daughter of the father of heroism, a displacement in which she overtly equates herself with heroic action, an equation acted out in her defiance of King Ḥanḍal.

As the hero's maiden daughter, Rayya is futhermore a primary conventional locus for her father's honor in quite ordinary, quotidian social terms. For though a man may achieve honor through his own heroic actions in raids and battles, his paramount social duty and function is to defend that honor which is physically resident in the women of his household, most particularly in the persons of unmarried women such as younger sisters and daughters.

As shown in figure 4, Rayya and the poet, sundered aspects of the hero/poet Abū Zayd, are repositioned as emblems of the complementary aspects of heroic honor: Rayya physically personifies her father's honor,

Figure 4. Bifurcation of the epic hero

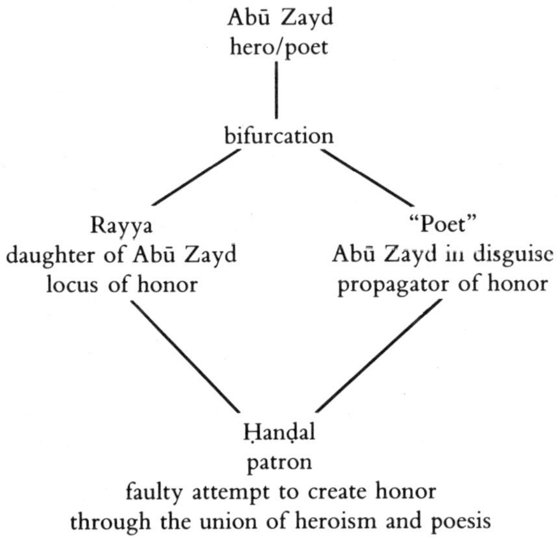

both in conventional social terms and through her genealogical descent from his heroism; the poet is the disseminator of that honor, honor that cannot spring independently from heroic deeds but must be given voice and form by the poet. Ḥanḍal's proposition is thus unthinkable on several levels:

(1) Quite obviously Rayya cannot be joined with the poet, for he is in fact her father; the tensions created by Ḥanḍal's incestuous suggestions are clear.

(2) This basic sexual taboo is furthermore overlaid with, and thus reinforces, Rayya's claim that she cannot be joined to the poet because she is the daughter of a "father of heroism." The father/daughter opposition therefore suggests a second antithesis, that of poet and hero who cannot be joined (incestuous union?) except in the original space created by the character of the epic hero.

(3) Poet and hero are joined in the figure of Abū Zayd; however, the union of Heroism (via Rayya) and Poesis (via the Poet) at the instigation of the Patron (Ḥanḍal) is rejected and held up as an object of comic parody. Ḥanḍal is a villain, a man without honor, and his attempt at largesse and generosity as patron cannot, in fact, bring about the desired union of heroism and poesis: he cannot create honor where none exists, even when fulfilling, at least in form, the obligations of patron. He only believes himself to possess the marks of honor, which we, the audience, recognize as stolen (the captured maidens) or counterfeit (a court poet

who is an enemy in disguise); inducing the poet to describe that captured prize produces a mocking, not a laudatory, poem. Abū Zayd literally sings and describes his own honor (his daughter), not that of the credulous patron.

On another level, however, the impossibility of this union also suggests that Rayya and the poet are two like forces. For the poet is to some degree a feminized male; he complements the hero (as do the hero's female dependents), and, although he is a necessary part of the hero's honor (as are wives and daughters), he is in fact dependent—on both hero and patron. He is a man dependent on men. He is a man who does not ride into battle where independent honor may be achieved, but rather carries his "weapon" (the rabāb), which is precisely *not* a sword, into the arena where such honor is vicariously celebrated. Such is the ambiguity of the panegyric poet: a figure with no heroic deeds on which to base his own honor, yet indispensable for the process of propagating the honor of heroes. He is both powerful and powerless. A union between two forces which are both essential complements to the male hero (female dependent and male dependent) is posed here as impossible, unmergable.

The act of publicly describing the maidens in poetry here represents a highly significant moment. Such descriptions occur fairly frequently within the epic, but they are usually presented to us in the voice of the performing poet, that is, in the narrator's voice, as background material presented for the benefit, or titillation, of the male audience. Such descriptions of women are only placed in the mouth of a character within the epic and sung publicly during scenes of humiliation such as the one we are examining. The poet in the scene has thus usurped our own poet's role; he is playing to Ḥanḍal and his men as our own poet usually plays to his patron and audience. We may therefore reread the poetic description of the maidens in still another manner, as an indication of an act of male alliance and bonding which takes place between the Poet, the Patron, and the Audience, a collusive bonding which excludes females and asserts the masculinity of the epic project. Poet and Patron conspire to dismember and assert power over the possessed women for their mutual entertainment; an act produced within the story for Ḥanḍal and his men, and reproduced by our poet for the men of al-Bakātūsh and their visiting male ethnographer. Though the act of describing beautiful maidens through poetic "blazon" is one that recurs with great regularity throughout the epic, no similar description of males, even when they are portrayed as devastatingly handsome (as in "Tale of ʿAzīza and Yūnus," for example), ever occurs.

From the audience's point of view, Ḥanḍal's proposal is framed, of course, as comic, a parody, for not only do we, the audience, and the maidens already know the true identity of the "poet," but Abū Zayd in addition signals to Rayya before she comes forward to sing her response. We are told that Rayya steps forward to "clinch the trick." This sham is being played out for King Ḥanḍal, and we are privy to it; we in the audience are led to understand that the scene is one of mockery—not, as Ḥanḍal intends, humiliation of the captive maidens and indirectly of their menfolk, but rather of the patron himself.

The dynamic is one of collusion, not only a collusion of males encircling possessed female objects, but also a complex maneuver in which the roles of poet, hero, and patron are being played out at several levels, for there are two poets here, one inside and one outside the narrative, and likewise two patrons and two audiences—a moment of complete duplication.

Abū Zayd and Rayya are in collusion within the tale, which produces the comic aspect of this scene and consistently focuses its impact on the patron, the butt of the joke. But the performing poet and the audience of this performance event in al-Bakātūsh are also positioned in parallel collusion against Ḥanḍal, the unworthy patron, whom we understand to be mocked.

The parallel collusions in figure 5 between Rayya and Abū Zayd, and the performing poet and his present audience, are placed in opposition to the performance Ḥanḍal believes he is presenting as entertainment to his male companions within the narrative. The father/daughter, poesis/heroism, and female dependent/male dependent oppositions, outlined earlier, all underline the impossibility of Ḥanḍal's desires to be a real patron and to have his honor publicly lauded. The result is a parody of the noble and meritorious act of patronizing poets with public displays of generosity.

Sīrat Banī Hilāl, as it is currently performed in the region of the Nile Delta, achieves a great deal of its force and popularity by commenting

Figure 5. Performance Collusions

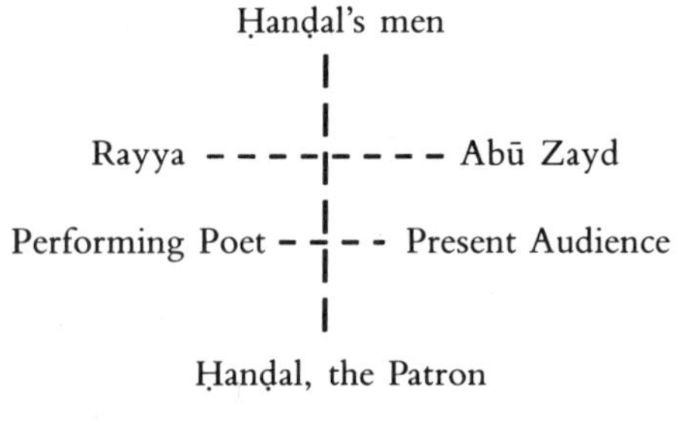

upon, and negotiating, the very situations, characters, behaviors, and morals that create it. The implications of this negotation are most sharply seen in the ambiguities that surround the public persona of the poet in the larger community, and the gap that exists between that persona and the private persona nurtured within the poets' smaller community. Although all representations may to some degree comment on themselves, as all narratives may at some level be read as autobiography, the intensity and form of the relationship(s) that obtain between the poet inside and outside the epic in this tradition suggest a particularly rich domain for examining and questioning our current conceptualization of the boundaries between "text" and "context."

Each of the elements cited earlier serve to link the poet to his poem; they do not, however, successfully counter all of the factors that constitute the mistrusted persona of the epic poet. The epic singer is usually a Gypsy with no known aṣl or origin. He owns no agricultural land, he is itinerant, he has specific customs which differ from those of the fellāḥīn, yet he bears a tradition the villagers claim as their own and he also wields power in performance by commenting on village affairs while singing the epic (as we shall see in later chapters), which makes him all the more a source of tension.[35]

Though music's position vis-à-vis official Islam has always been ambiguous, in the context of the village the poets' connection to music does not appear to contribute to the forces that set them apart.[36] Two family groups of professional musicians in al-Bakātūsh are from ordinary villager families rather than Ḥalab-poet families. One is a family of instrumentalists who perform at saints' festivals and other occasions; the other consists of a father-and-son team of singers who perform at local weddings. The members of these families are not perceived as outsiders (their extended families all live in al-Bakātūsh), nor are the performers ostracized because of their chosen profession. For them, music is a profession rather than an identity.

Given the socially negative connotations of being an epic poet, and the diminishing contexts for performance which we examine in Chapter 3, it is not surprising to find that the men of the youngest generation in the poets' community have abandoned the poet's profession and are openly seeking to assimilate. The youngest performing poets (with one

35. An example of this power to publicly criticize is examined in Slyomovics, *Merchant*, 110–11, 137–39. Several such incidents are also examined in this volume, Chapters 4 and 5.

36. See, for example, Lois al-Faruqi on the disenfranchisement of musicians in Islamic society: "The Status of Music in Muslim Nations: Evidence from the Arab World" (1981); and idem, "The Shariʾah on Music and Musicians," in *Islamic Thought and Culture* (1982). See also *Asian Music* 17, 1 (1985), a special issue on music and musicians in the Islamic world.

exception) are in their late forties and early fifties. The next generation, that is, men in their thirties and early forties, were trained as poets in their youth but have taken up new occupations. For example, during my first period of fieldwork in 1983 Ṣalāḥ ʿAbd al-Salām the Poet was still a performing poet. By the time I returned in 1986, he had given up the poet's trade to go work in construction and would no longer play or record. Men in their twenties, such as Ṣalāḥ's younger brother, have never learned the epic and cannot even play the rabāb. They spoke to me with pride of their lack of knowledge of the epic tradition and often added that they had hardly ever even heard their fathers perform. Nearly all of the male children and teenagers of the poets' community are currently enrolled in school. It is hoped that these young men will be able to provide for the others when *Sīrat Banī Hilāl* ceases to provide an income for the community.

Though I spoke many times with older poets about the disappearance of the epic and the abandonment of the poets' calling, their reactions were usually pragmatic: *Sīrat Banī Hilāl* is no longer in great demand and no longer provides enough money to feed a family. Thus it is considered a good thing that the young men are finding other jobs, and even better that the children are going to school (all of the performing poets are illiterate and never acquired any schooling other than rote memorization of sections from the Qurʾān). Only rarely were comments made expressing regret over this development. The fear lurking behind the disappearance of the epic lies much more with the possible complete dissolution of their community. As Shaykh Muḥammad Aḥmad said to me a few weeks before his death, "When no one is singing the sīra any longer, what will become of the 'children of Ḥalab' [*wilād ḥalab*]?

Social Context and the Performance Tradition

The most fundamental questions that remain to be asked about the relationship between greater and smaller communities in al-Bakātūsh are why social outsiders such as the Ḥalab have come to bear a narrative tradition that is seen as the history and property of the larger community and how their social role has affected that narrative tradition.

In many societies around the world, performers of various sorts are socially marginalized. As purveyors of music, theater, or dance, as itinerant elements in an otherwise fixed social pattern, they are often unofficially, sometimes even officially, disenfranchised. In some cases the performer may achieve some measure of respectability through association with a respected art form; in other cases a particularly interesting social tension arises from social sanctioning of the art form but not of the performer. The performance of *Sīrat Banī Hilāl* in Egypt is clearly a case of the latter situation.

We have no reliable data about the origins of the Ḥalab poets of the Nile Delta, nor about the date of their arrival in Egypt.[37] Given the strong parallels between the epic singers of northern Egypt and socially marginalized performers elsewhere, however, some speculation about the epic singers' situation seems possible.

Jozsef Vekerdi, examining the case of Gypsies in Hungary, has drawn some basic conclusions:

> [The Gypsies] live in less developed social and cultural conditions than their actual non-Gypsy environment. When they were settled in the neighbourhood of the villages or when their wandering groups came into contact with the peasantry of country, the contact being indispensable for their livelihood, they commonly adopted elements of the folk-culture of the non-Gypsy community. In the course of time the economic and social life of the village developed and the old traditions sank into oblivion. However, [they] . . . rarely participated in the overall social economic development experienced by the non-Gypsy community. They continued to live in the old manner and continued to preserve the peasant folklore which they had borrowed when arriving at the village. This creates a paradoxical situation in which the Gypsy groups ultimately become the conservators of non-Gypsy traditions.[38]

Here Vekerdi essentially expresses the argument of marginal preservation. He is particularly concerned with folk music and folktales; he is not, for the most part, dealing with genres that involve professional or semiprofessional performers. His writing is also marked by a strong desire to see all good examples of ballads and folk music as originally Hungarian, and he unfortunately couples his actual data with strongly negative views about the role of Gypsy tradition-bearers and more than a little romanticism about non-Gypsy transmission. Despite this marked bias, the concept of marginal preservation among Gypsy groups must be set forth and evaluated. In the case of the epic singers of al-Bakātūsh, however, the tradition appears to function within a different dynamic. Their attachment to specific customs and traditions seems to be involved in the poets' sense of separateness from the larger society, that is, an aspect of differential identity, and seems to be specifically engaged with

37. The lack of early references to Gypsies of any sort in Egypt prior to the late Middle Ages has prompted some scholars to posit a fourteenth-century, or later, migration. See, however, Paul Kahle, "A Gypsy Woman in Egypt in the Thirteenth Century" (1950).

38. Jozsef Vekerdi, "The Gypsy's Role in the Preservation of Non-Gypsy Folklore" (1976), 80.

the Arabic concept of aṣl, or origin, through the establishment of a persona that is more Arab than that of neighboring social groups.[39]

Marginal preservation, however, also does not fully explicate the development of a professional group for the performance of a single specific tradition, and there is little evidence for assuming that the performance of the folk siyar in Egypt was ever common among nonmarginal social groups. Margaret Beissinger has examined the marginality of performers of epic and heroic poetry in a number of Balkan and central Asian societies and argues that this very marginality, the liminality of the performer, is what enables him or her to guide the audience into the liminal world of the past, the underworld, or the fantasy world of acknowledged fictional tales.[40]

This argument strikes me as tenable within the context of the Nile Delta epic-singing tradition as well, for the *Sīrat Banī Hilāl* performance tradition clearly thrives on the symbiotic relationship that exists between the poet and the poem. The singer is perceived as a direct link to the tale he narrates; in a vague, undefined way he is somehow an extension of the very characters of whom he sings. The constant insertion of scenes where singer and hero conflate into a single performing poet continually strengthens this perception. Who better to narrate the world of rabāb-wielding poets and Arab heroes than an "Arab" poet wielding his rabāb?

There can be little doubt that the sociological interaction of these two communities, one essentially a community of purveyors of a tradition, the other essentially consumers of that tradition, has contributed greatly to the shaping and formation of the performance tradition itself.

To begin with, the moment of performance must be a moment of power reversal, for the outcast is now center stage and the dominant force in this social setting. In recent years this role reversal has become even stronger, for the performance, particularly the sahra, or evening gathering, realigns the roles of many audience members as well. Underlying the entire performance situation is a network of relationships created in the social environment of daily life, relationships of power and identity most visible in the reversals wrought upon them in the performance situation. The poet, in daily life an outsider, becomes central and powerful in performance. Though the poet is respectful to high-status or wealthy villagers as patrons or potential patrons, he may, as performing poet, cut off someone who is speaking (unacceptable in daily life) or wield poetry to comment on those present or current conditions in

39. See Abu-Lughod, *Veiled Sentiments*, 41ff.

40. Margaret Beissinger, "Balkan Traditional Singers and Non-Mainstream Figures" (1988).

the village or elsewhere. The poet literally obtains a voice in performance which he is denied in daily life.

A similar reversal of status and power takes place within the audience. In ordinary life the middle-aged educated and young highly educated villagers have seized status and power from more traditional groups. In a sahra of *Sīrat Banī Hilāl*, the lowest of the low, the poets, emerge on top, followed by their coteries of traditional-minded listeners—older men with little or no education, who are given outward respect but do not wield power in the village, men who practice traditional folk forms of Islam (confreres in the Sufi brotherhoods, kuttāb-educated men, etc.). Educated audience members are welcome, but their criticism, if voiced, is refuted through one or more channels during the performance (see Chap. 5). Though in an earlier period this might not have been true (that is, it does not appear that in the past the upper class of the village denigrated the epic but rather patronized it), the sahra of *Sīrat Banī Hilāl* currently is framed as a gathering of conservative, traditionally minded members of the community. To listen to the epic in a public recitation such as a wedding is a very different thing from organizing or attending a private performance (sahra).

This perception of *Sīrat Banī Hilāl* as ally to conservative and traditionalist forces in Arab society has been most poignantly expressed in the final line of one of the most famous poems of modern Arabic literature, Nizār Qabbānī's "Bread, Hashish, and Moon" (Khubz, ḥashīsh wa-qamar). The poet muses ironically on the power of the moon, here reminiscent of the floriated style of classical Arabic odes composed and addressed to the poet's Beloved, and the numbing force of hashish, traditional music, and fatalism, while misery and the daily search for bread occupy the lives of millions. The poem in full is a powerful statement about the modern Arab world's relationship to the Arabic artistic tradition, and its final passage (quoted here) exemplifies why the sīra is often regarded with suspicion and even disdain among intellectuals and in urban areas:

In my country
Where fools weep
And die weeping
Whenever the face of the crescent moon rises over them . . .
And their weeping increases
Whenever the sound of some lowly lute moves them . . .
or a voice intoning, "O Night!"
—that death we call in the East
Layālī—or the sound of song . . .
In my country . . .

In my country of simple people
Where we mull over our unending *tawāshīḥ* chants
—that consumption which ravages the East,
those lengthy refrains of the *tawāshīḥ*—
Our East that mulls over its history
Lethargic dreams
And empty legends
Our East that seeks all of its heroism
In Abū-Zayd al-Hilālī[41]

I posited earlier that the retention by the poets' families of certain dying domestic customs and traditions has more to with establishing a sense of aṣl than with mere marginal preservation. Another performance phenomenon may also be attributed to this same motivation. The poets do not publicly participate in the genealogical history of the village, that is, the villagers do not locate the poets within the on-going system of marital and blood relations. A poet is identified merely as a poet, not as an individual member of a larger family and clan. The older poets, however, are experts on the subject of the genealogical warp and weave of the village. Tea breaks during sahra-performances are often filled with detailed accounts of the families of every listener present. Shaykh ʿAbd al-Wahhāb Ghāzī, in particular, is able to amaze audience members with his knowledge of their relations once he has placed them, for he often does not recognize the younger men right away. When the sahra includes a group of older men, the conversation may fill an hour before there is any pause in the proceedings. This material is never requested by the audience and does not constitute a recognizable, named genre for either audience members or poets. It occurs with such regularity, however, that it must be accounted for as part of the overall performance tradition. Shaykh ʿAbd al-Wahhāb Ghāzī usually starts by asking some newcomer who he is: "Whose son are you?" And, after the initial response, the poet launches into the show.

Isn't your grandfather so-and-so, and your grandmother so-and-so? And your father's the youngest of the bunch, his brothers ——, ——,

41. My translation. Other English translations are available in Ben Bennani, ed. and trans., *Bread, Hashish and Moon: Four Modern Arab Poets* (1982), 5–7; Mounah A. Khouri and Hamid Algar, eds. and trans., *An Anthology of Modern Arabic Poetry* (1974), 174–79; Issa J. Boullata, trans., *Modern Arab Poets, 1950–1975* (1976), 55–57.

Layālī literally means "nights," but also refers specifically to evening gatherings that feature music (similar to sahrāt) and to an improvised song-form in which the singer uses only a few words such as "O night!" (*yā lēl*) while demonstrating vocal virtuosity. The *tawāshīḥ* is another song form, with roots in Islamic Spain, which usually deals with love or religious sentiments.

> and —— are all older, right? You're too young to have known your oldest uncle, eh? Well, I'll tell you, he was a fine man. The whole village wept when he died. And *your* grandfather [pointing to somebody else], he died the next day. That week we went to the cemetery four times, and each time for a fine man. Are you married yet? Whose daughter have you taken? She's your cousin that one, right?

Moving from one listener to the next he very often succeeds in linking every person present into his patter. There is no formalized tradition of reciting genealogy in Egypt; there are no griots or other figures who specialize in family lines or history. These displays of genealogical virtuosity are the only performances of their kind in this society.

Beyond its entertainment value, there are certain pragmatic reasons for the poets to possess this extensive genealogical knowledge. Listeners are pleased and complimented to find out that they and their families are known, and perhaps even more pleased to have this knowledge recited in public (usually with many compliments about deceased members of the clan). Also, this data is the raw material for a key genre of entertainment, *ḥitat baladī* 'bits of country stuff' or 'local color' (see Chap. 4). But the immense amount of detail and the enthusiasm with which this information is performed support the argument that this knowledge of village genealogy and history is also a vicarious participation in aṣl, a sense of roots and origins which, though not theirs in the eyes of the world, allows the poets to participate in and associate with the communal history and cohesion of the village. When the poet achieves his voice in performance, he often uses it to establish the idea that he belongs to, is a member of, this community.

Another common theme for tea break conversations is the narration of triumphal performances of the past, the poet's own heroic exploits, as it were. Several stories were well enough known that audience members would request them during tea and cigarette breaks. Common motifs are found in all the poets' repertories of such performance tales: audiences that refused to let them stop singing well past the dawn call to prayer; villages they visited where the audiences refused to let them move on and insisted that they stay on, performing every night for weeks on end; strange and unusual events that took place during performances such as deaths and omens; performances where other poets were performing nearby but the audience members refused to leave the narrator's performance. These and many other short narratives lasting from a few minutes to half an hour are told and retold between sections of the epic.

One such tale told by Shaykh ʿAbd al-Wahhāb G̲h̲āzī (and summarized from two tellings) is about the curious death of one of his patrons:

Shaykh ʿAbd al-Wahhāb used to perform for a very rich Christian landowner—he owned nine hundred faddāns (one faddān equals approximately one acre), his sister seven hundred, and his other sister seven hundred. Shaykh ʿAbd al-Wahhāb used to go to him every year during the cotton harvest; they would set up a *ṣīwān* 'pavilion', and Shaykh ʿAbd al-Wahhāb Ghāzī would play. This Christian had built a mosque for the Muslims where the coffee was free, and the tea was free, and the food and whatever one wanted. See how generous he was (*shūf il-karam*)! One year Shaykh ʿAbd al-Wahhāb did not come, but the patron sent a letter for him saying, "Why hasn't Shaykh ʿAbd al-Wahhāb come? Where is he?" And when Shaykh ʿAbd al-Wahhāb arrived, the patron met him with hugs and asked, "So where have you been?"

The government took all of the patron's land except for two hundred faddāns (in the land reforms of the 1950s) and his station in life changed (*ḥāluh itghayyar*). When Shaykh ʿAbd al-Wahhāb went to him he still set up a ṣīwān and everything, but not like the other years. There came a time (everyone was eating and listening and enjoying themselves), and he said, "Tonight I shall die." He told his servants, "Go tell the people who are outside." And he went to sleep and died. May God have mercy on him!

His wife was in Cairo, with the children. He had five sons—that's not counting the daughters. They loaded his body into a car and took him to Cairo. As soon as they arrived at the house the wife came out and she screamed, "My son, my son, they've brought your father dead! Your father has died!" She knew even before they told her.

Another such tale (summarized from numerous tellings) presents the encounter of Shaykh ʿAbd al-Ḥamīd Tawfīq with the famous Cairene composer, singer, and musician Muḥammad ʿAbd al-Wahhāb:

Shaykh ʿAbd al-Ḥamīd was down in Cairo, and Muḥammad ʿAbd al-Wahhāb's chauffeur was sitting in a café and heard the Shaykh performing outside in the street. The driver called him over and asked if he knew any music by Muḥammad ʿAbd al-Wahhāb. He knew a bit. The driver took him (around midnight) to Muḥammad ʿAbd al-Wahhāb's house in Zamalek, where there was a large circular stairway in a big building. When they arrived, Muḥammad ʿAbd al-Wahhāb was entertaining guests, so the driver sat him on a chair in the entryway. When they brought him into the room people laughed. Muḥammad ʿAbd al-Wahhāb came over and frankly laughed, then asked Shaykh ʿAbd al-Ḥamīd to play, but just music, not singing. Shaykh ʿAbd al-Hamīd played and eventually squeezed in a melody by Muḥammad ʿAbd al-Wahhāb, who laughed again and said, "What is this, have you stolen my music?" Shaykh ʿAbd al-Ḥamīd replied, "We are honored by it." Muḥammad ʿAbd al-Wahhāb gave him a large sum (large, that is, to

Shaykh ʿAbd al-Ḥamīd), and asked if he had eaten. He took him aside and had him served supper: "a big piece of fish with no skin and no bones [*shōk*]—like a piece of meat!" Then he left. But it was now two o'clock in the morning and the last trains had already gone. So he went and spent the night in a *ḥammām* 'a Turkish bath'. He bathed in hot and cold water and slept, all for five *taʿrifa* (2½ piastres, which is about one-fourth of a U.S. cent)![42]

In recent decades a much larger portion of the population of al-Bakātūsh has been out and about in the world—to Alexandria, Cairo, the Sinai, Yemen, the Gulf, and other places, for work, military service, or just travel. But it is easy to imagine that, only decades ago, the tales poets told of performances in strange parts of the country, and of strange sights seen and heard about, were part of the overall appeal of poets' performances. Such tales also clearly establish the credentials of the performing poet and serve as a form of self-aggrandizement—the norm in a performance situation where listeners only pay what they wish as they exit.

Another remnant of this role is found in the poets' expertise in local dialects. When the topic comes up in conversation, they often present a string of dozens of examples and usually remain unchallenged by other participants. Several of the poets have a habit of repeating verses that contain problematic vocabulary, offering different pronunciations and even complete substitutions in each repetition. Originally I took this clarification to be for my own benefit but soon came to realize that it was an integral part of the performance technique of the older poets.

There are many levels then at which the social role of the poet, outside the performance, shapes not only the text but the entire performance situation. Each of these informal genres of performed materials which fill the breaks between sections of the epic are tied intimately to social needs and realities outside the performance. This link becomes clearer later in the volume when I expand my analysis from the epic text to the entire sahra performance.

The Construction of Commercial Images

We can learn a great deal about the social role of the traditional poets by examining a small group of singers who managed to turn the epic

42. Each time I heard this tale, the ensuing discussion inevitably focused on the large boneless piece of fish, with some people asking for clarification. Others offered descriptions of similar dishes served in Alexandria, Iraq, or elsewhere. I was intrigued with this encounter between a *Sīrat Banī Hilāl* poet and the most famous composer of Arab music in the twentieth century; the audience never questioned the authenticity of this account, and I never heard anyone ask for further details except about the food.

into a commercial success precisely by distancing themselves from the mistrusted qualities of the traditional poets. Turning briefly to these commercial stars, we see how they have chosen to distance themselves from these suspect qualities and construct a commercially palatable image for *Sīrat Banī Hilāl* epic singing. Here I contrast such traditional performers of the sīra as the poets of al-Bakātūsh with the small number of singers who were able, from the late 1960s through the early 1980s, to disassociate themselves from the public persona of the traditional epic-singer and become commercial stars in the booming cassette industry, achieving a highly ambiguous role as epic singers who were not "really" epic singers.

The most famous of these singers in the western Nile Delta was Sayyid Ḥawwās, who died in the late 1970s. He was very successful commercially and commanded fees up to fifty times higher than did traditional poets for his live appearances. If one asks about the epic *Sīrat Banī Hilāl* in this region, the name Sayyid Ḥawwās is the first name on everyone's lips. Sayyid Ḥawwās was not of Gypsy origin, but rather from a peasant background, and nearly everyone agrees that he was literate, unlike the traditional poets. The following account is of Sayyid Ḥawwās's early relationship with the epic, as told by a Ḥalabī poet from al-Bakātūsh:

> Sayyid Ḥawwās was a great poet, but not from a poet's family. His family owned land—fifty faddāns! But when he was young he fell in love with the epic. He used to sit in a café and listen to the poets. He heard it from another great poet, Shaykh Sibāʿī from Kafr Ibra [Minufiyya Province], who was educated, an Azharī, who had left his studies to become a poet. Sayyid Ḥawwās's father used to beat him for listening to poets, because he was neglecting his studies to go listen at the café. He fashioned himself a crude rabāb but his father broke it. Still he persisted. (Shaykh ʿAbd al-Wahhāb Ghāzī, 3/17/87)

The poets of al-Bakātūsh emphasize in the story of Sayyid Ḥawwās's life the great power of the epic itself, that it caused a wealthy, literate man to leave all those things behind to become a poet. The villagers, however, emphasize the idea that Sayyid Ḥawwās was literate and cultured and that therefore his renditions were better—for his versions were in fact radically different from those of the traditional poets.

A brief list of these differences includes his use of large ensembles of up to eight musicians, his use of amplifiers and loudspeakers, his use of a completely different poetic structure, his reliance on sources other than the oral tradition, and his use of different costume. He also performed the epic on the Western violin (kamanja) rather than the traditional rabāb, which is the archetypal instrument of the epic. So strong is the presence of the rabāb in the poetic tradition, in fact, that Sayyid Ḥawwās retained it in his performance texts, often singing lines such as, "I will sing to you on the rabāb and entertain you," while in fact holding a violin in his hands.

The issue of poetic structure and the content of the stories is an important one. The traditional poets of *Sīrat Banī Hilāl* in the Nile Delta use a single end-rhyme, medial caesura form with long verses (up to twenty-six and even thirty syllables in length); they often maintain the same rhyme for upward of a hundred verses. This poetic form is used throughout most of Arabic literary history and is the form of the earliest-known Arabic poetry dating to the sixth century C.E. Sayyid Ḥawwās used short verses in varying rhyme schemes, most often in quatrains, though with constantly varying patterns more typical of southern Egyptian folk songs. With some justification, the traditional poets look down on Ḥawwās's poetry as mere ditties or jingles. It seems clear that Ḥawwās's short verses and ever-changing rhyme scheme appeal to new audiences no longer well acquainted with the epic stories and poetic form. His verses are simple, easy to listen to, and the rhyme scheme is readily apparent.

Traditional end-rhyme schema

---------------- ----------------A
---------------- ----------------A
---------------- ----------------A
---------------- ----------------A

Quatrain schema used by Ḥawwās

---------A ---------A
---------A ---------B

---------C ---------C
---------C ---------B

The importance of the costume adopted by Sayyid Ḥawwās becomes evident in testimonies from villagers and others about the difference between the traditonal singers and Sayyid Ḥawwās. One of the first elements used in making the distinction is that Sayyid Ḥawwās was *bitāʿ aṭ-ṭarbūsh* and the Bakātūsh poets are *bitūʿ ul-ʿimma*, that is, Sayyid Ḥawwās wore the tarboosh, the red felt hat often known as a fez in English, whereas the traditional poets wear turbans, which are lower class, rural. A similar observation is often made in testimonies where people point out that the traditional poets are not *bitūᶜ ul-mikrofonāt*: they are not "microphone poets," while Sayyid Ḥawwās was.

One of the key associations of the *ṭarbūsh* headdress and the amplified ensemble style for villagers of al-Bakātūsh is with religious singers known as *munshids*.[43] When asked if Ḥawwās was a *munshid*, villagers invariably answered no, for, it would be explained, he did not sing the religious repertory of the munshids. On further questioning, however, people readily agreed that he "looked like a munshid" (*shakluh kān shakl munshid*) and that he sounded "like the munshids" (*zayy il-munshidīn*).

What is clear is that these deviations from the traditional performance style were not random. The changes Ḥawwās effected were explicitly aimed at distancing himself from the low-status, "Gypsy-poet" associations of the epic and at rendering the performer of the epic respectable. Sayyid Ḥawwās, consciously or unconsciously, patterned his performances and his public persona after the religious singers who occupy such a strong role in Egyptian folk culture, the *munshidīn*. These shaykhs, by virtue of the religious material they perform, and by virtue of the education and erudition attributed to them (often falsely) by their audiences, are eminently respectable. In patterning his performances on those of the munshidīn by adopting their musical idiom and costume, Sayyid Ḥawwās succeeded in creating a new style of epic performance which allowed the performer as well as the material performed some degree of respectability.

Visually and musically, Ḥawwās's performances are distinct from those of the traditional poets. This new performance style, however, was not viewed by audience members in al-Bakātūsh as a break in the tradition. All of the various elements used by Ḥawwās are part of the greater musical environment of the region: the music, the instruments and orchestration, the rhyme schemes, the costume—all are familiar to the audiences, albeit from other genres of folk music. Since the essential aspect of the epic—that is, the story, the plot itself—remained virtually unchanged, audiences in al-Bakātūsh and elsewhere readily accepted the new patina of respectability and modernity.

One can validate these ideas by examining the careers of other poets who attempted to model themselves on Sayyid Ḥawwās. One such poet, Saᶜd Muṣṭafā, succeeded; many others did not. Saᶜd Muṣṭafā was in fact of Gypsy origin; there were no other epic singers in his immediate

43. From the form IV verb *anshada* 'to chant or sing religious verse'. See Earle Waugh, *The Munshidin of Egypt: Their World and Their Song* (1989); however, see also my review (1989) for a number of reservations concerning translations and other aspects of that work.

family, and I was unable to determine whether there had ever been any epic singers in his extended family. By performing on violin instead of rabāb, by adopting the ensemble-style performance used by Sayyid Ḥawwās and the musical idiom of the munshidīn as Ḥawwās had done, and by adopting the ṭarbūsh as headdress, Saᶜd managed to create an ambiguous public persona. Sayyid Ḥawwās was known as a non-Gypsy epic singer; Saᶜd performed in the same style as Sayyid Ḥawwās. As one might expect, confusion regarding Saᶜd's origins resulted. I encountered many different opinions about Saᶜd Muṣṭafā; the pattern basically broke down to a division between people who lived geographically close to Saᶜd's home near al-Manṣūra who knew that he was of Gypsy origin, and those who lived farther away who held the opinion that he was not, because he did not perform in the traditional style. In any case, alongside Sayyid Ḥawwās, he remains the most famous and most popular of the epic singers in the Nile Delta.

Two of the fourteen poets in al-Bakātūsh own Western violins and occasionally play them. When asked how and why they came to buy violins, each confessed that he had dreamt of becoming a commercial star like Sayyid Ḥawwās, and a person could only do that if he played violin instead of rabāb. Asked why they did not continue attempting to perform like Ḥawwās had done, each responded with mustered pride: *kalāmuh mis̲h̲ kalāmnā* 'his words are not our words'. The villagers, however, responded that the poets could not become famous like Sayyid Ḥawwās because they were ᶜarab.

In brief, because of the mistrusted persona of the Gypsy poet, we encounter in the Nile Delta tradition of *Sīrat Banī Hilāl* epic-singing a case where the art form has been respected (albeit by specific groups) and the performer has been endowed with little of the respect given his art. A small group of performers were able to shake off this handicap and become commercial successes by adapting elements of the performance style and the musical idiom of a known and respected folk music form. Since all of these elements are recognized and known, the audiences do not perceive this new combination of elements to be a break in the tradition. What, from our point of view, is clearly radical change is, for the audience, unremarkable continuity, since the essential thread—the story, the plot—has remained unchanged.

Conclusion

The preceding description of *Sīrat Banī Hilāl* epic-singers in the context of the village of al-Bakātūsh has sought to reveal the relationship between the performers, their artistic tradition, and their audience's reception and understanding of that tradition. Many factors within texts and performances of *Sīrat Banī Hilāl* are conditioned by who the performers are, or at least by who the performers are perceived to be. The poets of al-Bakātūsh are outsiders: perhaps performers because they are outsiders, perhaps outsiders because they are performers. They are marked most strongly by their Gypsy ethnicity, an ethnicity they themselves do not emphasize; rather, they seek identity and community in their formulation of the "poet" persona, a persona that embodies eloquence, graciousness, acumen, and an ancient "ur-Arabness." This image, however, finds only limited acceptance among the villagers.

The boundaries between the two groups, villagers and poets, are maintained and supported on both sides: on the side of the villagers most strongly by their social attitudes toward the poets; on the side of the poets by the preservation of certain customs, an identity closely linked to the epic itself, and a body of secret knowledge which includes powerful resources such as names and their own language.

Of the many social factors at play, it is perhaps the forged link of identity between poet and poem which most clearly shapes the textual and performance traditions. The poets inside and outside the epic are kin; the poet outside fashions a continuing commentary about his world by manipulating the poet within the epic. All artists speak to some degree through the characters and products they create, and to some degree there is an "I" embedded in any narrative. Here that voice is marked by direct mimesis—a poet creating the image of a poet.

In the performance situation, this set of social factors motivates the telling of tales of poetic prowess in between sections of the epic; the feats of the poet in past performances are recounted to add an aura of grandeur to the present performance. In addition, the poet's unusual knowledge of other places, other dialects, as well as his knowledge of the details of the village's own history and genealogy set him apart from other men. With this special status comes a certain form of respect from the villagers—the poet is accorded a liminality, an "otherness," which adds potency to his ability to narrate and continually re-create a nonexistent world of past heroes and their antagonists.

In the most recent past, the traditional poet has also stood in contrast to the commercial stars of the cassette studios, performers who distanced themselves from precisely these suspect qualities of the Gypsy epic-singer. Also in recent years, the small groups of devotees who still listen to *Sīrat Banī Hilāl* in private gatherings have emerged as a socially conservative and socially disenfranchised group, often with the poet at their center, a catalyst for their assemblies. The entire tradition, the epic itself, is perceived as partaking of the disappearing traditionalism represented by the members of its audience. This recent social realignment, more than any aesthetic or artistic criticism from other groups, may well augur the end of the *Sīrat Banī Hilāl* performance tradition in the Nile Delta.

CHAPTER 3

The Economy of Poetic Style

The café owner shouted in angry exasperation:

"Are you going to force your recitations on us? That's the end—the end! Didn't I warn you last week? . . . "

The old poet sweetened his tone a little as he tried to soothe the angry man and said:

"This is my café too. Haven't I been reciting here for the last twenty years?"

The café owner took his usual seat behind the till and replied:

"We know all the stories you tell by heart and we don't need to run through them again. People today don't want a poet. They keep asking me for a radio and there's one over there being installed now. So go away and leave us alone and may God provide for you"

Naguib Mahfouz, *Midaq Alley*

In Chapter 2 we examined a few of the many relationships which obtain between epic poets and the epic poem they perform. We now turn our focus to audiences and performance situations in order to examine the social economy of poetry and poetic style: Why do audiences patronize the poem (and by extension the poets)? How do they do so? How does the performance emerge from the poet's interaction with differing audiences and differing patronage structures? And finally, how do audiences, patronage, and performance situations affect the stylistic choices of the poet, the tone of the performance itself?

I use the term "social economy of poetic style" here as an image of my own understanding of the interaction of these disparate elements—that is, an economy consisting of the on-going interaction of multiple forces that translate the material power of wealth (patronage) through markets (audiences) via products (epic poetry) that possess aesthetic characteristics (style) that are in great part determined by the financial and market pressures that help create them. Poetry, power, social allegiances, and money are all part of the traditional performance process, though Western researchers often choose to divorce the "real" world of money and patronage from the "higher" realm of poetic form and artistic tradition. In this regard, that Western view of art and poetry which privileges certain forms of expression and distances them from their economic and sociopolitical dimensions is poorly adapted for the analysis of expressive culture in traditional societies. No epic singer in al-Bakātūsh would deny the direct influence of patronage and payment upon his performances; it is an accepted part of the profession. The difficulty in analyzing the interaction of money, power, and poetry lies primarily in the lack of a beginning or an end to the process; no a priori precedence exists for any one element over the others, for we are not examining a chain of causal relationships but rather an interacting whole. Any starting point must therefore be somewhat arbitrary, and though the relationships we highlight may be consistent, they cannot be exclusionary.

In this volume I focus on one specific performance context, the sahra, or private evening gathering, and on audiences drawn from a limited population (the inhabitants of al-Bakātūsh and their occasional guests). In order to achieve a fuller understanding of the role and characteristics of the sahra context, however, I map out the social implications of the context itself through comparison with other performance situations. Each of these contexts, I argue, represents a separate complex of interacting factors that influence both performer and listener. Expectations, behaviors, and evaluative frameworks all coalesce into definable and describable performance environments.

The problem of unraveling a complex set of interactions such as is presented to us in performances of traditional texts is not only one of identifying what actually takes place in a specific performance or even repeatedly within a specific performance context, but also in understanding what does not, that is, in understanding how each performance or context differs from other performances in other contexts. Performances and performance situations resonate with and against each other, and what is, by comparison, absent in a particular performance may be as eloquent and as significant as what is present.

The performances we study as folklorists possess a quality that, for lack of a better term, we choose to call "traditional." The term comes to us loaded with ideological baggage, but part of its connotative meaning is highly significant here. These performances invoke performances of the past, performances of identifiable and nameable texts of the past, and therefore they create a constant chorus of voices, a multivocality dependent upon re-iteration. As a methodology, then, it would be folly for a folklorist to examine a single avatar of a traditional text if other examples were also available. The comparison of different renditions of the same material by the same poet, and by different poets, becomes essential for understanding the "absences," the mute voices, of the epic within a given performance.

This chapter therefore first treats, as distinctly as possible, a series of contexts for *Sīrat Banī Hilāl* performances. By understanding the normative forms of performances in different contexts, we can come to a rough understanding of when and why the norms are broken, that is, how such "presences" or "absences" communicate in performance.

Next, focusing specifically on the sahra, we turn to audiences in al-Bakātūsh and assess their attitudes toward, and participation in, the *Sīrat Banī Hilāl* tradition in an attempt to flesh out as completely as possible the social background for the performance processes examined in the concluding part of this study. The differing tastes of various social groups within the village have engendered different acceptable performance styles; as a result, individual poets in al-Bakātūsh have established their own coteries of listeners. Four of these poets and their individual performance styles are introduced at the end of this chapter. These four were chosen as representative of the capacities and performance styles of the entire al-Bakātūsh epic-poet community. All of the texts in the remainder of this work are drawn from performances by these four artists so that the reader can acquire a sense of the interplay between the performers' personalities and their performance styles.

Traditional Performance Contexts

Before examining in some detail the contexts for professional performance of *Sīrat Banī Hilāl*, that is, performance by the epic singers, it is worth noting that the epic both exists and is transmitted in many nonprofessional contexts as well. Within the community of al-Bakātūsh there are adults who narrate portions of the epic as prose tales; these are often directed, at least superficially, to children. There are also a number of connoisseurs in the village, and even more in the surrounding hamlets, who can narrate extensively from the epic tales with varying amounts of intermittent poetry; these "reciters" narrate principally for informal gatherings of adult male companions. At least one older man in the region is capable of sustained poetic narration which he delivers in a high declamatory style, though he does not sing or use any musical accompaniment. Furthermore, at least two chapbooks, each representing only a fragment of the epic, have circulated in the village in recent years.[1]

In this one location and time period then, the epic of the Banī Hilāl is found in verse, cante-fable, and prose renditions, and in both written and oral forms; there is no evidence that this was ever *not* the case. We must assume that a researcher passing through this region doing primarily collection or survey work might well have encountered the epic in any of its various forms and then continued on unaware of its cognate performance forms. With this in mind, we must address with care not only the map of literary forms and performance modes which emerges from our sketchy data from most regions (see the Introduction), but also theories such as those advanced by Menéndez Pidal and others concerning the historical "breakdown" of epic into balladic and other simpler forms.[2]

Epic poets in the Nile Delta region have traditionally performed at nearly all local celebrations: at weddings, local saints' festivals, circumcisions, and at private evening gatherings (*sahrāt or layālī*). They have also maintained itinerant circuits of cafés and patron families over a wide geographic area through contacts built up over generations. For poets who are not gifted enough to attract significant patronage, or for any poet when economic needs dictate, there are less respected forms of income: playing in town squares (usually praise songs to the Prophet Muḥammad rather than epic) for whatever pennies are given by passersby, riding trains and singing for similar pittances, even sitting at the edges of fields to entertain villagers as they harvest or plant in return for a meal and some small payment. These latter activities are often viewed as "beggary" or "vagrancy" (*tasawwul*) by villagers. They are admitted to reluctanctly by the poets and referred to pejoratively by others. The poets, as might be expected, are pragmatic about this distinc-

1. I obtained and then xeroxed these two chapbooks. They were both incomplete, undated copies of the same edition of "Sīrat banī hilāl fī qiṣṣat abū zayd al-hilālī wa-l-nāʿisa wa-zayd al-ʿajāj" from the Maktabat al-jumhūriyya al-ʿarabiyya publisher in Cairo. Several poets and villagers stated that a number of chapbooks of *Sīrat Banī Hilāl* had been present in the village years ago; many of these were said to have been destroyed by the dampness that accompanies the annual winter rains.

2. "Briefly stated, Menéndez Pidal's theory of 'fragmentation' posits that as the old epic fell upon hard times, juglares found that their audiences displayed an affinity for hearing certain favorite parts of the old cantares, usually brief narrative episodes or dramatic exchanges of dialogues that marked moments of high tension in the tradtional epic songs, and that these sections lifted from the longer poems came to be sung independently." Merle E. Simmons, "The Spanish Epic," in Oinas, *Heroic Epic and Saga*, 229.

The most useful of Pidal's many presentations of these ideas is found in Ramón Menéndez Pidal, *Poesía juglaresca y orígenes de las literaturas románicas*, vol. 3 (1957), and idem, *Romancero hispánico* (1953).

tion: invited appearances are fine when they are plentiful and generate sufficient income, otherwise, poets, like everyone else, must seek God's bounty wherever they can find it.

A number of the traditional contexts for the performance of epic poetry, however, are rapidly disappearing or undergoing radical transformation. Urban areas rejected the epic tradition some time ago as rural, "hick," and provincial. Though performances in Cairo were common until the late nineteenth century, in the twentieth century performances of *Sīrat Banī Hilāl* have been primarily a rural phenomenon.[3] Now, even in the countryside, things are changing.

According to the poets of al-Bakātūsh, the cafés were the first site to change. The arrival of battery-powered radios, later cassette recorders, and now television has pushed out the poets and their stories.[4] At weddings it is no longer considered chic to bring in a poet or poets. As recently as the 1970s, villagers recount, a wedding was hardly a wedding if there was no poet to sing the deeds of the heroes of the Banī Hilāl tribe after the traditional wedding songs and rituals had taken place—and the performance had to go on till the dawn call to prayer to be a good one. Now many villagers prefer to hire a singer with an amplified band who sings a mixture of traditional rural wedding and religious songs along with renditions of songs by famous urban singers such as Umm Kulthūm and ʿAbd al-Ḥalīm Ḥāfiẓ. Private parties featuring poets are becoming rarer and rarer as the elder generation, those who still most appreciate the epic, passes on. The poets of al-Bakātūsh currently live mostly from their circuits of patrons, a few weddings, private gatherings, and "vagrancy."

The following discussion of performance contexts concentrates on three sets of features: (*a*) economic structures, that is, means of payment, patronage structures, (*b*) customary performance characterstics—choice of repertoire, use of auxiliary genres, and so forth, and (*c*) the attitudes of villagers and poets toward the context itself.

Weddings

The process of engagement and marriage in al-Bakātūsh, as in most of Egypt and the Arab world, unfolds in a sequence of ceremonial stages,

3. For nineteenth-century sources on performance of Arabic oral epics see Lane, *Manners* (1895); Yūnus, *al-Hilāliyya*; and Breteau, "Témoinages."

4. For an evocative description of the transformation of a café from a site for epic performance to a media-dominated context, see Naguib Mahfouz, *Zuqāq al-midāqq* (1947), 7–12; idem, *Midaq Alley*, trans. Trevor LeGassick (1981), 3–7; part of this translation is quoted at the opening of this chapter.

often spread out over several months or even years. These include the Reading of the *fātiḥa* (*al-fātiḥa*), the Writing of the Wedding Contract (*katab al-kitāb*), the Presentation of the Dowry (*shabka*),[5] the Night of Henna (*laylat al-ḥinna, SA ḥinnā*ʾ), the Carrying (*al-shayla*), the Procession (*al-zaffa*), the Consummation, literally, 'the Entrance' (*al-dukhla*), and the Morning Visit (*al-ṣubḥiyya*).[6] Each of these takes place on a separate occasion and is marked by traditions and ceremonies, several of which include music in the form of traditional songs or professional entertainment. The prime context for the performance of *Sīrat Banī Hilāl* occurs on the Night of Henna, which is usually the largest of the public celebrations, but on occasion poets may be called in for the Presentation of the Dowry and the nights leading up to the Night of Henna by families who wish to make a particularly notable event of the occasion.

On the Night of Henna the bride and groom are separately prepared for the wedding's culminating ceremonies, which take place the following day. In their respective groups of relatives and friends, they are bathed, their hair is trimmed and coiffed, they are dressed, and each is physically adorned with henna. In the case of the groom in al-Bakātūsh, the latter is usually decorated only on the palms—in each hand he holds a lump of henna mixture which will dye his palms bright orange. Once the groom has been bathed and freshly attired, he is led outside with much festivity and seated on a chair on a platform, while relatives and friends celebrate around him. A parallel celebration takes place around the bride, though this is held indoors.

The traditional songs sung at this point of the wedding reflect not only the activities that are being carried out at that moment but the entire complex of behaviors linked with marriage. Perhaps the most common wedding song in all of Egypt, with its myriad of different verses, is "The Henna, the Henna" (*al-ḥinna, al-ḥinna*). It is most commonly sung by women as they dress and coif the bride, though it is

5. Western terminology of dower, dowry, and brideprice does not often clearly distinguish between payments made from the groom to the bride and payments made from the bride to the groom. In the Egyptian case, substantial payments are made to the bride by the groom in the form of gold jewelry, which becomes the bride's private property and remains hers even if she is widowed or divorced. It could be considered a form of social insurance. The groom also provides housing and basic furniture; the bride brings into the marriage her personal belongings and all the household effects necessary for the beginning of their domestic life (linens, kitchen utensils, etc.).

6. The various rituals and traditions surrounding engagements and weddings differ in detail from region to region, though most follow this general pattern. A mark of both the diversity of these ceremonies and the importance attributed to them may be seen in a weekly radio program that has run for several years on the Voice of Cairo (Ṣawṭ al-qāhirah) radio station. The program discusses wedding rites and customs from around Egypt and the Arab world. Several of my close friends in al-Bakātūsh avidly followed this program throughout my stay.

heard and well known by the men as well. The recurring interjection "O my eye!" (*yā ʿaynī*) is a reference to the eye as the seat of emotion and love in Arabic poetry (along with the heart, the soul, and the liver):

The henna, O the henna, O drop of dew,
O the window of my beloved, O my eye, brings [a breeze] or
[love].[7]
O how I fear your mother when she asks me about you,
I'll hide you in my eyes, O my soul, and put kohl over you.
O how I fear your sister when she comes looking for you,
I'll hide you in my hair, O my eye, and pleat it over you.
And if evil-speakers come to me and ask me about you,
I'll put you in my breast, O my soul, and cover you with pearls."[8]

al-ḥinna [SA hinnā'] yā l-ḥinna yā qaṭr al-nadā,
yā shubbāk ḥabībī, yā ʿaynī jallāb al-hawà
yā khawfī min ummak lammā tas'alnī ʿalayk,
la-aḥuṭṭak fī ʿaynī, yā rūḥī, wa-ukaḥḥil ʿalayk
yā khawfī min ukhtak lammā tudawwir ʿalayk,
la-aḥuṭṭak fī *sha*ʿrī, yā ʿaynī, wa-uddaffir ʿalayk.
wa-in ja'atnī al-ʿawāzil [SA ʿawādhil] tas'alnī ʿalayk
la-aḥuṭṭak fī ṣadrī, yā rūḥī, wa-l-lūlī [SA lu'lu'] ʿalayk[9]

The song refers not only to the activities of the night of henna (putting on kohl makeup, braiding the bride's hair, putting on jewelry) but also to the behavior demanded from the bride—that she display no emotional involvement in the proceedings. The bride must traditionally appear distant and even morose; her muted emotions must display sadness at her departure from her family home, and she must show no happiness or joy that might be construed as anticipation of the sexual act which will initiate her into womanhood. She must conceal her emotions, metaphorically described in the song as hiding her beloved.

7. The colloquial Egyptian word *hawā* conflates the classical Arabic words for both "love" (*hawà*) and "air" or "breeze" (*hawā'*). See Hinds and Badawi, *Dictionary of Egyptian Arabic*.

8. Text adapted from Baheega Sidky Rasheed, *Egyptian Folk Songs* (1964), 8 (my translation). There are literally hundreds of verses to this song, many of which are made up spontaneously at weddings and are then passed from wedding to wedding and region to region. A similar pattern for improvisatory singing is found in the song "ʿAṭshān yā ṣabāyā" 'I am thirsty, O maidens', which is used in many different contexts and to which famous poets and singers have created versions ranging from the highly political to sarcastic parodies of the original.

9. This transcription presents standardized vocalizations and spellings consonant with Modern Standard Arabic, with the exception of those lexical items glossed in the text.

The song also refers to traditional village ideas about public relations between men and women before marriage. If a woman does indeed love her future husband, no one must know, for it may lead to accusations of misbehavior. In front of the groom's mother and sister she should appear indifferent, hence her fears about successfully hiding her emotions. In addition, she must fear the *ʿawāzil* (sing. *ʿazūl*), who are a major concept in Egyptian folk poetry, translated here as "evil speakers."[10] They are people who strive to separate couples in love by creating rumors and gossip which effectively doom their chances of getting married. They do so out of jealousy, envy, and pure maliciousness. In a tightly knit society such as the village, "people's talk" (*kalām al-nās*) is a powerful social force and one to be reckoned with.

The imagery of the song thus indexes (1) the intimacy and possessiveness of young love, (2) the activities involved in preparing the bride, (3) the bride's struggle to conceal her feelings and emotions and to maintain the expected passive demeanor, and (4) the necessity of publicly dissembling any affection or desire she may feel for the bridegroom.

As the culminating portion of this celebration, when all the other ceremonies have been completed, poets are brought out to entertain the guests. It is a cliché in al-Bakātūsh that they should sing "until the dawn call to prayer."

For the poets, weddings constitute the most respected context for their art. Private gatherings of aficionados might be more challenging and more rewarding in personal ways, but it is at weddings that the poets reach their largest audiences and most strongly establish their public reputations. Wedding performances almost invariably take place out of doors, with the poet often performing on a rough platform or stage, and sometimes beneath a canvas pavilion. At weddings, poets almost always perform in pairs, for the audience demands constant

10. From classical Arabic *ʿadhūl* 'rebuker' or 'critic'. Hinds and Badawi, *Dictionary of Egyptian Arabic*, 576: "jealous person who attempts to interfere between intimates or lovers." The role of the slanderer/reproacher who seeks the rupture of a love affair has been part of the Arabic tradition of love poetry since the earliest periods. It has been suggested that this figure is one of many motifs associated with "courtly love" which passed into European tradition during the seven hundred years of contact with Arabic literature and culture in medieval Arab Spain, Arab Sicily, and during the Crusades.

For the history of the *ʿadhūl* and other features of Arab "courtly love," see Alois Richard Nykl, *Hispano-Arabic Poetry and Its Relations with the Old Provençal Troubadours* (1946); Lois Anita Giffen, *Theory of Profane Love among the Arabs* (1971); Linda Fish Compton, *Andalusian Lyrical Poetry and Old Spanish Love Songs* (1976); A. Kh. Kinany, *The Development of Ġazal in Arabic Literature* (1951); and for criticism of studies concerning literary contact between Arab Spain and medieval Europe, see Maria Rosa Menocal, *The Arabic Role in Medieval Literary History* (1987).

entertainment. Usually only one poet will sing the epic itself while the second accompanies him on the rabāb and periodically sings other types of material so the lead singer may rest.

A poet may earn more at a single wedding than several weeks, perhaps even months, of other types of performances, for not only is he paid by the family involved, but he receives gifts of money (*nuqaṭ* or *nuqūṭ*) during his performance commensurate with the audience's appreciation and approval.

Nuqūṭ (sing. *nuqṭa*) are literally "drops," as of water. The term refers to small gifts of money given to the bride and groom at weddings, to children at births or circumcisions, and to musicians at performances, particularly in return for public greetings or salutations. On the Night of Henna the groom's barber is also present, usually seated next to but lower than the groom, and receives nuqūṭ as well. Though barbers receive semiannual payments from families in return for cutting hair and shaving the male members of the family, their largest profit is derived from wedding payments which accumulate into a considerable sum by village standards.

Nuqūṭ paid to the bride and groom are carefully recorded in a register, for they must be paid back in equal amounts at future weddings involving members of the giver's family. The entire system is a complicated economy of exchange which may provide newlyweds with several hundred dollars worth of gifts with which to begin their domestic life, all of which is then paid back in reciprocal gifts over the years.

Poets' families do not ordinarily give nuqūṭ at villagers' weddings, nor do villagers offer nuqūṭ at poets' weddings. Poets do, however, as mentioned earlier, receive nuqūṭ as performers. Audience members are at times moved purely by the excellence of certain moments in the performance to approach the poet and offer him a small amount of money or cigarettes, which is almost always acknowledged verbally by the poet, often in verse. More often, however, audience members hand small amounts to poets in return for public salutations to the bride and groom and their respective families, or to notable guests in the audience. The poet in this way acts as the official mouthpiece for public greetings and compliments paid back and forth between families and friends. These salutations are a means of calling attention to one's attendance at the celebration, an act that is an acknowledged duty (*wājib*) in village society, and a means of negotiating relationships among individuals, families, and clans in a public forum. The outsider status of the poet, the neutral intermediary, greatly facilitates such social negotiation. Traditional weddings thus act as moments for the transference of sizable economic resources from the larger community to (1) newlyweds, (2) poets, and (3) barbers.

Though the epic singer may always function to some extent as a crowd-pleaser and as a reflection of his audience's tastes and preferences, different contexts do, in fact, engender different critical relationships between the performer and his listeners. These relationships are ones the poets openly acknowledge and discuss among themselves. Such private discussion is often couched in the form of advice presented to younger performers and constituted one of the richest veins I was able to tap during my "apprenticeship." I consistently found that although I could never act as a true apprentice in many respects (particularly as a nonnative speaker of Arabic and as someone who had not absorbed the complex narrative elements of the epic in childhood), I could act successfully as a catalyst for discussions about the ways of dealing with different types of audiences in different contexts, the sorts of episodes to perform when, the preferences of different social groups for sad versus comic sections of the epic, and so on. In such discussions the poets of al-Bakātūsh stressed the following characteristics of wedding performances:

⋆ The episode chosen should be a light and happy one from the epic, preferably one that ends in a wedding (examples include "The Tale of Shāma, Queen of Yemen" and "The Tale of the Maiden Badr al-Ṣabāḥ"). At weddings the poets are rarely asked to perform a specific episode and thus are usually free to present a story they feel is appropriate for the celebration. Should a patron request a certain section of the epic, however, poets almost always acquiesce. The final wedding scenes within such episodes can be elaborated and manipulated so as to include blessings and best wishes for the bride and groom and their families. The same scenes when performed in private sahras rarely take more than a few verses to describe.

⋆ At a wedding performance one should not begin singing the epic until at least midnight, when all the other singing and dancing has died down. In this manner, whoever wants to listen can listen, and the others can go home. Several times I was told that the commercial star, Sayyid Ḥawwās, never sang from the epic before one o'clock in the morning, after his son had already played for an hour or so to warm up the audience.

⋆ The poet should intersperse the performance regularly with praise songs to the Prophet (*madīḥ*), comedy routines (*ḥitat baladī*), lyric pieces (*mawāwīl*, sing. *mawwāl*); and (*adwār, sing. dōr*), and the like. People at weddings want to be entertained, "and that is what is required of us" (wi-dā huwwa l-maṭlūb minnā.)[11]

I might add one further element to this list based on my own observa-

11. Shaykh ʿAbd al-Wahhāb Ghāzī, 3/18/87.

tions rather than on specific statements by poets. At wedding performances, poets usually do not argue with audience members about details of the story or any other disputed aspect of the performance; if an audience member disagrees with him, the poet often cedes the point in the greater interests of the celebration. If there are requests for other materials such as mawāwīl or ḥitat baladī, the poet will generally comply. Since the story of the epic, particularly in the early part of the performance, is often interrupted by the presentation of nuqūṭ and accompanying salutations, there is little objection to further interruption for the performance of other materials. Whatever sense of authenticity the poet may evince in other contexts, whatever personal sense of loyalty he may posses to the tradition as he has learned it, this is usually suppressed in wedding performances so as to avoid conflict.[12]

Wedding performances possess an additional feature which strongly marks them: they represent one of the few contexts which female listeners and children may attend freely and openly. Although the listeners seated immediately in front of performing poets are almost invariably adult and male, on the edges of this central group, on porches, balconies, rooftops, and other marginal spaces, female listeners also assemble. Children at weddings are often running about and playing, but performances of epic are primarily late at night when the number of children still energetic enough to cause a disturbance is small. The children are, in any case, kept out of the area occupied by the adult men.

One result of this heterogeneous audience is that certain highly erotic sections of the epic are avoided or toned down during wedding performances (such as "al-Jāzya at the Wall of Tūnis"; see Chap. 5), or are performed, at minimum, with heavy censorship and repression of certain lines and jokes. This suppression of erotic themes is in direct contrast to some of the other elements of the celebration. The songs sung by the young, for the most part unmarried, men at weddings are almost all highly erotic and bawdy in nature.[13] (I have no parallel knowledge of the songs sung by the women celebrating round the bride.) The comic potential of the epic, on the other hand, seems to be routinely highlighted and emphasized at such large, outdoor performances.

Despite the increasing popularity of urban-style music at village weddings, an interesting set of circumstances can conspire to promote epic poets at weddings, at least temporarily. When there has been a recent

12. For references to the critical discussions within epic performances, see Taha Hussein, *An Egyptian Childhood* (1982), 2; and Slyomovics, *Merchant*, 110–11.

13. Typical songs sung by the young men include "Why Have All the Girls Gotten Married?" (Kull il-banāt itgawwizū lēh?), "What Is This Boy Scared Of?" (Il-wād dā k͟hāyif lēh?), "I'm Thirsty, O Maidens" (ʿaṭs͟hān, yā ṣabāyā), and others.

death in the village where a wedding is planned, and family members are still sitting the first seven days of mourning, it is considered disrespectful and inappropriate to have loud amplified music. In this case people often bring in the epic poets as a substitute form of entertainment. Even if they are less chic, they are traditional, and since they can perform without loudspeakers, the wedding may take place as planned.

A special atmosphere thus pervades the wedding context, one that demands light-heartedness (*khiffat damm,* lit. 'lightness of blood') and joy (*faraḥ*). The most common word in al-Bakātūsh for wedding is in fact *faraḥ* 'joy'.[14] This does not mean there will be no drama or tragedy in the performance. On the contrary, almost all episodes from the epic contain deaths of heroes and painful reversals of fate. A number of episodes, in fact, deal almost exclusively with the death of a major hero. The requirement is only that the tale resolve happily, preferably with a wedding scene. The "The Tale of Ḥanḍal al-ʿUqaylī," for example, is considered a light (*khafīf*) tale for it resolves happily and is easy to sing, though it also contains the deaths of the fathers of the main heroes at the hand of Ḥanḍal during his treacherous night-raid on the Hilālī camp. It is not, however, considered particularly appropriate for a wedding for it does not end with a great wedding scene.[15] Such wedding episodes are considered preferable for they have numerous comic sections and conclude with the desired wedding motif.

One wedding occasion outshines all others as a context for *Sīrat Banī Hilāl*: the wedding of a poet's son, when epic singers from all over the Nile Delta come together to celebrate. Traditionally on these occasions there are no recitations of complete episodes, but rather, poets take turns performing highlights from the epic, striving to outdo each other in humor, pathos, or eloquence. The accounts of several famous weddings of poets figure prominently when the al-Bakātūsh poets discuss great poets and performances of the past.

Clearly no other desired experience could have figured higher in my hopes during fieldwork than to attend such a wedding. Two in fact took place during my 1986–87 stay and I was invited to each. The first was to take place in al-Buḥayra Province, west of the Nile. Three weeks before it occurred, however, another poet's family in the same community celebrated their son's circumcision with a large celebration. At this

14. The term may refer to either the *shabka* or *laylat al-ḥinna* (the two large festivities) and is thus tied to the idea of the public celebration of nuptial rites.

15. Two characters do in fact get married at the end of the tale, but they are very minor figures; the celebration at the end of the tale is for the return of the hero, Abū Zayd, who had been thought dead, not for the acquisition of a new bride by a Hilālī hero or for the reunion of two separated lovers as in the other typical wedding episodes.

celebration a fight broke out which rapidly degenerated into a grand melee; shots were fired, the police were called, and several participants landed in jail. As a result, the al-Bakātūsh community decided not to attend the wedding en masse, but rather to send a single male representative from each household. I was asked not to attend.

The second wedding took place in al-Bakātūsh itself, and, as it fell toward the very end of my stay in the village, it seemed the perfect culmination to a year of fieldwork. To my initial surprise, however, the groom's uncle insisted that the entertainment be an amplified band from the provincial capital of Kafr al-Shaykh. Though everyone enjoyed the modern glow of the celebration, at the wedding meal a heated argument broke out about the use of a band rather than epic singers for entertainment. The dispute wove back and forth between the desire to show the larger community that they were not backward or too poor to have city-style music and the desire to maintain the tradition of a large gathering of singers to mark a poet's wedding. Emotions ran high, and eventually several men who most strongly supported the traditional wedding stood up and left.[16]

A wedding still constitutes the most respected context for the performance of *Sīrat Banī Hilāl* in al-Bakātūsh. As a performance context it has intrinsic constraints, and it dictates a specific performative framework. Furthermore, weddings represent a major financial resource for the poet community and also embody a specific style or mode of performance which every successful poet must master.

Circumcision Ceremonies

Grand, public celebrations of a son's circumcision—celebrations large enough to merit the hiring of a poet—are rare and restricted to families of considerable financial means. (Traditionally circumcision ceremonies were carried out when the son was anywhere between a few months to nine years old, but in recent years they have been held most often well before the son reaches the age of five or six.) The performance setting is quite similar to that of a wedding in that the occasion is large, public, and held outdoors, and payment is received from both the host family

16. In the period between my departure in 1987 and a later visit in 1988, no poet weddings had taken place, so it remains uncertain how the community will choose to celebrate these occasions in the future. It is possible that the wedding described here marked the loss of a major performance context, particularly since the sons of poets whose weddings are now being celebrated are not themselves performing poets. These young men have much more tenuous attachments to the epic singing tradition, and a number of them regard it as a disreputable aspect of their families' past which they would prefer to ignore completely.

and from listeners. The latter contribute in the form of nuqūṭ. Again, auxiliary genres are frequently used to liven up the festivities, and similar constraints of propriety are maintained in view of the mixed audience.

No episodes in the epic recount the circumcision of young heroes or their sons, so the poets' preferred choice of scenes for a circumcision is to sing an episode or sequence containing acts of heroism by one of the main heroes or one of their sons. Their motivation for singing about acts of heroism as part of a ceremony marking a boy's symbolic entrance to manhood and to fuller participation in the religion of Islam seems clear: the poets consciously sing about heroes in order that young people may learn by example. This idea is also reflected in testimonies by audience members about the importance of the epic.

Cafés

The epigraph at the beginning of this chapter exemplifies the disappearance of the café or coffeehouse as a context for *Sīrat Banī Hilāl* performance. Although that scene was set in Cairo in the early 1940s, similar scenes, according to the poets of al-Bakātūsh, were occurring in their region by the late 1960s. Prior to that period poets could depend upon a warm reception and an opportunity to sing for an evening or more at cafés that regularly attracted epic poets. Poets would set out from their home villages on circuitous routes through the Nile Delta region, stopping at cafés, at the villages of known patrons, and exploiting whatever other opportunities turned up.

Upon a poet's arrival in a village, his rabāb would be hung on two nails over or near the door to the café to indicate that there would be epic singing that evening. Though the café owner might pay the poet a small fee, more often he only fed him, supplied him with tea and cigarettes, and sometimes housed him during his stay. Either listeners handed the poet small gifts during the performance or a small bowl or other container was set up near the door and patrons dropped in a few coins as they came or left.

The following description, given by Edward Lane of coffee-shop performances of *Sīrat Banī Hilāl* and other siyar in Cairo during the 1830s, is echoed by descriptions given me in the 1980s by al-Bakātūsh poets:

> Reciters of romances frequent the principal kahwehs (or coffee-shops) of Cairo and other towns, particularly on the evenings of religious festivals, and afford attractive and rational entertainments. The reciter generally seats himself upon a small stool on the mastab'ah, or raised seat, which

> is built against the front of the coffee-shop; some of his auditors occupy the rest of that seat . . . most of them with the pipe in hand, some sipping their coffee, and all highly amused, not only with the story, but also with the lively and dramatic manner of the narrator. The reciter receives a trifling sum of money from the keeper of the coffee-shop, for attracting customers; his hearers are not obliged to contribute anything for his remuneration; many of them give nothing, and few give more than five or ten faddahs.[17]

One interesting aspect shared by both coffeehouses and patronage circuits is that audiences in particular locales apparently often ask the visiting poet for the same episode, year after year—perhaps owing to the pleasure of knowing and anticipating the story, perhaps owing to an association built up between certain poets and certain tales. Several of the al-Bakātūsh poets mentioned this phenomenon, which they chalk up as one of the quirks of the *fellāḥs* 'peasants', 'villagers'. Another characteristic attributed by poets to the fellāḥs is their supposed inability to remember the names of characters other than the main heroes. Poets often joke about the villagers' manner of asking for a particular episode ("Sing the story where Abū Zayd's son goes out to fight and then doesn't obey his father and he sends him on a journey to punish him,") rather than referring to the main character or to the "title," such as "The Story of Badr al-Ṣabāḥ," as the poets do.

One key characteristic of the café context which is now only extant in the sahra, which we examine in some detail when considering audience/performer interactions, is a sense of defending the integrity of the epic tradition. In most performance contexts, poets, when challenged about some aspect of their performance, will accommodate the audience's point of view to some extent, though they may comment on it and even laugh and joke about it afterward. In the sahra, and this was apparently true of the café as well, the poet assumes he is addressing a knowledgeable audience, "those who have an understanding of the epic" (*illī biyifhamū fi l-sīra*), which sets up a markedly different dynamic between poet and audience, one which supports and even thrives on criticism and discussion.

Patronage Circuits

During my fieldwork (1983, 1986–87, 1988), patronage circuits still represented the largest single source of performance income for the poets

17. Lane, *Manners*, 386.

of al-Bakātūsh. In a number of poet families, income from the activities of wives, daughters, and nonperforming sons has equaled or surpassed that brought in by the poet head of household. This was apparently not true in the past, though these additional sources of income may always have been essential. Commercial activities of other family members currently include buying and selling vegetables in the local markets and trading odds and ends such as plastic kitchenware and inexpensive t-shirts and socks. Various labor arrangements involving sons range from apprenticeships in nonpoet crafts to full-time employment in such occupations as carpentry, construction, plumbing, and even the police force. Such alternative employment for sons has only existed as a major factor in the economic life of the community for the past ten to fifteen years, according to the poets.

Relationships with patron families whom the poets of al-Bakātūsh visit have for the most part been maintained over several generations. As mentioned earlier, patron families are usually visited twice a year during the periods immediately following the major harvests. The poet's role of entertainer at the harvest festivities was probably at the heart of the patronage system of which we can observe only sparse remains today. Many narratives of past performances recounted by the poets (such as those presented in Chapter 2) include descriptions of poets arriving in time for the end of harvest celebrations at which they would then perform. These descriptions, however, are of the period before the Nasserite land reforms of the 1950s, which broke up major landholdings and redistributed them to the fellāḥs. There are no longer estates of hundreds and thousands of acres which require small armies of workers, and thus there are no longer enormous celebrations to which the poets are summoned to perform. Here, by contrast, is the summary of an account of a contemporary visit:

> Shaykh Ṭāhā and his eldest son, al-Sayyid, went on a four-day trip to an area near Sīdī Sālim to visit *nās ḥabāyib* (literally 'people who are loved ones', that is, patrons). Shaykh Ṭāhā recounts that they arrived about ten in the morning and the men were out planting rice, but the women greeted him by name and told him to come in and sit, telling him, "You're not a stranger! The house is your house! Come in and sit!" They sang for two nights and received six *kīla* of wheat[18] and four packs of cigarettes (above and beyond what they were given during the two nights and smoked there). During the two nights they performed they also received nuqūṭ (i.e., from the audience). The family slaughtered chickens and ducks

18. One *kīla* = 1/12 *ardabb*; 1 ardabb = 5.45 bushels; thus, 6 kīla = approximately 2¾ bushels.

> for them. They have been going to this family since before Shaykh Ṭāhā's father's time.[19]

As with narratives of past performances, these accounts of recent travels consistently reiterate several key motifs:[20] first, the poet and his son were going to visit "loved ones" or "friends"; second, these people knew their visitors by name; third, they were welcome (so welcome and trusted in this case that they were ushered into the house, even though the menfolk are not present); and fourth, their patrons were generous. These recurring motifs all seek to preserve the same essential distinction—the difference between visiting a patron's family and begging or vagrancy.

The "greeted-me-by-name" motif in particular is extremely common, for it is by this particular topos that the poets distinguish in their narratives between traveling done on their patronage circuit from traveling done in search of any opportunity to sing. The first is totally respectable; the latter smacks of vagrancy.

The lack of harvest celebrations is not the only aspect of the patronage circuits which has changed. One poet confessed that in recent years, his patrons have asked him to sing less and less often. Nowadays, he said, he ended up watching television with them as often as he sang—but they still give him remuneration as before.

I was never able to speak with the head of a family that was currently patronizing one of the al-Bakātūsh poets, though I was three times able to speak with sons of men who had or still did patronize epic poets. The first felt that his father genuinely loved to listen to *Sīrat Banī Hilāl*, though he, the son, did not care for it much and usually left the house when the poet began to sing. The second, however, felt that his father continued to patronize the epic poet who visited them once or twice a year out of a feeling of duty: it was something that his father before him had done, and the poets are, after all, needy (*ghalbānīn*).[21]

This second viewpoint was upheld and clarified by a folklore researcher in Cairo whose father had patronized not only poets but dervishes and sufis. The researchers felt his father did not do so out of any real interest in poetry, yet he put aside a portion of his crops every year for these groups. The reseacher felt his father's desire had been to preserve

19. Summarized from Shaykh Ṭāhā's account, 7/9/87.

20. I elicited these accounts. They are not an acknowledged genre, although they turn up regularly in narratives of "past performances" recounted commonly during breaks in sahra performances.

21. The term ghalbānīn is used to express a spectrum of ideas ranging from wretched and poor (in worldly terms) to unfortunate or miserable (in emotional terms).

somehow the "balance" of society, that these marginal groups represented something that should continue, a tradition to be preserved.[22]

In a hamlet about an hour's walk from al-Bakātūsh, a friend recounted that a long time ago his father had patronized a poet for several years. This relationship grew not only from the father's love of *Sīrat Banī Hilāl* but from an incident in his life. When the son was still very young, the father fell ill and was bedridden for several months. During that time he sent for a poet to come and live with the family, and to play for him in the early morning when he first woke up and late at night as he went to sleep. At other times of the day the poet would sing and entertain, but in the morning and late at night he was asked just to play the rabāb. In 1987, nearly thirty years later, the father, now in his eighties, could still recite for me lengthy sections of the epic from memory.[23]

Though the demand for actual performances is dwindling, the income the poets derive from this system does not seem to have dropped off drastically. Some of the patron families seem to share a will to secure for these traditional artists a basic livelihood with a certain amount of dignity, even when the art form they purvey is less and less in demand. The patronage circuits are a respected context for performance of *Sīrat Banī Hilāl*, with one drawback: they must be carefully distinguished from "vagrancy," for a poet leaving the village with his rabāb on his shoulder to visit a patron looks exactly like a poet going to the nearest town to play in the marketplace. The motifs of being greeted by name and being ushered into homes as honored guests serve not only to build the image of the poet as respected artisan, but also to differentiate between what the poets know in the outside world are judged to be licit versus illicit sources of income.

Saints' Festivals

The poets of al-Bakātūsh attest that there is no longer an audience for *Sīrat Banī Hilāl* recitation at the saints' festivals (*mawālid*; SA sing. *mawlid*, EA *mūlid*) of the Nile Delta region. At first this seems surprising, for the festivals attract to a great degree the same traditionally oriented social groups who constitute the most enthusiastic patrons of the epic. Furthermore, the festivals occupy a focal role in the religious life of the rural areas of the Delta. Al-Bakātūsh is within an hour's drive of the two largest festivals in northern Egypt, that of al-Sayyid al-Badawī in Ṭanṭa, and that of Ibrāhīm al-Disūqī in Disūq, and there are practicing Sufi

22. Conversation with ʿAbd al-Ḥamīd Ḥawwās of the Folklore Institute in Cairo, 7/5/87.
23. Father of ʿIṣām Abū Ḥumayd, hamlet of Abū Ḥumayd.

brotherhoods in al-Bakātūsh from the orders of both al-Badawī (the Badawiyya order) and al-Disūqī (the Brahimiyya or Burhāniyya order).[24]

The festivals are now dominated, however, by performers using urban-influenced performance styles—singers with large ensembles and loudspeakers. Instruments present at a mūlid currently include violin, lute (ʿūd), electric keyboard, and accordion, none of which exist commonly at the village level of "folk" music. Performers include shaykhs (*mas̲h̲āyik̲h̲*) who sing moral song-tales, munshids who sing praise songs to the Prophet Muḥammad (*madḥ al-nabī or madīḥ*), and accounts of the lives of the Sufi saints, as well as singers (who may also be called munshids) attached to local Sufi brotherhoods who exclusively lead *d̲h̲ikr*s (the musically accompanied repetition of one of the names of God or other short phrases which forms the heart of Sufi worship) and do not sing any of the longer narrative genres.[25]

Saints' festival celebrations have over the past few decades evolved toward a more modern, amplified, louder, soundscape. The traditional poet, singing solo or with a single accompanist, would undoubtedly sound thin and out of place. Although Edward Lane, in his description of Cairo in the 1830s, states that during the nights of religious festivals, epic singers performing at coffeehouses were particularly common, he does not mention epic singers performing out in the squares, the streets, and the open spaces that form the heart of the festival. It appears that even at that time, epic singing may have taken place on the margins of the overall celebrations, in smaller, enclosed spaces rather than in central, open spaces.

Though performances of this kind may still occur in other areas of

24. For descriptions of the Sufi brotherhoods and their festivals see J. Spencer Trimingham, *The Sufi Orders of Islam* (1971); Joseph W. McPherson, *The Moulids of Egypt* (1941); Annemarie Schimmel, *Mystical Dimensions of Islam* (1975). For a fictional and moving account of the al-Sayyid al-Badawi festival, see the novel *Ayyām al-insān al-sabʿa* (The seven days of man), by ʿAbd al-Ḥakīm Qāsim (n.d.); a summary and analysis of this work in English can be found in Roger Allen, *The Arabic Novel* (1982), 120–31.

25. These categories are not mutually exclusive; they are, however, the common terms and associated repertories used by the inhabitants of al-Bakātūsh. Much work is still to be done on the various genres associated with folk Islamic practice in living tradition. The moral song-tales of the shaykhs (*qiṣaṣ al-mas̲h̲āyik̲h̲*], for example, are perhaps the single most common genre of musical entertainment at festivals and celebrations but have received little attention from Western or Arab scholars. For the muns̲h̲id tradition, see Waugh, *Muns̲h̲idīn* (1989). Although this work is marred by numerous errors, it is at least a sympathetic introduction to the practitioners of modern Sufism and their art forms.

An additional category, not fully separable from either the mas̲h̲āyikh or the mus̲h̲idīn, is that of *maddāḥ*, literally 'one who sings *madīḥ*'. In the region of al-Bakātūsh, this seems to imply a less accomplished singer, usually performing alone, who cannot lay claim either to a particular level of religious education or to the level of musicianship associated with singers who perform with full ensembles.

Egypt, and there is some evidence that this context may still be alive in Upper Egypt, in the Nile Delta *Sīrat Banī Hilāl* appears to have irrevocably lost its place in the celebration of saints' festivals.

"Vagrancy": Squares, Trains, Fields, Marketplaces

From the viewpoint of the most villagers, the presence of the poets in al-Bakātūsh is uncomfortable because of their Gypsy origins and because of their association with *tasawwul*—vagrancy and begging. Indeed, all of the images and stereotypes propagated about the poets by the outside world relate to these two central issues. The villagers consider any uninvited performance "vagrancy." And this in turn means that the poets' income is always suspect, for it is always tainted with the possiblity of illicit provenance.

Trains, marketplaces, town squares, the edges of fields, and numerous other locations are all possible sites for performances. The income derived from these performances is minimal; however, it tides the poets over between other performances and as such plays a critical role. This type of performance, since the disappearance of the café circuits, is the only performance context fully controlled by the poet; all other contexts are contingent upon either the time of year (for visits to patrons) or an invitation to perform. This issue of control may in fact be the underlying cause of the deep-rooted antipathy villagers feel for these performances.

Such performances are marked by a strong reliance on the religious portions of the poets' repertory; rarely do they sing from the epic in these performances. There is no question of maintaining the integrity of the epic tradition here; these activities are undertaken with a single purpose—to earn money. The performances carry great psychological weight with the other inhabitants of al-Bakātūsh: The shame of the "beggar" poet is the counterweight to the fame of al-Bakātūsh as residence of the region's best singers of *Sīrat Banī Hilāl*.

The Sahra: Private Evening Gatherings

The sahra or *lēla*[26] is one of the fundamental evening pastimes of village men, from adolescence onward. It connotes time spent with companions in the evening or nighttime, usually with some diversion

26. The word *lēla* (SA *layla*) literally means "night," and the two terms are used interchangeably in the sense of an evening gathering; however, since *lēla* denotes a number of different things as well (night, Fate, a girl's name, etc.), the unambiguous term *sahra* is used throughout this work. A third though less common term used in the village is *ḥaflit samra* 'an entertainment party', which usually implies a larger, more organized activity than just a sahra of friends.

or pastime as a focal point. The verb *sahara*[27] may be used to designate time spent in cafés or other public places playing backgammon, listening to the radio, watching television, conversing, smoking on the *gōza* 'waterpipe', or simply staying awake late. *Saharnā sawā* means "we spent time together in the evening/night." But the noun, *sahra*, refers to a gathering that has been organized to some extent, for which there is a host and a venue. In the context of the village, this term invariably refers to a gathering held in someone's home. The same activities may take place (backgammon, television, etc.), but drinks such as tea, juice, hibiscus infusion (*karkadē*), or sweetened salep drink (*saḥlab*), and possibly food, are offered throughout the evening by the host. In addition, the host may provide entertainment in the form of a poet singing an episode from *Sīrat Banī Hilāl*. The host may pay a flat fee to the poet, or it may be understood that the guests are to contribute nuqūṭ as in other performance contexts. In any case the poet is offered numerous cigarettes by audience members, who place them directly in front of the poet or off to one side.

Only a handful of men in al-Bakātūsh now host such performances of *Sīrat Banī Hilāl* with any regularity. The friends they gather round them at these parties are almost always fellow enthusiasts of the epic tradition, though there are usually a few men in any such gathering who are not as well acquainted with the epic as the core group. These latter tend to take little part in the debates and discussions that break out frequently—this is not their bailiwick, and they usually defer to the acknowledged devotees in conversations about the performance.

The sahra represents the one contemporary context where the poets feel they are performing for aficionados of the tradition, although this is not always true, for the group may be constituted primarily of young men who are seeking more entertainment and pleasure than "authenticity." But at a sahra, even a lighthearted and convivial one, a listener may challenge the poet for having left out an important element, for having forgotten a certain passage, for having made a mistake, and the poet in this context (depending on whether he deems the point valid or not) will counter with a defense of his version, or amend it in light of a correction he thinks sound.

The performance structure of the sahra is quite stable.[28] After initial greetings, a glass of tea, and a cigarette, the poet unwraps his rabāb and

27. Not to be confused with the root /ṣ ḥ r/ with emphatic /ṣ/ and pharyngeal /ḥ/ which generates the word "desert" (*ṣaḥrā'*, pl. *ṣaḥārā*), the origin of English "Sahara."

28. The description which follows and numerous references over the next chapters are culled from seventy-six recorded sahrāt and several unrecorded performances, all from my 1986–87 stay in al-Bakātūsh. Performances from 1983 or 1988 are specifically cited as such.

begins to warm up by playing short instrumental passages. He then opens the performance with a praise song to the Prophet Muḥammad (*madīḥ*), usually one that recounts an event from his life such as "The Prophet and the Gazelle," in which the Prophet saves a mother gazelle from a hunter by offering himself as ransom; this acts so moves the hunter that he converts to Islam.[29] The poet then stops playing the rabāb and in rhymed prose rapidly sets the scene for the episode the audience is about to hear. He might explain where in the epic this episode occurs and which adventures have already taken place; sometimes he introduces the main characters. He breaks off the rhymed prose at a point when one of the characters is about to speak; then the poet admonishes his listeners to harken carefully to his words, and, after all have wished God's blessings on the Prophet Muḥammad, the character begins to speak. This speech is the speech of heroes—rhymed epic verse, sung to the accompaniment of the rabāb.

At this point we have moved fully into the domain of epic-singing proper. Once there, the narrative voice, characters' voices, and asides to the audience are nearly always in sung, rhymed verse. At intervals the poet stops and narrates a brief section in rhymed, spoken prose (with no musical accompaniment), usually so that he may smoke a cigarette or rest his voice, and then continues on in sung poetry. Also at intervals of a half hour to one and a half hours, the poet stops entirely, enjoining the listeners to wish God's blessing on the Prophet again, and takes a full break—long enough to sip a glass of tea, smoke a cigarette, and let the audience discuss and evaluate the performance so far.

The transition back into the epic is accomplished in the same manner each time, though the prefatory sections will now be quite brief: praise to the Prophet, rhymed prose scene-setting, then the movement into the sung, epic voice. Throughout the evening, as guests come and go, as listeners offer cigarettes, as the host offers refreshments, the poet also composes rhymed greetings and compliments to the audience members. Several other auxiliary genres often play a role in the sahra (see Chap. 4).

The sahra thus presented itself to me as an excellent context for study. It is the most common of the performance contexts actually taking place in al-Bakātūsh. It is also a context to which it was relatively easy for me as researcher to gain access. I could also, and did at times, host my own sahrāt to repay the generosity of friends, and, as host, I earned the right to determine which episode we were to hear. Finally, the relationships between the poet and his listeners in the sahra are intensified and made accessible to scrutiny by an outsider in the discussions and

29. Texts of this and other examples of madīḥ are given in Chapter 4.

conversations that frame and fill the gaps in each performance. The poets' conceptualizations of the tradition, the listeners' conceptualizations, competing concepts of "authenticity," the boundaries of acceptable variation—all these were far more observable in the sahra than elsewhere. We must bear in mind, however, that this is but one of many different contexts for the performance of this tradition; the connoisseurship we encounter in our analyses of poet/audience interactions and other topics is, at least in present days, found almost exclusively within the frame of the sahra.

Audiences of the Sahra

Within the population of al-Bakātūsh, only a small percentage of people ever listen to performances of *Sīrat Banī Hilāl* in any context other than the large public performances given at weddings and other celebrations. Though I recorded seventy-six sahrāt over the course of my 1986–87 fieldwork, in the presence of audiences that ranged from six to twenty listeners, these were attended primarily by the same core group of less than fifty listeners.

Even within the small group of people who do regularly listen to *Sīrat Banī Hilāl* performances in private evening gatherings, a variety of attitudes can be found regarding the value of the epic and its importance or lack thereof. These attitudes tend to vary with two main factors: age and level of education.[30] In many cases these two factors function in tandem and together define fairly distinct social groups within the village population. Until the 1960s, reading and writing in al-Bakātūsh were taught primarily in the kuttāb, the traditional Qurʾānic schools in

30. The generalizations that follow are derived from an informal survey I conducted over several months which eventually included responses from nearly 150 individuals. My aim was to determine basic attitudes concerning the epic and to determine roughly the frequency of *Sīrat Banī Hilāl* performances in al-Bakātūsh over the past few years. I posed a series of questions, usually within conversations; only with close friends did I ask the questions overtly as a survey. For this reason, many responses were incomplete, when conversations were interrupted or took different turns, when the setting was not appropriate for asking questions about education and personal background, and so forth. The basic format is as follows: What is your (1) name/age/occupation/education? (2) Did you listen to *Sīrat Banī Hilāl* before I arrived in the village? A lot? A little? (3) Which poets have you actually seen perform? (4) Has a poet performed at any weddings or other occasions in your family recently? Which occasions? Who performed? (5) Have you ever seen poets performing elsewhere?

Positive responses were followed up with a series of secondary questions about the evaluation of poets, the importance, if any, of the epic, and personal reasons for listening to the epic.

which the alphabet, memorization of portions of the Qurʾān, and some other basic religious texts are taught by religious shaykhs.[31] Men who received their entire education in this system differ markedly in attitudes toward many aspects of village life from younger men who were educated in government schools. Only a handful of men over the age of sixty in al-Bakātūsh are literate, but these few share an essentially traditionalist viewpoint that was reinforced rather than contested by their education.

Men in al-Bakātūsh over sixty years of age are the strongest public supporters and patrons of the tradition, and several of the educated men of this generation are among the most active public patrons of the tradition. These men grew up in a society where the epic played a highly visible and respected role. In discussions with me, they approached the value and worth of the epic primarily as history, history they considered both ancient and veracious. They also lauded the heroes as models of manly virtue and honor, explained that the epic contains "big ideas" (*afkār kabīra*), and contended that although the poets embellish and take liberties with the story in order to make the poetry entertaining, the epic is indeed the history of the Arabs.

Another primarily age-generated set of attitudes is found in the testimonies of men aged thirty to sixty or so. In this group, also largely illiterate though literacy is more common among men forty years old and younger, the epic is viewed with a certain amount of respect, but it is approached and patronized for the most part as entertainment. In conversation, educated men of this age group often at least initially derided the epic as it exists now as fabulous history with little connection to the events it describes. They often blamed the element of exaggeration and fantasy directly on recent generations of poets (including present-day poets). Several times I was told that if I had come fifty years ago, I would have heard the "real story" (*al-qiṣṣa al-ḥaqīqiyya*) of the Banī Hilāl. The sīra as it is told now, I was informed, is not "history" (*tārīkh*). The predominant opinion among literate men of this age group is that real history underlies the epic; but that the facts have had been warped into fantastic form by generations of poets, who added to and embellished the tales. The educated men of this age group rarely initiate performances of *Sīrat Banī Hilāl*, though they may regularly attend such gatherings. In contrast, less educated men of this group still occasionally host sahras and actively patronize the poets. Several men of this group

31. For a detailed narrative account of this education system see Hussein, *Egyptian Childhood* (1982); also Sayyid Quṭb, *Ṭifl min al-qarya* (A child from the village) (1945); see also the detailed descriptions given in Muḥammad ʿAbd al-Jawwād, *Fī kuttāb al-qarya* (In the village school) (1939).

told me, however, that they did so as an act of charity toward the poets who are poor and needy (*ghalbānīn*). A characteristic that these men cited several times in favor of listening to the epic was that it is "useful talk" (*kalām mufīd*), that is, one benefits and is improved by the examples of the heroes who possessed "high morals and manners" (*akhlāq*) and were of noble character (*aṣīl*). Active patronage of private evening gatherings for this age group seemed to vary more with factors of education than economic factors, though I do not have anything near a complete economic portrait of audience members.

Finally, I encountered only a handful of men under thirty who had ever attended a private performance of *Sīrat Banī Hilāl*. A large number had never even heard a public performance, though an equal number had on one or more occasions heard at least a portion of a wedding performance. Almost all members of this age group in al-Bakātūsh have attended several years of government schooling. Many young men of this group attended performances out of curiosity during my stay in the village. Though some found it interesting, when I returned briefly in 1988, none of these young men had attended further performances in the intervening eleven months. For most of these men, the epic evokes images of provinciality, illiteracy, and lack of sophistication.

Furthermore, those who favor contemporary revisionist and fundamentalist interpretations of Islam, almost all of whom are from this youngest age bracket, reject the epic as part of the matrix of folk or uneducated practices that they view as basically un-Islamic. These practices include the veneration of saints, the celebration of saints' festivals, the Sufi mystic brotherhoods, women's lamentations at funerals, the use of magic in any form, and other aspects of folk belief systems common in rural areas and in certain classes of urban society as well. Though outsiders may find little in the epic texts themselves which would seem objectionable (though saints and supernatural characters do appear in the stories), the epic is at present patronized almost entirely by those social groups against whom these young men have set themselves in opposition. In current social terms, the epic is strongly associated with traditionalist forces. The entire epic tradition is viewed by some groups as intrinsically bound up with the religious, social, and political views of its main body of appreciators.

These differing attitudes toward the epic are often discussed by poets in the privacy of their own homes. Cast in terms of advice to younger performers, their comments contain views such as the following: For old men, sing of the deaths of heroes; they like the sad parts, they like to hear *shakwa* [complaints sung about the vissicitudes of fate]. For the younger men sing light stories with lots of funny parts; entertain them.

For the *shabāb* [young men in their late teens and twenties] sing love stories with beautiful women.[32]

The poets speak in particular of the younger men's lack of understanding and lack of patience with the serious parts of the epic. But this disinterest is not attributed to any lack of character among the young, nor do the poets often relate it to social changes; rather they simply remark that the epic is a taste one acquires with years. According to Shaykh Biyalī Abū Fahmī, "They are not yet 'up to the epic' " (mish ʿalā qadd is-sīra). And Shaykh ʿAbd al-Wahhāb Ghāzī tells us, "This type of talk is strange to them; their age is not yet up to its age" (ik-kalām dā gharīb lahum; sinnihum mish ʿalā sinnuh).

Later we examine in detail aspects of texts that have been manipulated by poets to fit their audiences. No example could be clearer though than the following brief descriptions of a young maiden, as sung by the same poet to three different groups.[33] In the first instance the poet was singing to a mixed audience of men, women, and children. The maiden in question had a head as small and delicate as that of a dove, eyes like almonds, cheeks like roses, lips like cherries, and a neck as fine as that of a silver chalice (*kaʾs*)[34] in the hand of a sultan.

The second time I heard this section I was in a group of young men: the description now began with the maiden's feet, which were as small as those of a dove, and then climbed to her legs which were like pillars of marble. Her thighs were smooth as silk and on them you could see the veins as in the finest Italian marble; these two pillars supported a lush garden in which there was a fountain, above which her belly pleated like a fold in a length of silk. In the midst was her navel, like a fine silver cup out of which a sultan might drink. This description was performed to whoops from the young men and cries for more.[35]

The final time I heard this description from the same poet, he was performing for a group of elderly men and I was the youngest person present. Gone were the romantic images and the eroticism; now all was sarcastic—her eyes struck him like two arrows, little did he know she would soon be striking him with her two slippers!

32. Paraphrased from views expressed many times by Shaykh ʿAbd al-Wahhāb Ghāzī and Shaykh Ṭāhā Abū Zayd.

33. I paraphrase these versions because only one was recorded on tape, unlike the examples presented in detail in Chapters 4 and 5. When I discussed with the poet all three descriptions, he readily acknowledged they were tailored to fit his listeners.

34. The standard word for "cup" in Egyptian Arabic is *kubbāya*, but I use the more poetic term "chalice" to communicate a similar feeling of archaism.

35. Even from this paraphrase the stability of certain elements can be perceived: we begin each time with something small which is likened to that of a dove, and we end with the image of the cup.

The concept of differing audiences within the village context, then, reveals itself not only in the larger artistic choices but also in the finest of details. The poets speak not only of the difficulties they experience in playing to different audiences, but they recognize and discuss which members of their community are most talented at dealing with various age groups.

Individual Performance Styles

Varying audience attitudes toward the epic have helped differentiate the styles of the poets performing in the community of al-Bakātūsh; all of these styles, however, are part of the tradition. Although each poet has an individual repertory of devices for dramatizing or enlivening a performance (as I discuss in more detail in the ensuing chapters), each poet also leans toward a general style of performance and toward certain audiences with whom he is most comfortable. The following briefly describes the styles of four al-Bakātūsh poets as they perform in the sahra context:

Shaykh Biyalī Abū Fahmī is a showman par excellence. Heavyset, gregarious, sporting a black walrus mustache, and still in his fifties during my fieldwork (b. 1931), he is the preferred poet of the young men (*shabāb*) of the village. In performance he sways back and forth, waves his rabāb in the air, employs a wide repertory of facial gestures and humorous voices for such characters as old women, religious judges, Christians/Jews, and villains; the punch lines of his jokes are accompanied by a loud snap of the bow on the neck of the rabāb, a shout, or a deep-throated, hearty laugh. He has a powerful voice, clear enunciation, and is capable of singing, unamplified, for a large crowd. Shaykh Biyalī's performance style is one of rapidly changing textures: volume, melodies, gestures, facial expressions, quick switches from poetry to rhymed prose (*saj*ᶜ) to unrhymed prose, all conspiring to form a lively, highly entertaining kaleidoscope. His rhymes are ragged, his verses vary widely in length; he often misses a rhyme two and three times in a row before catching it again in a new sequence. Transcribing his texts proves difficult: his many digressions and excursions into jokes with the audience and commentaries leave many verses unfinished, and therefore much is left unsaid. I find it a formidable task to portray here the frenetic activity of these performances. He performs the complete *Sīrat Banī Hilāl* repertory as it is known in al-Bakātūsh, but his renditions often lack the detail found in the older poets' versions. When he first recorded the sīra for me, it ran thirty-seven hours, with two episodes from his repertory not

Shaykh Biyalī Abū Fahmī (shown performing on Western violin)

recorded. When I heard him in unrecorded gatherings, several of his episodes nearly doubled in length.

Shaykh ʿAbd al-Wahhāb Ghāzī is considered the doyen of the al-Bakātūsh poets. Small, thin, frail-looking but spry, he was nearly seventy (b. 1919) when I recorded his repertory. Though he walks with a cane, his energy belies his years. He is lively in performance and also uses comic effects, though perhaps less often than Shaykh Biyalī. He is the preferred poet of the older men of the village, among whom he has a staunch and loyal following. His stage presence bespeaks more dignity than a "showman" partially owing to his age and partially to his great store of knowledge about the history and genealogy of the village. During pauses in performances for tea and cigarettes, he entertains as much as while he is singing the epic; one way or another the audience is rarely disappointed. His repertory of facial expressions is more comic though perhaps more limited than Shaykh Biyalī's, and he is famous for his "shout" (*shakhṭa*) which he utilizes several times in a given performance, an effect anticipated by his listeners, something like the "surprise" in Haydn's Surprise Symphony. Two major problems, however, affect Shaykh ʿAbd al-Wahhāb's performance style: the loss of many teeth has resulted in often unclear pronunciation, and with age his voice has lost much of its power—it is often difficult to hear him over the sound of the rabāb. As a result he can now only effectively perform in small groups, and these are often made up of people who have been listening to him and his renditions of the epic for years and even decades. When recording his performance I was able to ameliorate this condition by placing a microphone directly in front of him aimed to capture his voice rather than the rabāb. His poetry and rhymes are more regularly structured than Shaykh Biyalī's. I recorded only about two-thirds of his repertory from the sīra (fifty-six hours); however, I also played with him in "lessons" (where we both played while he sang) for many additional hours and thus know his repertory better than that of most of the other poets except Shaykh Ṭāhā Abū Zayd. I never observed him in an unrecorded performance situation, however.

Shaykh Ṭāhā Abū Zayd, previous to my arrival, had not played in al-Bakātūsh itself for many years, preferring to play only on his extensive patronage circuit and at invited performances; he therefore had no following to speak of within the village. He is well over seventy (his date of birth is uncertain) but has a strong, sweet voice; his rabāb playing is considerably more controlled and coordinated with his singing than either of the poets described earlier. When, at my request, Shaykh Ṭāhā performed in a series of sahras, he surprised all present. His rhymes fell into place like clockwork, and his vocabulary was poetic, with more

Shaykh ʿAbd al-Wahhāb G͟hāzī

Shaykh Ṭāhā Abū Zayd

"borrowings" from standard Arabic than the other poets use. His performance style is stark and even severe, for he employs virtually no facial expression, no gestures, no voice changes, and even eschews rapid melodic changes. He prefers not to "clutter" his performances with the other smaller genres usually used to fill out an evening: he never added a mawwāl, ḥitat baladī, or more than a couple of lines of praise poetry to Muḥammad except at the direct request of an audience member. His performance style might be termed monotonous, but mesmerizing would certainly be a better characterization. I recorded what he described as his complete repertory from the epic (fifty-three hours), though he acknowledged that he could expand any of the episodes upon request. Once, in a discussion between Shaykh Ṭāhā, his son-in-law, and myself about adding detail or summarizing, he stated, "I can kill off the seven kings of the ᶜUqayla tribe in thirty minutes or I can take three hours doing it!" (6/22/87). Some listeners were very impressed with Shaykh Ṭāhā's renditions; others found his performance style too unchanging in delivery. My two college-educated assistants who helped with the transcribing of tapes both preferred Shaykh Ṭāhā's texts to those of all other poets.[36]

Shaykh ᶜAbd al-Ḥamīd Tawfīq is the youngest of these four poets (b. 1935); he has a fine voice and is a good rabāb player. He uses little facial expression, no body movement, and little variation in tone, volume, or tempo. The result in this case, however, *is* monotonous, for he is generally unable to create any interactive relationship with his audience: his performances are completely devoid of jokes or commentary; when disturbances occur, he plods on with his singing, rather than incorporate the disturbance with a comment as other poets are wont to do. His repertory is limited: he knows only three episodes from the epic (Ḥandal al-ᶜUqaylī, the Daughters of the As̲h̲rāf, and Manṣūr al-Ḥabas̲h̲ī), which together total just under ten hours of performance. This repertory is virtually memorized; recordings from 1983 and 1987 show less variation than similar recordings from the older poets completed only a few minutes or days apart.

Of the fourteen poets who were living in al-Bakātūsh in 1983, five can be ranked as having full command of the entire epic as it is known in local repertory. Seven have much smaller personal repertories ranging

36. Shaykh Ṭāhā's unusual phraseology and style can probably be traced to the fact that he is, both in clan affiliation and geographical origin, distinct from the other poets. His is the only family to have come to al-Bakātūsh, albeit nearly one hundred years ago, from the eastern province of al-Sharqiyya. The others came either from the south or west.

Shaykh ʿAbd al-Ḥamīd Tawfīq

from eight down to two episodes. Three of these lesser poets whom I had the opportunity of working with have died since I began my work in 1983. In addition, Shaykh Ṭāhā Abū Zayd, my primary teacher and colleague in this research, suffered a stroke in 1988 and then died just before I completed this work. He was an extraordinary human being and a gifted poet. His modesty, despite his truly prodigious poetic abilities, is perhaps best summed up in my last conversation with him before leaving al-Bakātūsh after my 1986–87 fieldwork. Shaykh Ṭāha remonstrated me for paying so much attention to the poets of al-Bakātūsh rather than just the poems and asked that I not make "a big deal" of them in my book in America. There were far better poets a generation ago, and no one from his generation could compare to them, he said. I countered that the poetry they sang had been around for centuries and was rapidly disappearing, and that it is beautiful poetry of "big ideas." Besides, I told him, there is not a single poet in America who can sing even a few hours of poetry, let alone night after night for a month or more! "Not one?" he asked. "Not one." "Okay, well then go ahead and write what you have to write and God grant you success" (ṭabb iktib baqa illī ʿandak w-allāh yinajjaḥak). I have been unable to bring myself to rewrite into the past tense the passages in this work which concern Shaykh Ṭāhā Abū Zayd.

There exists among the poets of al-Bakatūsh, and has probably always existed, a spectrum of differing abilities and of plain versus dramatic performance styles which includes a wealth of individual techniques such as the use of different voices for characters within the narrative, use of key melodies to mark joyful, tragic, or suspenseful scenes, facial expressions, hand and arm gestures, sudden shifts in volume, use of different "modes" of speech (prose, rhymed prose, and verse), and so on. Several researchers have been tempted to postulate that the plain, unadorned performance style is the oldest and most authentic manner of Arabic oral epic-singing and that the embellishing dramatic effects are modern accruals and basically compensatory techniques used by epic singers who cannot achieve high levels of eloquence.

Though this hypothesis initially sounds tenable, Lane, one of the earliest Western documenters of this performance tradition, clearly speaks of an animated performance style when he records that audiences are all "highly amused, not only with the story, but also with *the lively and dramatic manner of the narrator*."[37] This description is from the 1830s. Another early description, from Ṭāhā Huṣayn's autobiography referring to the 1890s, seems to evoke just the opposite style. Here the poet

37. Lane, *Manners*, 386 (emphasis added).

performs calmly and staidly, though the listeners (as today in al-Bakātūsh) clearly have their own opinions to express: "the poet would begin to recite in a wonderfully sweet tone the doings of Abu Zaid, Khalifa and Diab, and his hearers would remain silent except when ecstay enlivened them or desire startled them. Then they would demand a repetition and argue and dispute. And so the poet would be silent until they ceased their clamour after a period which might short or long. Then *he would continue his sweet recitation in a monotone.*"[38]

These accounts and other evidence of pre-twentieth century performances do not clearly indicate that either one of the two ends of the spectrum are older or more authentic. A spectrum of styles has existed for at least the past 150 years and probably much, much longer.

In this chapter I have linked traditional contexts, patronage structures, typical audience composition and attitudes, and individual poets' styles into some semblance of a larger interacting whole—a performance tradition. The challenge in analyzing specific performance texts now lies not merely in assimilating and including these domains as raw information, but also in delineating the balance and the relationships which concatenate among these various factors, neither shunting them aside as mere background description nor leaving them undifferentiated and univalent in their relationship to specific processes in actual performances.

38. Hussein, *Egyptian Childhood*, 2 (emphasis added).

PART TWO

TEXTUAL AND PERFORMANCE STRATEGIES IN THE SAHRA

Different performance situations in al-Bakātūsh draw different audiences. Large public performances such as weddings create mixed, complex groups which poets attempt to satisfy, and to some extent control, as best they can. Audience expectations are dictated to a great degree by the air of festivity and celebration inherent in such situations; consequently, the poet's choice of text, his manner of performance, and the balance between segments of the epic and auxiliary genres are usually keyed toward the successful realization of these expectations. Financial arrangements with patron families are usually completed previous to such performances; however, a potentially large amount of additional income resides in pleasing specific, usually high-status, members of the audience, or in creating a lively performance atmosphere in which listeners begin to vie with each other in offering nuqūṭ. Poets rarely dispute audience input in such public performances unless they deem it disruptive and inappropriate; such occasions, moreover, are minimally exploited for direct social or political criticism.

The sahra, or evening gathering, offers a counterpoise to this situation in several respects: First, the audience is likely to be more homogeneous and cohesive. Although listeners may come and go during a performance, and men of different age groups may join the gathering for all or part of the evening, there is almost inevitably a core group attached in some way to the host. A sahra is essentially a "private" gathering, though in terms of village mores and hospitality, once the sahra is under way, virtually any adult male may enter as a guest. The audience is also more likely to be more focused in their desire to listen specifically to *Sīrat Banī Hilāl* as a primary activity, though their reasons for doing so may differ, for different social groups in al-Bakātūsh approach the epic with different basic expectations.

Second, poets generally feel that in the sahra setting they are addressing the aficionados of the tradition, their own most loyal supporters. In contingent discussions during the evening, poets vigorously defend their interpretations and their performances of the sīra; listeners, particularly older men, regularly evaluate the performance and draw parallels from the sīra to everyday life. In the sahra, the epic is a contested tradition, a text open to interpretation and negotiation, and therefore, also to conflict.

Third, the sahra juxtaposes a series of genres of verbal art which differs substantially from those performed regularly in other contexts. Though all of the performance events cited in Chapter 3 feature performances from *Sīrat Banī Hilāl*, the epic is in each case set within a different sequence of verbal art. It thus becomes necessary to recognize that a complex of interacting genres may form a larger whole, the individual parts of which may be understood more fully in light of each other, as an interacting dynamic. For this reason in part 2 I gradually broaden my focus, step by step, so as eventually to include the entire sahra as the basic unit of analysis, rather than restricting us to the performance of *Sīrat Banī Hilāl* texts, or even only to those genres of verbal art culturally recognized and labeled "performances." It is my basic contention here that, despite the possibilities for examining the various segments of the sahra in isolation as independent texts, an understanding of the sahra as social action (the "why" rather than the "how" of social participation in, and support of, these events) must lie in a broad-based analysis of the multivocal, interacting, and conflicting aspects of the event.

CHAPTER 4

The Interplay of Genres

"Tell him how the people inside are suffering. Tell him how Israel's blown up twenty thousand homes and four whole villages. Tell him how the detention camps are as full of young men as a cheap public bath's full of cockroaches. Tell him what happened to al-Bahsh's son and to al-Shakhshir and to al-Huwari's daughters. But the worst thing is that all of us, every last one of us, are forced to work in their brothels just in order to live!"

Usama stood up abruptly: "Goodbye all!" he said.

Adil didn't move. Zuhdi got up and put out his hand: "Where are you off to, my grumpy sir? Why such a rush? We haven't finished. . . ."

"Well, why did he get so upset?"

"He just doesn't want to hear it."

Abu Sabir smiled wanly: "I get it. He only wants to hear nice Abu Zayd stories."

Sahar Khalifeh, *Wild Thorns*

A sahra in al-Bakātūsh begins in a very basic sense with the arrival of the poet at the home of the sahra's patron. The patron and some of his guests may already be present, but many people will not enter until they hear the music begin, that is, until the performance has begun. The poet may be served tea and cigarettes before he begins to sing, and the host may spend quite a bit of time in extended greetings, salutations, and conversation with the poet and his guests. After tea and cigarettes, the poet begins to unwrap and ready his rabāb, an act often drawn out for several minutes: he carefully folds and sets aside the cloth cover, adjusts the fit between the body of the rabāb and the neck, applies rosin to the bow and then directly onto the strings, and finally tunes the instrument.

At some point the poet utters the *basmalah* ("In the name of God, the All-Merciful, the Compassionate"), puts bow to string, and commences playing. Conversation at this point often continues unabated, the musical introduction serving only marginally to attract the attention of the listeners. Over the next few minutes, guests who have been lingering outside awaiting the start of the performance enter, passing in turn around the entire room to greet and shake hands with all present. If the entering guest is a person of rank and status, the host and other guests (except for the most elderly) rise to greet him and wait till he is seated to resume their places.

Madīḥ (Praise to the Prophet Muḥammad)

When most of the hubbub has died down, the poet begins to sing his "Praise to the Prophet" (*madīḥ* or *madḥ al-nabī*). If the praise song is to be short, it consists entirely of laudatory epithets and brief allusions to well-known tales; if it is to be long, it moves rapidly from a chain of epithets to a full narrative or a chain of narratives from the life and works of the Prophet and/or his companions. The madīḥ poems are usually constructed on various quatrain patterns (aaab cccb etc. being the most common), though repetitions in actual performance often obscure to some extent the four-line structure. The following examples demonstrate both narrative and nonnarrative types. All repetitions have been retained.

Text 4.1 Brief Madīḥ
Shaykh ʿAbd al-Ḥamīd Tawfīq, tape 83–718 (4/28/83)

ḥabīb il-ḥabīb illī yiṣallī ʿalā n-nabī 1
nabī ʿarabī ashhar linā l-adyān

law-lā n-nabī wa-lā kān shams^{in} wa-lā q'amar 2
wa-lā kān khulūq ganna ganna wa-lā nayrān

Beloved of the Beloved is he who wishes blessings upon the
Prophet— 1
An Arab Prophet who made known to us the religions.

Were it not for the Prophet there would be no sun or moon— 2
Nor would there have been created a paradise, [neither] paradise
nor [hell]fires.

In the tale of the Prophet and the Gazelle, the Prophet offers to be held captive in place of a gazelle who has been trapped by a Jewish hunter so that she may return to her children and feed them one last time before she is killed.[1] Released from her shackles, she rushes to her young, only to find that they refuse her milk and urge her instead to return to the hunter so that the Prophet may be released (and thereafter intercede for them on the Day of Judgment). When the hunter sees that the gazelle has kept her word and returned so the Prophet might go free, he is convinced of the Prophet's calling and converts to Islam. This version is in quatrain form (aaab cccb etc.), though the poet has missed several rhymes and has inserted a pseudo-refrain which recurs three times ("Said the Prophet, 'You hear these words, O Gazelle' "). The poet alludes briefly to two other narratives about the Prophet ("for whom the rose did open," line 7) and ("the camel came to Him and spoke," line 9), before actually recounting the tale of the gazelle:

Text 4.2 Narrative Madīḥ "The Prophet and the Gazelle"
Shaykh ʿAbd al-Ḥamīd Tawfīq, tape 87–035 (3/2/87)

anā abtadī amdaḥ fī muḥammad
an-nabī l-ʿarabī l-mumaggad
<u>kh</u>ayr^{u} <u>kh</u>alQ allāh huwa aḥmad
an-nabī badr il-tamām

I begin by praising the Prophet Muḥammad,
The Arab Prophet, the Revered,
The best of God's creation is Aḥmad,
The Prophet, the Perfect Full Moon.

man yizūr in-nabī yasʿud
ibn zamzam wi-l-maQām-I
man lahu al-ward-I fattaḥ
man ʿalēhi rabbuh sallam

He who visits the Prophet is made joyful,
Son of Zamzam[2] and the Kaʿba,[3]
For whom the rose did open,
And upon whom the Lord granted peace.

1. See G. Canova, " 'Muhammad, l'ebreo e la gazzella': Canto di un *maddah* egiziano" (1981).

2. Zamzam is the name of a well in Mecca, the waters of which are believed to possess great powers of healing; in certain folk traditions it is with the waters of Zamzam that the Prophet is purified during a visitation by three heavenly figures. See Annemarie Schimmel, *And Muhammad Is His Messenger: The Veneration of the Prophet in Islamic Piety* (1985).

3. In the Arabic, *maqām*, literally 'site, location, or erected building' such as the tomb of a saint; here it is used in reference to the Kaʿba.

wi-l-baʿīr gā luh wa-takallim
wi-stamiʿ yā khillī wa-fham
wi-l-maʿānī wa-l-niẓāmī

And the camel came to Him and spoke.
So listen, my friend, and understand,
The meanings and the compositions.

gāt ghazālt il-barr-I tashkī
gāt ghazālt il-barr-I tashkī
bi-n-nabī ḥakam wa-tabkī
wa-tiqūl luh inta makkī
kun shafīʿī yā tuhāmī

The gazelle of the desert came to complain,
The gazelle of the desert came to complain,
To the Prophet, an arbitrator, and she cried.
And she said to Him, "You are Meccan,
Be my intercessor, O Tuhāmī.[4]

yā nabī iṣ-ṣayyād ṣadnī
ba-l-Qiyūd wi-kān rabaṭnī
wi-l-madāmiʿ sālit minnī
ʿalashān awlādī l-yatāma
ʿalashān awlādī l-yatāma

"O Prophet, the hunter hunted me,
With shackles he did bind me,
And the tears did pour forth from me,
For the sake of my children, the orphans,
For the sake of my children, the orphans.

kān murādī arūḥ wi-asʿud
naḥwihum wi-rjaʿ bi-surʿa
asQīhum law kān garʿa
q'abl-I mūtī wi-nʿidāmī

"It was my wish to go and take heart,
Near them and then return quickly,
To suckle them if but a mouthful,
Before my death and my annihilation."

4. One of the common epithets of the Prophet, literally 'from the region of the Tihāma', the coastal plain along the southwestern edge of the Arabian peninsula.

Qāl il-yahūdī mā-asībhā<u>sh</u>
Qāl il-yahūdī mā-asībhā<u>sh</u>
izā l-<u>gh</u>azāla mā-tgīnā<u>sh</u>
yibqā kalāmhā ʿalēnā maḥāla⁵

Said the Jew, "I'll not let her go."
Said the Jew, "I'll not let her go.
If the gazelle does not come back to us,
Her words to us will have been but a trick."

Qāl in-nabī sāmʿa l-q'ōl yā <u>gh</u>azāla   30
sāmʿa l-kalām wiyyā l-maḥāla

Said the Prophet, "You've heard his talk, O Gazelle,   30
You've heard the words and the condition."

lakin taʿālā yā nabīnā
ʿind il-yōm anā rahīnhā
lammā n<u>sh</u>ūf il-<u>gh</u>azāla lam tijīnā
yibq'ā kalāmhā ʿalēnā maḥāla   35

(But come, O our Prophet!)
"For this day I am a hostage in her stead."
"If we see that the gazelle doesn't return to us,
Her words to us will have been but a trick!"   35

q'āl in-nabī sāmʿa l-q'ōl yā <u>gh</u>azāla
sāmʿa l-kalām wiyyā l-maḥāla

Said the Prophet, "You've heard his talk, O Gazelle,
You've heard the words and the condition."

ḥallihā min da l-Quyūdī
ḥallihā min da l-Quyūdī
sārit il-<u>gh</u>azāla f ī l-barr-I tanḥā   40
naḥw awlādhā al-yatāma

He released her from the shackles,
He released her from the shackles,
The gazelle went off into the desert heading   40
Toward her children, the orphans.

5. The term *maḥāla* is used here with several different connotations: an impossible thing
(*mustaḥīl/istiḥāla*), a trick (*ḥīla*), a condition or obligation (*ḥāla/maḥāla*).

lammā l-ghazāla ḥaṣalithum
taltaqī l-gūʿ q'ātilhum
bakit wi-damʿ il-ʿēn sijāmī

When the gazelle did reach them,
She found that hunger was killing them,
She cried and the tears of her eyes were streams.

Qāl in-nabī sāmʿa l-q'ōl yā ghazāla
sāmʿa l-kalām wayyā l-maḥāla

Said the Prophet, "You've heard his talk, O Gazelle,
You've heard the words, O Gazelle, and the condition."

lakin taʿālā yā nabīnā
q'āl il-awlād yā umma
kittim dārī mā bīnā
yōm il-q'iyāma mīn yashfaʿ fīnā

(But come, O our Prophet!)
Said the children, "O Mother,
Keep quiet, conceal our condition,
[Else] on the Day of Resurrection who will intercede for us?"

man Qālhā ḥurum labanki
Qālhā ḥurum labankī
wa-ḥurum ash-shurb-I minkī
wa-rjaʿī li-llī ḍamankī
ballaghī minnā s-salāmī

[One of them] said to her,
"Your milk has been forbidden [to us],
He said to her, "Your milk has been forbidden [to us],
And forbidden it is to suckle from you,
So return to Him who vouched for you,
And extend to Him our greetings."

ragaʿit il-ghazāla ilēh
tiltaqī l-anwār ʿalēh
taq'addamit bāsit īdēh
taq'addamit bāsit īdēh
shāfhā l-yahūdī hamm

The gazelle returned to Him,
She found there were lights upon Him,
She advanced and kissed His hands,
She advanced and kissed His hands.
The Jew saw her and grew uneasy.

shāfhā ṣ-ṣayyādī.
lammā shāfhā ṣ-ṣayyādī al-yahūdī
qāl yā muḥammad inta aʿẓam
innī amint-I bak yā tuhāmī
wi-āmin bi-n-nabī ʿalēh is-salām

The hunter saw her.
When the Jewish hunter saw her,
He said, "O Muḥammad, you are mighty!
I believe in You, O Tuhāmī."
And he believed in the Prophet, Upon Him be Peace.

There is nothing surprising about the religious frame invoked with both the uttering of the basmalah at the very beginning of the evening and the deployment of the madīḥ as the first genre in the performance. The basmalah is commonly repeated by many observant Muslims at the outset of any action no matter how small or quotidian (eating, getting into a car, getting up to leave, etc.). The mobilization of the religious figuration, in the form of the madīḥ, is also noteworthy in that it foreshadows some of the religious overtones of epic performance in what might otherwise be perceived as an essentially secular heroic narrative.

In pragmatic terms, the madīḥ assists in unifying the attention of the listeners and effectively brings an end to other on-going activities through the repeated references to the Prophet Muḥammad, to which the listeners respond with one or another form of the nearly obligatory traditional blessings, "May God bless and preserve Him" (ṣallā llāhu ʿalayhi wa-sallam) or "Upon Him be God's blessings and peace" (ʿalayhi al-ṣalāt wa-l-salām). Such socially approbated group responses also move the audience for the first time in the evening into the participatory role of providing the expected verbal responses and other vocal forms of encouragement which are an integral part of the sahra. The attention and emotional involvement of the audience members at this point are usually still limited, betraying the auxiliary nature of the madīḥ in this setting. A similar performance of madīḥ at a saint's festival (mūlid; SA mawlid), for example, would typically evoke a much stronger and energetic reaction; here, however, the madīḥ is a prefatory genre and not the emotional highpoint of the performance.

The madīḥ, in addition, reemphasizes the conceptual bond noted in Chapter 2 between the performing poet and the hero-poets within the epic, for the most commonly mentioned repertory of the poets within the epic is precisely praise poetry to the Prophet. However, the vision of Islam propagated in these performances of madīḥ, and further supported by narrative elements within the epic, is decidedly anti-institutional and is informed by the various beliefs and practices of folk Islam. This vision of Islam is strongly focused on the person of the Prophet as perfect model for human existence, in a world peopled by the interceding figures of Sufi dervishes and shaykhs, al-Khiḍr, al-Quṭb, and other figures.[6] Institutionally oriented Islam is represented within the epic only by figures such as the teachers in the kuttāb (Qur'ānic school), referred to as fiqīhs, whom Abū Zayd kills as a young boy when subjected to their cruelty, and the *qāḍī* 'religious judge', Badīr of the Banī Hilāl tribe, who is distinguished by his physical cowardice in battle and his ofttimes pretentious mannerisms in speech and dress.

The transition from the madīḥ to the epic can be direct and even abrupt. When the poets of al-Bakātūsh perform in the *sahra* setting, however, they are more likely to precede the movement into the epic narrative itself with a mawwāl or even a series of mawwāls.

Mawwāl

The Egyptian folk mawwāl is the genre of poetry most often performed in conjunction with the sīra by the poets of al-Bakātūsh. The term is slightly confusing in that in Egypt it is used to refer at times to the poetic form of the mawwāl, at times to the singing style used in performing mawwāls, and at times in reference to the typically sad and aphoristic content of the folk mawwāl. In the realm of classical Arab music, for example, the term most often refers to a specific style of singing in which the text is fixed, but in which the singer takes great liberties in modifying the melody, rhythm, and vocal embellishments—in essence, freesong—whether or not the text in question has the poetic form of a mawwāl. This performance style is in fact used by the poets of al-Bakātūsh when singing mawwāls. In literary usage, however, *mawwāl* refers to a specific polyrhymed form of colloquial poetry, usually in five, seven, or nine lines, though sometimes the lines are "chained" together to create long narrative poems. Even at the folk and popular

6. For further information on the role of these interceding figures see F. de Jong, "al-Ḳuṭb," EI², and A. J. Wensinck, "al-Khaḍir (al-Khiḍr)," EI².

levels there exist conflicting ideas about the identification of a mawwāl; many of the texts and statements recorded from literate authors of popular chapbooks of mawwāls, for example, are not applicable to the conceptualizations expressed by the epic singers or the audience members in al-Bakātūsh.[7]

The most common theme of the folk mawwāl, and perhaps the most ubiquitous and enduring theme in all of Egyptian folk poetry, is that of *shakwà*, literally 'complaint.'[8] Shakwa, however, is specifically a complaint that addresses the forces of the world: Time (*al-zaman*), the Days (*al-ayyām*), the Nights (*al-layālī*), the Era (*al-awān*), Fate (*al-dahr*), Destiny (*qadar*), the World (*al-dunyā*), and Separation (*al-bēn*; SA *al-bayn*). Shakwa is not addressed directly to the Almighty; that is rather the domain of prayers, supplications, and pleas. It would, in any case, be sacrilegious to complain to God, for all matters in the world move only by His will. For the pious, the relationship between worshiper, worldly states, and God, may be summed up in the common expression *nashkur li-kull-I ḥāl* 'We give thanks for every state (or condition).' The cause of troubles (and therewith the focus of "complaint") is thus displaced onto Time, Fate, and Destiny, and it is these forces which are to be endured.

Text 4.4 Mawwāl 1
Shaykh Biyalī Abū Fahmī (2/11/87)—Pattern aa b aa

iṣ-ṣabr ʿuqbuh farag li-llī nshaghil bāluh 1
Patience—its result is release for he whose mind is occupied (with cares and troubles),

aḥsan min illī yifaṭfaṭ[9] yiḥuṭṭ il-fikr fī bāluh 2
(Which is) better than he who grumbles and puts thoughts in his mind.

7. The most thorough examination of the mawwāl's various forms and roles in Egypt is Pierre Cachia, "The Egyptian Mawwāl" (1977). For additional information, see Serafin Fanjul, *El mawwāl egipcio: Expresión literaria popular* (1976); idem, "Le mawwal blanc," (1977); idem, "The Erotic Mawwāl in Egypt" (1977); Sami A. Hanna, "The Mawwāl in Egyptian Folklore" (1967); Aḥmad Alī Mursī, *al-Ughniyya al-shaʿbiyya: Madkhal ilā dirāsatihā* (The folk song: An introduction to its study) (1983); Nada Tomiche, "Le mawwāl égyptien" (1970).

8. The mawwāl form has become so irrevocably associated with the theme of shakwa 'complaint' that for many people it can refer to any type of sad song. The term has become nearly proverbial in this sense in phrases such as *balāsh kull il-mawwāl dā*, which, loosely translated, means, "Don't give me a song and dance about it!" or "Don't make a big fuss about it," or *aqallihā mawwāl yinizzih ṣāḥbuh*, "The smallest mawwāl [= ditty] gives its composer pleasure."

9. *Faṭfaṭ*, also *faḍfaḍ* 'to sit and brood, then complain and talk about one's troubles', to get something off one's chest (usually derogatory)'.

mā fīsh aḥsan min illī yiṣbur 3
There is nothing better that he who is patient

li-ḥikam iz-zaman wi-awānuh 4
(and endures) the judgments of Fate and his Era;

min ḥusn ʿaql il-gadʿ biyiʿdil aḥmāluh 5
From the good sense of the stalwart fellow he is able to balance
his loads.[10]

Though the singer of a mawwāl may be moved to sing by specific trials and tribulations, in poetic form these must be expressed in the abstracted imagistic world of folk symbols: the camel (*jamal*) is a stalwart man; the crow (*ghurāb*) is an omen of death and separation; the eye (*al-ʿēn*; CA *ʿayn*) is the soul; the doctor (*ṭabīb*) is the source of spiritual cures or the Beloved who alone can cure the yearning lover; the camel's burdens (*aḥmāl*, sing. *ḥiml*) and wounds (*ajrāḥ*, sing. *jarḥ*) are human troubles and woes; the lion (*asad*, also *sabʿ*) is a figure of authority; mosquitoes (*nāmūs*) are petty interlopers. The foregrounded virtues in both the real and poetic world are patience and endurance (*ṣabr*); the ability to be someone who conceals (*mughaṭṭī*) one's worries and troubles, one who does not babble (*halwas*), grumble (*faṭfaṭ*, also *faḍfaḍ*); who empties his mind of whisperings (*wiswās*) and thought or brooding (*tafākīr*); and who, above all, submits to the will of God (*ḥukm allāh*):

Text 4.5 Mawwāl 2
Shaykh Biyalī Abū Fahmī (2/11/87)—Pattern aa bbb a

yā qalbī fiḍḍak min il-wiswās wi-t-tafākīr [2x][11] 1
O my heart, empty yourself of whisperings and thoughts;

iṣbir li-ḥukm iz-zaman il-ayyām tiwarrī ktīr 2
Be patient with the judgment of Fate, the days reveal much;

iṣbir yā q'albī bass-I mā tihimsh-I [2x] 3
Be patient, O my heart, but do not Go Astray[12]
Worry Yourself

10. Literally 'to balance loads as on a beast of burden, so as to make them easier to bear'.

11. The repetitions of the first and third lines once again display alternation between differing dialectal pronunciations: *yā qalbī* becomes *yā q'albī* in the repetition of line 1, and in line 3 the process is reversed, *q'albī* becoming *qalbī* the second time.

12. Double entendre formed from the verbs *hām* 'to wander, go astray', and *hamm* 'to worry, be anxious'.

allāh khalaq lak naẓar [2x] bīh iṭ-ṭarīq timshī 4
God gave you sight [2x] with which to walk the path

gher ḥikam il-ilāh yā ʿubēd mā tiqdar allā tmashshī 5
Without the judgments [wisdom] of God, O little slave,
you couldn't even make your way,

wi-ēh yiʿmil il-ʿabd law kān luh jināḥ wi-yiṭīr 6
So what would the slave do if he had wings and could fly?

The shakwa theme represents a poetic discourse in which one may express feelings and emotions which it would be dishonorable to express in action or in everyday speech. It is a poetry that constructs a world of un-acted-upon impulses, unspoken voices, unrealized desires. The poetic form, by social convention, allows the speaker to disavow actual responsiblity for the contents expressed; the process of symbolization within the tradition allows statements to be couched in a language at once one level removed from the real world and yet completely comprehensible. This distance lies at the heart of the tradition, for the texts of these "complaints" admonish us, in fact, not to complain; these complaints are rhetorically structured so that they in fact *avoid* the direct expression of personal complaint. This rhetoric is part of the general tenor of Egyptian folk poetry and extends far beyond the mawwāl and even into the epic.[13] When Khaḍra al-Sharīfa is cast out of the Banī Hilāl tribe in the episode of the Birth of Abū Zayd, for example, she sings the following:

Text 4.6 Shakwa from within the Epic
Shaykh Ṭāhā Abū Zayd, tape 87–101 (6/1/87)

anā in shakēt wallāhī rubʿ mā biyy 1
wi-l-baḥr il-jārī yinshif māh

anā in shakēt wallāhī rubʿ mā biyy 2
il-ḥajar il-jalmūd yiṭīr shatāh [2x]

anā in shakēt wallāhī rubʿ mā biyy 3
il-jabal il-ʿālī yihidd-I ʿulāh

13. See Abu-Lughod, *Veiled Sentiments*, for an analysis of a body of women's poetry (*ghinnāwa*) as a discourse which allows expression in artistic forms of thoughts and feelings that it would be wholly unacceptable to act upon in real life. Her insightful examples provoked my own thoughts about the functioning of the mawwāl, and of shakwa in general, in Egyptian folk poetry.

I, if I complained, by God, of even a quarter of my situation, 1
The flowing sea, its waters would dry up.

I, if I complained, by God, of even a quarter of my situation, 2
The solid stone, its splinters would fly. [2x]

And I, if I complained, by God, of even a quarter of my
situation, 3
The high mountain, its heights would crash down.

To complain, and yet not complain, is the paradoxical situation of all honorable characters within the epic—and in real life.

The mawwāl is constructed most often on a five-, seven-, or nine-line pattern involving at least two different rhymes, and often three or more. It is quite distinct from the rhyme structure of epic verse:

Epic Verse

-------------- --------------A
-------------- --------------A
-------------- --------------A
-------------- --------------A
(etc.)

Seven-Line Mawwāl

----------A
----------A
----------A
------B
------B
------B
----------A

In musical terms the two genres are equally distinct; the mawwāl possesses a sound and ethos quite separate from that of epic verse. Epic verse is in general mesmerizingly rhythmic, the same melody often being used for dozens of lines before a change occurs. Although the poet may throw in a large number of devices such as extending certain notes, accenting the melodic line differently, adding musical embellishments, and such, these rarely become the focus of the audience's attention. The overall effect is one of regularity. The mawwāl, on the other hand, is a genre used to demonstrate vocal virtuosity. It has no regular rhythm and is often sung with a great deal of melisma, heavy rubato, and in an emotionally heightened style.

The mawwāl often displays an additional feature that distinguishes it from other forms of Arabic folk poetry: an extremely artful and complex technique of paronomasia and double entendre. Briefly, the final words of all the lines that share a common rhyme are pronounced almost exactly alike in performance, though they would be quite distinct in conversational speech. This leaves to the listener the activity of choosing between the various similar-sounding possibilities and the selection of those meanings foregrounded by the poet.[14] Providing a written transcription of a mawwāl often conceals much of the artistry of the genre. In the text below, for example, the final words in lines 1, 2, 3, 4, and 7 are close puns, not only because the words themselves are similar (i.e., standard puns) but because the poet has deliberately obscured differences in pronunciation, "leveling" the differences to a single pronunciation in his performance.

Text 4.7 Mawwāl 3
Shaykh Biyalī Abū Fahmī (2/11/87)—Pattern aaaa bb a

qāl: il-ʿajab ʿalā jamal majrūḥ wi-**mighaṭṭī** 1
He said: What a wonder is the camel who is wounded but CONCEALS IT!

yifūt ʿalā l-iʿād miḥammil ghulb wi-**mighaṭṭī** 2
He passes by his enemies bearing misfortune and is COVERED BY IT.

yiqūl: anā fī zamānī kunt ashīl aḥmāl wi-**akhāṭī** 3
He says: "I in my time used to bear burdens and TRAVEL ON."

yā ʿēnī *kh*udī lik rafīq zēn min khiyār il-nās wi-law **khadtī** 4
O my eye, take for yourself a fine companion from the best of people, if you must TAKE ONE.

14. Pierre Cachia (in "The Egyptian Mawwāl") has found that although a single term in a mawwāl may suggest many different interpretations, composers of mawwāls and some of the more literate singers focus on a single specific meaning in each line. In addition, it appears that although a rhyme *word* may appear more than once in the same poem, traditionally it should never refer to the same *meaning* twice. This is quite probably true of the mawwāl as a literary genre; audiences and epic poets in al-Bakātūsh, however, do not always seize upon some of the more recherché wordplays and often interpret the poem using the same meaning for more than one line.

yibqā dā khēra wi-law 5
This will be good and if

ḥakam il-zaman wi-māl 6
Fate judges and "leans,"

yuqʿud yidamdim ʿalā l-ʿibād wi-**yighaṭṭī** 7
He will sit with you and say only "hmmmm" and
"HURRUMPH"[15] to others (concealing your troubles).

This example encapsulates much of the worldview and style of the mawwāl complaint. The voices are detached, nameless; we must fill in the unspecified subject of the third-person verb ("he said,"; "he says,") that introduces the first and third lines. Even when a direct address, to the "eye" (= soul) is introduced in line 4, we remain but eavesdroppers to the internal dialogue of an unknown speaker. The ideas are expressed in depersonalized symbols, terms with no specific antecedents. The virtue extolled is that of concealing pain and worries in the presence of enemies and rivals. If possible, troubles and concerns should not be expressed to anyone; failing that, the mawwāl exhorts us to choose a companion to confide in only with great care, someone who will conceal our secrets from others. The result of a bad choice is in fact another major theme of the folk mawwāl—deception and betrayal by friends and trusted companions.

In the following example, the final word of lines 1, 2, 3, and 9 (all pronounced *khaṭābī* or *ḥaṭābī* in this performance) can be broken down into a number of possibilities:

Sung Pronunciation		Common Spoken Pronunciation(s)	Translation(s)
khaṭābī	=	khaṭā biyya [SA khaṭiʾa]	he/it wronged me
	=	khaṭā biyya	he/it walked with me (i.e., carried me) he/it walked on me (i.e., trod on me)
	=	khaṭa biyya [SA khaṭāʾ]	a fault in me
ḥaṭābī	=	ḥaṭabī	my kindling

15. From ghaṭṭ, yighuṭṭ, literally 'to snort', which I have tried to capture with the translation "Hurrumph." My thanks to Pierre Cachia for this explanation.

=	ḥaṭṭ biyya	he/it pushed down on me (i.e., humbled, abased me)
=	ḥāṭṭa biyya	she/it is pushing down on me (i.e., is humbling, is abasing me)

In performance the poet can sing [kh] and [ḥ] so that they are nearly indistinguishable, which means that in theory all of the listed translations are possible interpretations for each of the lines. In the translation that follows, when more than one possibility functions with ease in a line, they have been capitalized and retained.

Text 4.8 Mawwāl 4
Shaykh Biyalī Abū Fahmī (2/11/87)—Pattern aaa bbb a

wi-yikūn jamalī ʿind shēl il-ḥiml **khaṭābī** 1
And my camel at the carrying of the burden WRONGED ME
CARRIED ME

mā kān ghurāb il-naya shālnī wa-**khaṭābī** 2
In spite of the Raven of Separation, [Fate] bore me and
CARRIED ME ACROSS
TROD ON ME

yā nār qalbī ʿalēhum qidīnī **ḥaṭābī** 3
O Fire of my heart, against them light MY KINDLING.

anā asʾalak yā rabb [2x] yā mugrī l-laban fī l-bizz 4
I ask you O Lord, O you who cause milk to flow in the
BREAST!

titaʿtaʿ il-bakr min taḥt il-ḥimūl wi-yifizz 5
You stir the young camel 'neath his loads and he SPRINGS UP!

wi-tisalṭan il-ʿizz 6
And you have authority over all PROSPERITY!

wi-layālī il-ʿizz bitdūm lī lakin il-layālī maʿa l-ayyām **ḥaṭābī** 7
Let the nights of prosperity continue for me; But the nights,
along with the days, PUSH DOWN ON ME
(HUMBLE ME)

Paraphrase:

1) As a strong man, when the time comes, I should shoulder life's burdens,
2) Yet Fate seized me, despite my intentions, and bore me away from what I had hoped my life would be.
3) O my heart, strengthen yourself against the difficulties of life [or: against your enemies],
4) I ask you, O Lord, I ask you, O Lord, You who cause milk to flow in the breast,
5) You who give the young hope despite their troubles,
6) You have the power to grant me prosperity,
7) Let me continue to prosper. Yet all the forces of the world are trying to overcome me!

The shakwa theme whether expressed in the form of a mawwāl, such as above, or in epic verse, such as in Khaḍra's shakwa also above, is one that attempts to conceal what it in fact actively reveals: the subject's discontent and lack of *ṣabr* 'patience, endurance'. Though mawwāls are composed about many different subjects, the examples interpolated into performances of *Sīrat Banī Hilāl* by the poets of al-Bakātūsh almost all deal with shakwa; as a body they may be taken to consititute a subgenre of sorts, intimately associated with the epic. As the examples above demonstrate, at the level of basic imagery the motif of "concealment" is a common one in the genre. The technique of paranomasia within the mawwāl differs, furthermore, from other types of punning, and may be read as a formal extension of the strategy of "concealment." Puns are at times used by the al-Bakātūsh poets within the body of the epic; however, in these cases they rely upon the closeness of the common pronunciation of words to indicate the pun, which furthermore may be located anywhere in the verse. In short, in this form of wordplay it is up to the listener to create the link between two or more terms based on the similarity of pronunciation (though poets often mark the pun as well with paralinguisitic cues such as musical marking with sudden pause, accentuation, sudden change in volume or tempo, etc.). In the mawwāl, the normally different pronunciations of the verse-final words are deformed and suppressed: they are pronounced the same and are all located in the verse-final rhyme, and nearly every rhyme is a pun. In the mawwāl then, the listener knows that there are puns structuring the poem, knows where they are to be found, and most significantly, must wrest the "words" from within the "pronunciation."

In the first form of punning, the listener supplies the connection between two signifieds because of the relation she or he perceives between two signifiers (similarity of pronunciation), while in the second, the listener must forcibly bifurcate a single signifier (based on its structural location) into two or more separate signifiers and then connect the possible signifieds.

Standard Punning

Signifier A		listener's		Contrast-		Signified A
	→	perception of	→	comparison	→	and
Signifier B		similarity		between:		Signified B

Mawwāl Punning

Signifier A		listener splits		Signified A
	→	single signifier		
Signifier A		into possibilities,	→	Signified B
	→	then foregrounds		
Signifier A		one or more, thus:		Signified C

The basic strategy of concealment within the mawwāl thus emerges at several different levels through (1) use of a timeless and spaceless rhetoric (distanced from singer and listeners); (2) suppression of any specific identity for the "speaker" within the poem; (3) expression of ideas in nonhuman images and abstractions which are nonetheless easily understood (displacement, for example, onto animal imagery) and; (4) concealment of key words within the poem through the deformation of normal pronunciation.

At all levels then (speaker, time, images, puns, rhymes) the shakwa-mawwāl asks its listeners to comprehend what it pretends to conceal—a strategy directly rooted in the social norms which have created a genre of poetry, the "complaint," which bears the message that the greatest fault in a human being is to complain. To sing a mawwāl is thus precisely to complain without complaining, an extended use of *praeteritio*, to reveal emotions in a form that pretends to conceal them, to seek release (*faraj*) while still laying claim to endurance/patience (*ṣabr*).

The location of the mawwāl at the transition point of the sahra performance between the opening praise to the Prophet Muḥammad and the epic narrative fundamentally rearranges the axis of identification of the listeners. First of all, the mawwāl itself marks an increased attention within the performance to poetic form and likewise demands from its listeners an increased level of concentration if they are to grasp the various implications of the poem, particularly the punned rhymes. Perhaps more significant, however, is the shift away from the *ideal* (embodied in the person of the Prophet Muḥammad) toward the level of *identification* with the human heroes of the epic, heroes who are as torn as we are between suppression and expression of troubles and emotions, but in order to be human heroes they must have faults: one cannot become a prophet; one can, however, aspire to the heroic.

These two common auxiliary genres of epic performance, madīḥ and mawwāl, should in any case attract our attention by dint of their constant proximity to the epic; their significance becomes even more telling as we become aware that both genres are constantly replicated in miniature *within* the epic as well, at particularly crucial junctures.

Sīra

At the end of the madīḥ-mawwāl sequence, a new sequence is set into motion, one repeated by the poets of al-Bakātūsh whenever they begin to sing the epic itself, whether this be at the beginning of an evening or after an interruption, however lengthy or brief. A musical interlude is presented first, followed by a spoken passage in rhymed prose (*saj*ʿ). This spoken prose section, known among the poets as *kalām al-rāwī* 'the words of the reciter', or as the *qa*ʿ*da* the 'base' or 'foundation', provides either introductory information regarding the scene-setting (such as introducing characters or alerting listeners to which episode or which part of an episode is about to be sung) or actual narrative material which carries the story forward. The subsequent poetry at times re-presents narrative material from the prose passage; at other times the story continues forward with no substantial repetition of material.[16]

The critical juncture between prose and poetry is always effected in the same manner: a character within the epic must be emotionally moved to speak. Situations and emotions must reach a confluence that impels a character to stand up and sing: "and he sang, saying verses which you shall hear, and all who love the beauty of the Prophet, wish God's blessings upon Him," or, "he rose and gestured, saying words, and all who love the beauty of the Prophet wish God's blessings upon Him." Alternatively, the poet entreats the audience to harken to what a character is about to say: "and he wept: Listen to what he shall say, and all who love the beauty of the Prophet, wish God's blessings upon Him." The moment of transition is one of highly charged emotions, and each time a poet moves back into the epic, he must do so in the same manner, through the vehicle of a character within the epic who is *moved* to speak.

16. In some older manuscripts of *Sīrat Banī Hilāl*, the poetry consistently re-presents in dialogue the plot material summarized in third-person voice in the prose sections. See Anne Blunt and Wilfred Blunt, *Stealing of the Mare* (1892), for an example of this style translated into English.

Once the transition has been accomplished, once the epic-verse mode has been broached, various voices may be deployed, including extensive sequences in third-person narrative voice. The actual transition, however, is effected with the introduction of first-person voice, and this first-person utterance is usually motivated by emotional conditions. Thus typical transitions occur at moments of grief, joy, fear, anxiety, or in formal, public speech-acts:

Music → Rhymed Prose → Emotional Crisis → Verse

The final line of the rhymed prose section is invariably an invocation of God's blessings on the Prophet. As audience members whisper one of the appropriate responsary blessings upon the Prophet Muḥammad, the poet plays another brief musical interlude, tunes the rabāb if necessary, and selects his recitation melody. The very first verse is accorded a great deal of importance by the poets, for it "sets" (*tabbit*; SA *thabbata*) the rhyme; the words are not hard to find, however, for this introit is one of the most formulaic of sequences in the epic. The poet's first line of sung verse (*kalām al-shāʿir* 'words of the poet') will once again be a mention of the Prophet, often couched in the poet's own first-person voice:

A. anā ʿabd-I mīn yaʿshaQ jamāl-I muḥammad
ṭāhā l-lāzī ḥajj il-ḥajīj wi-jāh
I am the servant of he who adores the beauty of Muḥammad,
Ṭāhā for whom the pilgrims pelerinated and came.

B. anā ʿabd-I mīn yaʿshaQ jamāl-I muḥammad
nabīnā l-hudā sayyid wilād ʿadnān
I am the servant of he who adores the beauty of Muḥammad,
Our Prophet of True Guidance, Lord of the Sons of ʿAdnān.

C. awwil kalāmī fī madīḥ il-muṣṭafā
il-hāshimī mā linash shafīʿ siwāh
The first of my words are in praise of the Chosen One,
The Hashimite. We have no intercessor save He.

This brief panegyrical opening is at times expanded to two or even three lines, but rarely further. The next line invariably includes one of several formulae for announcing the speaker whose words we are about to hear, usually coupled with another formula indicating his or her charged emotional state:

D. qāl il-amīr barakāt wi-l-qalb-I fī l-wajal
wi-nār-I qalbuh fī l-fu'ād yikawūh
Said Prince Barakāt, and his heart was in dread,
And the fire of his heart in his soul did sear him.

E. qālat khaḍra ʿindimā māl bihā z-zaman
wi-ḥayāt-I rabbī, lā ilāh[a] siwāh
Said Khaḍra when Fate leaned upon her,
"By the life of my Lord [God], there is no god but He."

F. qāl il-malik faḍl-I min mā aṣābahu
dunyā daniyya ammā z-zaman jabbār
Said King Faḍl from what befell him,
"[It's] a wretched world and Fate is a tyrant."

After this verbalized quotation marker, and the commonly attached expression of strong emotionality, comes the shakwa sequence or a sequence of aphorisms, sung directly by the epic character or in an unattributed voice. This aphoristic preface to epic narration has a number of parallels in other epic traditions. A suggestive parallel can be found, for example, in the heroic songs of the Mande hunters which Charles Bird breaks down into three separate modes: proverb-praise mode, narrative mode, and song mode. The proverb-praise mode acts as an introduction, establishes the veracity and authenticity of the singer's performance, and is often found at all major divisions in the story.[17] An additional, and even closer, parallel is found in the opening passage to "The Wedding of Smailagić Meho" as sung by Abdo Međedović. The epic poet, a Muslim, first invokes God's assistance, then sings a series of aphoristic sentiments ("Rain will fall and the year will bear its fruits, and the debtor will free himself of his debt, but never of a bad friend, nor yet at home of a bad wife. . . . Roof over your house and it will not leak. Strike your wife and she will not scold."), then addresses his listeners, sets the scene, and finally begins the narrative itself.[18]

Finally, at the conclusion of the shakwa passage, the epic narrative is engaged.

17. See Charles Bird, "Heroic Songs of the Mande Hunters," in *African Folklore*, ed. Richard Dorson (1972).

18. *Serbo-Croatian Heroic Songs Collected by Milman Parry, Volume Three: The Wedding of Smailagić Meho*, trans. Albert B. Lord (1974), 79. My thanks to Albert Lord for directing me to this parallel.

	Musical Introduction
	Rhymed prose
Spoken	Emotional crisis
	Invocation for the Prophet
	Music
	Poet's introit/mention of the Prophet
Sung	Illocutionary marker/emotional state
	Shakwa (aphoristic mode)
	Epic narrative

One variation on this sequence is common among some of the poets: a mawwāl may be sung between the rhymed prose passage and the beginning of the sung epic verse. Since the mawwāls used at this point in the performance invariably deal with the shakwa theme, no shakwa passage is then heard between the announcement of the speaker and the commencement of the story itself. (The mawwāl, once again, is a poetic form based on a poly-rhymed sequence of verses in which most verses end with a particular form of paronomasia, sung in a very distinct manner; the shakwa is a theme that can be couched either in the form of epic verse or in that of a mawwāl.)

Paired below are parallel passages taken from Shaykh Ṭāhā and Shaykh Biyalī Abū Fahmī which demonstrate these two typical transitions (with and without mawwāl).

Text 4.9 Transition into Epic Verse 1
Shaykh Ṭāhā Abū Zayd, tape 87–101 (6/1/87)

Spoken:
. . . qām ʿusarat ʿalēh nafsuh min ʿadam zikrat iṣ-ṣubyān, fa-qaʿad Rizq yinshid ʿalā ʿadam zikrit iṣ-ṣabī kalām tismaʿ ilēh wi-ʿāshiq jamāl in-nabī yikattarum iṣ-ṣalāt^{u} ʿalēh:

[Music]

Sung:
anā ʿabd-I mīn yaʿshaq jamāl-I muḥammad, 1
Ṭāhā l-lāzī yashtāq lahu kull-I rāyiḥ.
ismaʿ mā qāl rizq ish-shajīʿ ibn^{u} nāyil, 2
dam^{ʿin} jarā min muqlit il-ʿēn sāyiḥ.
āhēn min id-dunyā wi-d-dahr wi-z-zaman, 3
kull-I mā shuftuh bi-l-ʿēn rāyiḥ.
mā mdaḥsh fī l-ayyām yawm^{an} yisirranī, 4
illā yijī ʿuqbuh nakād wi-shaḥāyiḥ.
yā bēn ṣaliḥnī kifā mā faʿalta biyy, 5
armēt silāḥī ilēk wa-bi-l-ʿuzr wāḍiḥ.

mālī kitīr yā rijālī min ghēr zikrā, 6
mål^{in} balā zikrā baʿd il-ʿumr^{u} rāyiḥ.

Spoken:

. . . His soul grew greatly troubled over the lack of an heir, so Rizq sat and sang, of the lack of a male heir, words which you shall hear, and he who loves the beauty of the Prophet wishes God's blessings upon Him:

[Music]

Sung:

I am the servant of all who adore the beauty of Muḥammad, 1
Ṭāhā, for whom every pilgrim yearns.
Listen to what said Rizq the Valiant, son of Nāyil, 2
A tear from the orb of his eye did flow.
"Ah! Ah! the World and Fate and Destiny! 3
And all I have seen with my eyes shall disappear.
I do not praise among the days one which pleases me, 4
But that its successor comes along stingy and mean.
O Fate make peace with me, 'tis enough what you've done to me, 5
I cast my weapons at you [but] my excuse is clear.
My wealth is great, O men, but [I am] without an heir 6
Wealth without an heir after a lifetime disappears."

Shaykh Ṭāhā, in his opening transition into the epic-verse mode, moves, as we have detailed above, at a moment of emotional duress from spoken prose to sung verse, commencing with his own statement that he is a servant to all who adore the Prophet. He then marks the following utterance as that of Rizq the Valiant, son of Nāyil, and portrays Rizq's emotional state with the description of his tears. Shaykh Ṭāhā rarely interpolates a mawwāl at the juncture between prose and poetry, a habit he attributes to personal taste. The shakwa theme in his rendition is placed directly in the mouth of the speaking hero. Shaykh Biyalī Abū Fahmī, in contrast, nearly always inserts a mawwāl in his transitions. It is clear from his own statements that he feels he possesses a good singing voice and that audience members are pleased when he takes these opportunities to demonstrate it. The flowing, freesong style of the mawwāl allows much more room for the demonstration of vocal skill than does the more rhythmically restricted epic verse:

Text 4.10 Transition into Epic Verse 2
Shaykh Biyalī Abū Fahmī, Tape 87–003 (2/11/87)
Spoken:

. . . ṣār Rizq ibn-I nāyil yanʿī ʿalā nafsuh wi-ʿalā qillit wi-khilifit iṣ-ṣubyān bi-hāzā l-abyāt. anā wi-antum nuṣallī ʿalā n-nabiyy sayyid il-karamāt:

[Music]

Mawwāl (sung):
Mawwāl 4 (text 4.8 above)

Epic Verse (sung):

tuḥiyā l-layālī bi-ṣ-ṣalātu ʿalā n-nabī 1
nabīnā il-hudā nūruh min il-Qabr lāyiḥ

wi-smaʿ mā ghannā rizq ibn-I nāyil 2
yāllah salāma wi-mi-z-zaman il-makāfiḥ

tizawwijt-I min in-niswān yā ʿēnī tamanya: 3
khallift-I minhum ḥidāshir ṣabiyya
abadan mā nabnī min warā l-ḥarīm rabāyiḥ

Spoken:

. . . Rizq, son of Nāyil, began to lament his state and the lack of siring boys, in these verses. I and you, we wish God's blessings on the Prophet, Lord of Miracles:

Mawwāl (sung):
And my camel at the carrying of the burden wronged me,
In spite of the Raven of Separation, [Fate] bore me and carried me off;
O Fire of my heart, against them light my kindling,
I ask you O Lord, I ask you O Lord,
O you who cause milk to flow in the breast!
You stir the young camel 'neath his loads and he springs up!
And you have authority over all prosperity!
Let the nights of prosperity continue for me;
But the nights, along with the days, humble me.

Epic Verse (sung):
The nights are greeted with our wishes for God's
blessings on the Prophet! 1
Our Prophet of True Guidance, His light from the
Tomb shines forth.
Now listen to what sang Rizq the Valiant, son of Nāyil, 2
Come now Salāma [=Rizq], time only brings struggles!
"I have married of women, O my Eye, eight: 3
I sired with them eleven maidens,
No profit comes from siring only daughters."[19]

19. Literally, 'we can never build profits behind females'.

Such is the association between the transition from prose to poetry and deep-felt emotions that at times the poets must supply a passionate impulse where the narrative provides only sparse emotional motivation. In Shaykh Ṭāhā's performance cited earlier, the second shift from the prose "words of the reciter" to the verse "words of the poet" occurs when the Banī Hilāl tribe has arrived in Mecca, after Rizq has announced his desire to marry the daughter of the sharīf of Mecca. The qāḍī (religious judge) of the tribe, Fāyid, stands and faces the Meccans to declare what the Banī Hilāl are willing to give as a brideprice. This clearly constitutes a formal speech-act: The emotions described by the poet, however, seem completely overblown given the situation in the narrative; they should be read as part of the intensified framing that surrounds the transition from prose to verse, speech to song, from performance to "performance within the performance."

Text 4.11 Transition into Epic Verse 3
Shaykh Ṭāhā Abū Zayd, tape 87–101 (6/1/87)
Spoken:
. . . wi-ḥaḍar il-qāḍī, fāyid illī huwa abū bedīr. fa-qāl luh tikallim yā qāḍī wi-tkallim ʿan ṣiyāq iṣ-ṣabiyya (iṣ-ṣiyāq dā yaʿnī il-mahr). shūf il-qāḍī hayiqūl ēh, wi-ʿāshiq jamāl in-nabī yiṣallī ʿalēh:

[Music]

Sung:
anā ʿabd-I mīn yaʿshaq jamāl^{a} muḥammad 1
ṭāhā l-lāzī ṭalib ish-shifāʿa wi-nālhā
ismaʿ mā qāl il-qāḍī fāyid wi-mā nishid 2
maṭrūfat^{an} wa-lā ya'lif in-nōm ḥālhā
tibāt ʿalā niyya wi-tiṣbaḥ ʿalā ḥazir 3
ka-mā in kalālīb il-ʿamar fī majālhā
wi-in mālit il-aḥmāl bi-yadī ʿidiltihā 4
wi-in mālit id-dunyā ʿalā llāh iʿtidālhā
hanī'^{an} bi-ʿēn^{in} tinʿis il-lēl kāmil^{an} 5
tibāt mastirīḥa mā ʿalēhā wa-lāmhā
wi-ʿēnī wajīʿa tishar il-lēl kāmil^{an} 6
tibāt tisallīnī ʿalā llī jarā lhā
ismaʿ li-qōlī āh yā Qirḍa wi-iftaham 7
kalām amāra āh mā hum ʿayyālhā
niʿūz minnak ṣabiyya munassiba 8
aṣīlit il-jaddēn ʿamm^{in} wi-khālhā

Spoken:
. . . And the Qāḍī Fāyid, father of Badīr, came forth. So [the sharīf of Mecca] said to him, "Speak, Qāḍī, and speak of the brideprice for the

maiden." (*Poet's aside*: The brideprice, that is, the dowry.) Listen to what the Qāḍī will say, and he who loves the beauty of the Prophet wishes God's blessings upon Him:

[Music]

Sung:
I am the servant of all who adore the beauty of Muḥammad, 1
Ṭāhā, who asked for [the power of] intercession and obtained it.
Listen to what the Qāḍī Fāyid said and what he sang: 2
"[My eye] is pained and sleep frequents it not in this state.
It goes to sleep with [good] intention, but awakes filled with caution, 3
As if the [all the] hooks [?] of life were in its [sleep's] domain.
If my burdens lean, with my own hand I set them straight, 4
But if the world leans, only God can set it straight.
Happy is the eye which sleeps the whole night through, 5
It passes the night in comfort, no blame is upon it.
But my eye is in pain, it keeps vigil the whole night through, 6
It passes the night troubling me with all that has befallen it.
Listen to my words, O Qirda, and comprehend, 7
These are the words of princes, Ah! they are not [mere] children.
We wish from you a maiden high-born and of noble ancestry, 8
From both grandfathers, paternal and maternal uncles [too]."

If my conjecture that the emotional core of the epic tradition lies in the speeches of its heroes is true, then the intensified framing that accompanies the "breakthrough into performance" of these speeches seems comprehensible.[20] The obligatory shakwa seems equally comprehensible when we read it as establishing the emotional space within which characters are moved to speak or, more properly, moved to *sing* their words.

We can approach this sequence of minute genres in a different manner, however, if we focus upon the formal features of each. This general sequence from the real world into the world of the epic is accomplished through the step-by-step accrual of formal features, features that set epic verse (*shiʿr*) apart from normal "talk" (*kalām*). As we move from "talk" into the epic, we encounter first music alone, and then rhymed prose (*sajʿ*) without music, which introduces the feature of rhyme as well as the narrative element; the mawwāl then combines instrumental music, vocal singing, and rhyme but is neither narrative nor rhythmically regular; the brief lines of madīḥ at the beginning of each "speech" set into

20. See Dell Hymes, "Breakthrough into Performance," and "Breakthrough into Performance Revisited," in *"In Vain I Tried to Tell You": Essays in Native American Ethnopoetics* (1981).

motion the regular rhythm of the general recitation but does not yet integrate the narrative thread; and finally as we hear the character speak and begin to tell his or her story, we have entered fully into the epic world where utterances are musical, sung, rhymed, rhythmically measured, and narrative. The following chart illustrates this progression of formal features.

	Musical Intro	Rhymed Prose	Mawwāl[21]	Madīḥ	Shakwa	Epic-Verse Narrative
Musical	+	−	+	+	+	+
Rhymed	−	+	+	+	+	+
Sung	−	−	+	+	+	+
Measured	−	−	−	+	+	+
Narrative	−	+	−	−	−	+

Each of these genres, or modes of presentation, thus marks a transitional set of formal features which eventually move us into the world of epic utterances, a poetically differentiated world. If, as the Formalists would have it, the poetic function emerges as the conscious marking of language with features deployed to distinguish it from other, more ordinary, language use, then this tradition displays great concern not only to mark the utterances and narratives of heroes, but also to provide carefully organized transitions from the world of "unmarked" language use to the "marked" world of epic song.

Our deductions in this case can be partially substantiated by the poets' habit of using this same pattern to reenter the epic after all interruptions. In many instances the poet is forced to rework the material in order to deploy this traditional sequence of genres and formal features when reentering the sung, epic-verse mode. If interrupted at an inconvenient point, the poet may have to resort to a lengthy prose introduction until he arrives at a moment in the narrative with enough emotional impact to trigger the movement into song, covering ground in the story which is, in uninterrupted performances, usually performed in sung poetry.

This traditional sequencing of formal features carries additional significance beyond the general increase in complexity of the formal marking: such marking is also used to indicate allusion to a variety of speech-acts and to other local genres of verbal art exterior to the epic. Scholars of a number of cultures have remarked that some epic traditions tend to assimilate and absorb other genres of verbal art found in their proximity. I have argued elsewhere that this phenomenon is true of the *Sīrat Banī*

21. Any given sequence includes either a mawwāl or a shakwa section, but not both.

Hilāl epic-singing tradition of northern Egypt.[22] A close study of these features, the genres of verbal art alluded to within the epic itself, and the import of the various means poets utilize for marking speech-acts within the epic would help us understand the *how* involved in the process of signification—how various figurations are deployed and interpreted in epic performance.

One final general observation worth exploring concerns the short transitional sequences we have examined above: these sequences frame the utterances of epic heroes precisely as the sahra itself is framed. As the sahra progresses from (1) the opening mention of the Prophet to (2) praise of the Prophet to (3) a lyrical interlude on the vicissitudes of Fate and Destiny, and only then to (4) the narrative element of the sīra, so within the sīra, heroes' speeches progress in the same way from an initial mention of the Prophet, to words in His praise, to shakwa, and finally to the narrative. This observation is further supported by noting that poets who regularly sing mawwāls in their epic performances do so *both* in the initial sequence of the evening and at the juncture between rhymed prose and epic verse, while poets such as Shaykh Ṭāhā, who generally prefer not to include mawwāls within the epic, also do not perform them at the beginning of the evening. Whichever sequence the poet observes, the progression is parallel.

The heroes' words are thus marked in the same manner as the poets' words. Both the madīḥ and the theme of shakwa (in the form of the mawwāl) which opened the greater sahra performance reappear in miniature within the sīra when heroes speak. The speech of heroes and the speech of poets are once again equated by a tradition that has clearly evolved in a social context where poets over generations have bound their profession, and with it themselves, to the fictional characters who are accorded the respect which the poets in real life are consistently denied; in this sense, the sahra performance replicates itself over and over again within the sīra.

Other Genres

The three genres we have examined—the sīra, mawwāl, and madīḥ—constitute the three most clearly recognized genres of performance within the sahra. As alluded to in Chapters 2 and 3, however, poets do not confine themselves to these three genres, although the three are performed only by poets. Though the audience may have a great deal of

22. See Reynolds, "Interplay."

input, the genres are not primarily dialogic forms. In the sahra two other recognized genres occur repeatedly which we can examine together in that they appear to share a single function in incorporating audience members directly into the "text" of the performance. They are (1) "greetings and salutations" (*taḥīyāt wa-salāmāt*) and (2) "bits of country stuff" or "local color" (*ḥitat baladī*). The first is a genre that plays a much greater role in large public performances where listeners offer small payments (nuqūṭ) to have themselves, friends, or family members mentioned by the poet in a sequence of traditional greetings and well-wishing. In the sahra, these greetings are usually reserved for guests as they arrive or depart from the gathering and are usually restricted to one or two verses. The second genre, the "bits of country stuff," is a sahra genre par excellence in that the poet must possess detailed knowledge of the social life of his listeners.

The following example of ḥitat baladī was performed at the request of an audience member, Ustādh Bakr, who possesses a great deal of personal and family-based status. As a government employee in the provincial capital, he commands an observable degree of respect from other inhabitants of the village; in the sahra context he is a listener who receives attention from the poets through greetings and salutations as well as other references to his presence during the performance. This request for "a bit of country stuff" was made during an intermission in which cigarettes were offered around but tea was not served; the not very veiled comments that surface in this text concerning hospitality and the offering of food and drink helped successfully initiate a substantial round of tea at the next break in the performance. In this case the poet chose a basic traditional pattern that contrasts good and bad fortune; in particular he amplified and emphasized the role of the wife in the presentation of hospitality to guests (directed at the "missing" tea in this gathering). Within the treatment of this motif, he embedded several further cutting remarks aimed at the shortage of flour in the village and the evils of hoarding food.

Audience members burst out with applause and laughter at many points, but the strongest response occurred after the poet's criticism of the supervisor of the government-subsidized food outlet (line 28), a criticism he picks up again (line 32) in more allegorical terms with references to the timing of the Nile flood (before the building of the Aswan High Dam): if the flood came too late, it did no good, for the cotton was already dead; likewise hoarded food does no one any good if it is stored and not used.

The primary qualities of this form of entertainment are (1) the pervasive comic tone, (2) the mention within the text of members of the audience, either directly by name or obliquely through land they own or other well-known attributes, and (3) an intersticial social commentary concerning either the immediate performance situation or the general sociopolitical situation of the village at large. Clearly there is an element of excitement and tension situated in any performance of this type, for no one knows who or what will be the target of the poet's wit. To attend such performances and participate in them is a form of social roulette: the entertainment gained at the expense of others may well be at the cost of one's own public embarrassment.

There is little or no adherence to a strict verse form in this performance genre, though a single end-rhyme is used to mark each cluster of phrases. The poet even overtly mentions his use of rhyme when he turns to me to explain (line 30) why he is using the far less common word *zaʿbūṭ* instead of the usual word for men's apparel, *galabiyya.* (I did not know the word at the time, and my confusion doubtless registered in my expression.) Although one might line out this text in many ways so as to highlight differing formal features, here I address only the techniques by which the poet involves and implicates the audience members into the text. I have therefore chosen to group the phrases into "clusters" based on the occurrence of the end rhyme. Shaykh ʿAbd al-Wahhāb in this performance jumped rapidly from full singing voice, to speaking voice, and from shouts to whispers; he imitated the "bad wife's" voice with a deep threatening growl and mimicked the "good wife" in soft, sweet tones.

There are, however, many features that link together various portions of this text and provide a certain cohesion to some units as well as a sense of balance to the overall development, despite the rapid-fire shift from topic to topic. The most obvious pattern is the juxtapositioning of positive versus negative images. These oppositions at first occupy the space of a single line (2, 5), then a pair of lines (3–4), and are then expanded to occupy much larger segments (the "good son" in 6 and 7 versus the "bad son" in 8–10; the "good wife" in 11–16 versus the "bad wife" in 17–31). As the size of the oppositions increase from line, to couplet, to larger segments, so the "lines" themselves become looser and looser clusters of phrases sung or spoken very rapidly with only occasional punctuation from the rabāb rather than full musical accompaniment. The poet returns to measured, rhythmical verses only at the close of the performance.

The section most clearly developed here, concerning the "bad wife," takes up a full half of the performance; there is within it a consistent movement back and forth from the image of the "bad wife" to the poet's other concerns, as shown in figure 6.

Figure 6. Thematic movement in Ḥitat Baladī performance

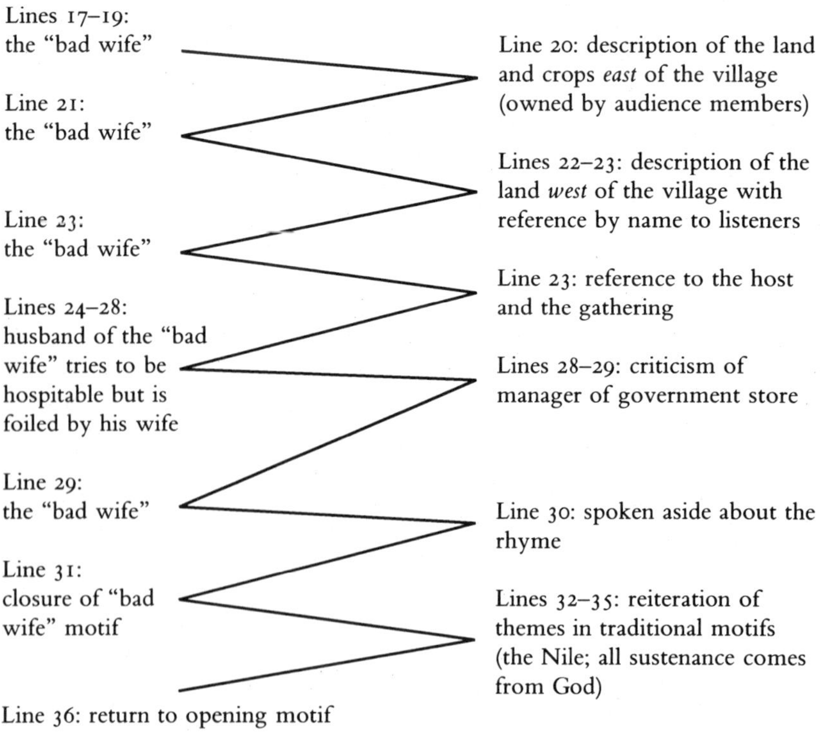
Lines 17–19: the "bad wife"
Line 20: description of the land and crops *east* of the village (owned by audience members)
Line 21: the "bad wife"
Lines 22–23: description of the land *west* of the village with reference by name to listeners
Line 23: the "bad wife"
Line 23: reference to the host and the gathering
Lines 24–28: husband of the "bad wife" tries to be hospitable but is foiled by his wife
Lines 28–29: criticism of manager of government store
Line 29: the "bad wife"
Line 30: spoken aside about the rhyme
Line 31: closure of "bad wife" motif
Lines 32–35: reiteration of themes in traditional motifs (the Nile; all sustenance comes from God)
Line 36: return to opening motif

Text 4.12 Example of Ḥitat Baladī
Shaykh ʿAbd al-Wahhāb Ghāzī, tape 87–044 (3/15/87)[23]

Sung:

He whose goal is heaven wishes God's blessings on the Prophet; 1
An Arab Prophet, He has a permanent sanctuary.
And sustenance from God is sometimes [good] fortune
and sometimes [bad] fortune [lit. fortunes and fortunes].

And there is he who is given, yes, generosity and nobility, 2
and there is he who is given stinginess till he dies.

And there is he who is given ornamented gardens, 3
and in them are mangoes, and in them are pears,
and in them are grapes, and in them are dates,
and in them are pomegranates,

23. The rhyme is -ūṭ/-ūt. Transliterated Arabic text is found in the Appendix.

glorious fruits, O my brother;
And sustenance from Our Lord is sometimes [good]
fortune and sometimes [bad] fortune.

And there is he who is given a single acacia tree, 4
by God, O my eye, or a male mulberry tree.

And there is he who is given caftan and broadcloth, 5
and there is he who is given a rag of a garment.

And there is he who is given a son, 6
clever, polite, a well-bred son;
When the boy is mentioned in conversation in the gathering,
it pleases his father;
O my brother, he holds his head high [lit. his neck is long]
and he sits contented.

This is a son who takes after his maternal uncle; 7
The boy's maternal uncle is a man from the noblest of houses.

And there is he who is given a son who is a 8
disappointment and a good-for-nothing;
Yes, O my eye, foul-mouthed [and] rude.

He brings his father problems and misdoings; 9
And the stores and the cafés and the fields
and the buses and the train, yes, and all the houses.

Because his father is a man of reputation and well-meaning, 10
they all come back to the father to collect the money and the bills;
O my brother, a son who grew up a good-for-nothing,
taking after his maternal uncle,
for his maternal uncle is a worthless man.

And there is he who is given a beautiful, comely marriage; 11
Very pretty, O my brother, comely, beautiful,
noble, from the noblest of houses.

And her face is fair and her cheek glistens like a jewel [i.e., a
ruby]. 12

When he has guests who are friendly with him [lit. who lean
toward him], 13
all "requests" come to the guests while
her husband remains seated (with them),
without him sensing it or knowing it;
He doesn't have to say,
"O my daughter, bring this, pass that."
All the "requests" come to the guests
while her husband sits among the guests contented.

Pickled dishes and rice dishes. 14
A noble [woman], beautiful, very pretty,
from the noblest of houses,
her husband sits among the guests contented.

He calls for something: "Yes, right away" 15
[Whispers:] "Yes, right away, yes, right away."
And her teeth laugh from her fair face like jewels.

Her husband, if he lives with her eighty years, 16
ninety years, or completes one hundred,
(and all lifespans are in the hand of God!)
he will live and die in happiness, yes, contented.

And there is he who is given a marriage, O my brother, 17
Our Lord does not grant it success, nor grant success
to those who bore her or sired her or recommended her
A marriage which has become today a destructive affliction;
Lazy! Stingy! Lazy! Stingy!
From the laziest of houses,
she has a neck that resembles a catfish!

God is great! God is great! 18
And when a guest goes near their house,
she gets up, O my brother, clutching a wooden club!

"I was coming [to visit] Uncle So-and-so." 19
She says, "He's at the doctor, O brother.
He's dying, he's dying, he's dying, he's dying"
[i.e., she lies so as not to offer hospitality].

I asked about him as I was coming along 20
the Salamōniyya [irrigation canal] from the East;
that is, over by the contractor's from the north,
along the path from that train station of ours.
This is a very good year,
and the cotton is producing twelve qinṭārs this year,
and that's in the rented lands,
and in the reform lands,
and in the private lands it's at nine and a half or ten or so,
and the credit and the agriculture are good,
and they filled up the goverment subsidy store—
Boy, was I content!

[The wife says:] "O if only, O my father— 21
Five minutes before you came the car came and took him off,
he's going to die, he's going to die."

I asked about him as I was coming from near the 22
Fazāʿiyya over in the West;
Sirahna village, from the house of Abū Ṣuḥb,
paternal uncle of al-Ḥājj Muḥammad,
a prince of a man, people of nobility,
nobility and "contentedness" [= here "well-off"].

I asked about him at Aḥmad Muṣṭafā's place, 23
a good man, and at al-Ḥājj Kāmil's, as well,
[I asked about] my Uncle So-and-So;
They said, "It's a very good year."
The woman says, "He's dying, he's dying."
I wish he would, I wish he would:
"He's going to die!"
She's just the daughter of misers!
The man is sitting in the guest room!
Like this one of Aḥmad Bakhātī's that we are all
sitting in this evening for a happy gathering!
If God wills, let it be a gathering for good purposes
wishing God's blessings on the Prophet Muḥammad,
the Light of the Prophet, yes, fills the crypt!

If he [the husband] is worried about his reputation 24
he runs out the back door which faces east,
and around to meet the guests:
"O welcome! One thousand million welcomes! O welcome!
Please, come in, come in, please!"
He shakes out the couch, and the cushions,

and the pillows, and arm-rests, and bolsters.
The story, praise be to God,
has become good, all over!
Lots of cushions, lots of armrests,
and beautiful houses!
Absolute satisfaction! Praise be to God!
He said, "Praise be to God!"
He's become the richest of people,
those who live contented.

So he sits and greets them, 25
and he sprinkles on them a few cigarettes,
a few drinks, a few sweets,
and then afterward, when he gets alone with the evil, hairy one,
that daughter of disasters says to him:
O such hostility! O such hostility!
"Whadya want?" "A bite for these guests to eat,
they've been two hours sitting here."
"I was going to go to the clinic today,
but when I saw them from the eastern door,
I went quickly [to invite them]."
He even goes along with what she said,
the words of the evil-tempered one; what does she say?
"I have a postponement for the clinic,"
(that is, he goes along with what she said,
that is, so he can live contented).

We are their children, O my brother, āh— 26
"I had a check-up appointment today,
but when I saw these guests,
my health got better, praise be to God, much better.
Bring us some lunch."
Two hours pass, I don't know, perhaps three . . .
Food in a rush!
She goes to bring out the food, O my brother,
and she places it in front of him, and lets loose in a very loud voice;
Oh what great news, she's brought them bitterness!
So she's even managed to ruin this, what will they eat?
They leave the food, it's become a funeral,
and he who seeks refuge in God . . .[24] his friends.
Because she is miserly and the daughter of misers,
from the laziest of houses.

24. Unclear on recording.

The guests leave, and the man, O my eye, 27
is not feeling good,
afterward he is not content.

He goes back and says to her: 28
"Why, O why! Why, O why!
You've ruined my reputation,
and the reputation of my grandfathers!
The generous man is never treated unfairly.
The generous man is never treated unfairly.
And these people have been in the habit of coming to
us since the days of our fathers and our grandfathers.
And this house has been open [to guests] from long, long ago.
She says to him: "It's none of your business!
Shut up! So you've opened the main door?
Sit down, sit down and keep quiet."
And Our Lord's munificence is great,
and the guest, before he comes, his sustenance comes before
him;[25]
And she hoards and conceals so!
All day long I've been looking for flour in the shops,
I went to Abū Sulēmān's [private shop]
and to Ustāz Jalāl [manager of the government store].
I found all their flour was locked up tight!

"Okay, so here's a little bread, take it!" 29
"Quiet! Am I a baker? Do I pat out the loaves?
And my arm is tired—I sit down and—
Get away, get away!
And a word from her,
And a word from her husband and she starts a quarrel.
She tears his *zaᶜbūṭ* [men's outer garment].

[*Aside to me*: That is, you say *galabiyya* from 30
beginning to end, but *zaᶜbūṭ* is for the rhyme!]

She tears up his zaᶜbūṭ, she shreds his zaᶜbūṭ. 31
"O woman, leave me, go back to your people's house!"
"By God, I'll never leave you, I'll be here till you die!"

25. That is, God provides the wherewithal to feed guests, for all guests are first and foremost "guests of God" (*iḍ-ḍēf ḍēf allāh*).

And when the Nile would come to us in [the month of] *misrā*,[26] 32
When the Nile used to come to us in [the month of] misrā,
And there is no good in the Nile if it comes in *tūt*.[27]

The planting, it's life would already have passed, 33
after twenty-five days the water would come,
all the cotton would have died, and all of it gone.
And when the Nile would come in misrā,
there is no good in the Nile which comes in tūt.

The *fatta* and bread were no more expensive than zucchini. 34
And there is no good in provisions that are hoarded.

And he who dies, yes, whence does he pass. 35
And sustenance from God, yes, is sometimes [good]
fortune and sometimes [bad] fortune.

And there is he who is given generosity and nobility, 36
and there is he who lives in stinginess till he dies.

Yes, and there is he who is given of life his fill, 37
and there is he who is given a year and then dies.

And sustenance from God, yes, is sometimes [good] 38
fortune and sometimes [bad] fortune.

And the best of these words are 39
(I and you together, O listeners to these words)
Wish God's blessings on the Presence of the Prophet,
an Arab Prophet, He has an enduring sanctuary.

This is a "high-context" performance.[28] It is densely contextualized, an insider's text, and a text that "alludes to" far more that it "indicates" or "states," a text that does not create a narrative "story world." To achieve even the most basic understanding of this performance we would be forced to discuss the following:

Implications of landownership, the fact that only a few powerful families in al-Bakātūsh own gardens with fruit trees, and which of these families were represented in this audience;

Stereotypes of close emotional relationships between boys and maternal

26. Twelfth month of the Coptic year.
27. First month of the Coptic year.
28. See Edward Hall, *Beyond Culture* (1976), chap. 7, "Contexts, High and Low."

uncles versus more severe, disciplinarian-style relationships between boys and paternal uncles;

The performing poet's middle son, who has been a constant disappointment to him and caused a great deal of trouble in the village, and who is particularly known for his misbehavior at gatherings;

The reputation of the house where the performance was taking place, which was one distinctly lacking in hospitality;

The topography of the village, which lands are owned by members of this audience, and the relationships between those mentioned by name and those not;

Basic tensions common in village households which arise from the wife's responsiblity for domestic expenditures and the husband's desire to display public hospitality (which can result in effective female control of certain types of male displays of honor); and

The role of government-subsidized foods, the distribution system by monthly ration booklets, and the way this system functions within the local political and social context.

A full explanation of this brief text would, in short, lead to a detailed ethnographic portrait of the community. If this be a "text," then it is a text that imitates the relationships it portrays. There is of course a narrative thread, but it is scarcely more than a thread: the narrative proceeds in leaps and bounds, and what holds it together is not an internal narrative logic, but the external structure of the performance. The poet moves rhythmically back and forth between the "narrative structure" and his poetic forays out into the audience and their reality.

The epic poem is certainly open to contextualized interpretation (and I argue below that it in fact necessitates such interpretation); there is a level, however, at which the epic is consciously performed as a "complete" text, a separate world, one in which the tradition itself does not recognize or perpetuate interpretation according to performance context. The ḥitat baladī, however, displays a marked contrast in its relation to the world: it makes no pretense of "completeness," it is woven directly out of the performance context, and its story world exists only as a mechanism by which to implicate the audience directly into the performance.

In Chapter 2, we briefly examined a series of typical "conversational genres" that are commonly deployed by epic poets in the sahra context: (1) narratives of past performances, (2) discussions of village history and genealogies, and (3) dialect stories. I have suggested that beyond their basic function as entertainment, these genres represent negotiations of social status by the poet vis-à-vis his listeners. His recitations of village history and genealogies, in much the same manner we have just observed with the ḥitat baladī are a maneuver of inclusion. In the historical and genealogical performances, one does move not between a story world and the real world, but rather is firmly situated spatially in "real life." Such a pendular movement is, however, inherent in these performances: rather than implicating his listeners into his text, the poet in a display of genealogical or historical mastery, insinuates himself into the village community and identity, a role he is in other contexts denied.

Narratives of past performances and the dialect tales do not serve quite this same purpose of allowing the poet to impinge upon village history and identity but serve to differentiate his métier from that of beggary or vagrancy. And of course they also bolster the image of the poet as a respected and accomplished performer.

The performance activities of a poet during a typical sahra might include any or all of the following:

Formal Genres	Informal Genres	Conversation Genres
1. madīḥ	1. taḥīyāt/salāmāt	1. genealogies
2. mawwāl	2. ḥitat baladī	2. dialect tales
3. sīra		3. past performance narratives

This tripartite division is empirically justifiable only from the performer's point of view: the poets recognize the "formal" genres as those one learns through apprenticeship, they are all "arts" (*funūn,* sing *fann*). The "informal" genres are accepted as part of the craft (*il-mihna*) of being a poet but are not among the accepted funūn and are thought to be acquired through experience (*khibra*) rather than training. When pressed, poets were willing to label these "informal" genres as ḥashw 'filling,' though this term was elicited in response to my questions and is probably not otherwise an operative conceptual category. The final category of "conversational" genres is not accepted as part of the poet's craft at all, and any of these "genres" might be performed by audience members as well. Only poets can perform genres from the first two categories.

Our examination of the typical content and formal features of these genres provides us with a working model of the interactions of "texts" within the sahra; it remains now to expand our examination of these genres into performances which implicate and necessitate the participation of an audience.

CHAPTER 5

The Sahra as Social Interaction

> The people listened to the storytellers in the cafés; they heard about Sayf ibn Dhi Yazin, who left no stone unturned all over the world looking for the *Book of the Nile*. Their hearts were aflutter with love for the Princess Dhāt al-Himma. They followed the stories of the Barmacides with the Abbasids, Abū Zayd and Diyāb and Zanātī Khalīfa, Solomon and how he controlled the jinn, the martyrdom of the dearly beloved Husayn at Karbala. Nobody knew that one thread ran through what all the professional singers, chanters, and storytellers in Egypt did.
>
> Gamal al-Ghitani, *Al-Zayni Barakat*

Sīrat Banī Hilāl is not merely a textual tradition; it is also a performance tradition. The genres of verbal art which we examined in Chapter 4 are not only formally, that is, textually, marked as different genres, they also motivate markedly different processes of interaction between performer, audience, and text. During a sahra, audience members are at times implicated directly into the performance; at times they respond to and fuel the performance with their comments and interjections; at times they are completely silent while an aesthetic space is created for displays of vocal or instrumental artistry; and in the interstices of the poet's professional performances, audience members may take the floor with evaluative and interpretive discussions as well as with their own performances of various conversational genres of verbal art.

We have expanded our examination of the sahra from the confines of its major performance genre, *Sīrat Banī Hilāl*, toward the inclusion of a wide variety of genres, and have laid the groundwork for the examination of these elements as a dialogue of forms that contribute to a larger interacting whole. We have so far examined each of these forms as a unidirectional presentation; now we address them as multivocal, interactive performances created through the participation of poets and audience members.

In expanding our analysis to include the interactive processes of performance, we must first examine the audience's role in the performance of those genres which we have just discussed before turning to audience activities more independent of the poet's professional role as performer.

Audience Reactions and Participation

The opening madīḥ of a sahra typically provokes affirmatory and responsory reactions from listeners. We have already noted that the madīḥ obliges the audience to move into an active mode of listening with multiple mentions of the Prophet by name or epithet, each of which is acknowledged by listeners with one of a limited number of traditional blessings. Little if any direct appreciation of the aesthetics of the performance is overtly evident from audience reactions; poet and listeners generally appear equally focused upon the content of the poetry, the evocative and emotional images of Muḥammad and His companions, the Prophet's beauty, His generosity, and overall perfection as a human being. When interjections from the audience do well up and seize the attention of those present, they are expressions of the emotional impact these reflections on the Prophet have had upon the speaker, usually evinced in supplications to God or invocations of one of the saints or of the Prophet Himself.

The mawwāl is, in contrast, the most highly compacted and cohesive aesthetic form of the evening's activities: it is a space for displays of vocal artistry. Its imagery, complex rhyme schemes, intricate wordplay, and general rhetoric of abstracted truths demand immediate and active interpretation by listeners. Appropriately enough, mawwāls are often listened to in nearly complete silence with a minimum of affirmatory backchanneling. Comments and responses are delayed until the mawwāl's conclusion; it is responded to as a single unit—a short but complete whole—a fact further indicated by the frequent calls to hear a mawwāl again (*tānī*) or for an additional mawwāl to be sung (*kamān*). Comments about mawwāls, unlike those about madīḥ, are most often directed toward the poet as artist and toward the aesthetic qualities of the performance ("Your voice is golden!"; "May God lengthen your life for our sakes!" etc.) and only secondarily to the content of the song ("Ah yes," "So true," etc.).

Both madīh and mawwāl, however, are performances that explicitly state that the text is relevant to our daily lives, the first through the life of Muḥammad and the Companions as a guiding example of human perfection (*qudwa*), and the second through a rhetoric of proverbial, enduring truths. Their constant propinquity to the epic further provides an invitation to approach the epic in a similar manner, as a text that possesses significance beyond its perceivable boundaries. This relationship is confirmed in audience discussions of the sīra and in their reactions and interjections during performances of the sīra.

A transcribed performance of *Sīrat Banī Hilāl* does not resemble the orderly, neat lines we are accustomed to seeing on the pages of the *Iliad* or *Beowulf.* Instead, audience members voice approval or disapproval, take advantage of the brief pauses between lines to shout compliments and exclamations, at times even compete with the poet for attention with jokes and witty remarks. Text 5.1 illustrates some of the simplest and most common forms of vocal interaction between poet and audience members.

The example is taken from the epic's opening episode, "the Birth of Abū Zayd," the hero. Rizq, son of Nāyil, has been married to nine different women and has fathered twelve daughters. After an omen from God, he marries Khaḍra al-Sharīfa, daughter of the sharīf of Mecca, hoping at last to sire a male heir. Seven years pass, however, and Khaḍra does not give birth to any children, male or female. Rizq and Khaḍra quarrel, and Khaḍra, seeking solace, goes to visit Shamma, another barren woman in the tribe. The two women and the servant Saʿīda go into the desert where they make special requests to God for sons; each woman requests that she bear a son with specific qualities. Meanwhile, King Sarḥān convinces Rizq to seek reconciliation with his wife after their quarrel. Rizq's willingness to be reconciled and Khaḍra's fervent prayers result that night in the conception of a son, the future hero of the Banī Hilāl tribe, Abū Zayd. Due to the nature of Khaḍra's request, however, her son is born black, though his parents are both white, which later causes the expulsion of Khaḍra (who is accused of adultery) and her son from the tribe. Eventually, Abū Zayd, raised in another tribe and ignorant of his true origins, faces his father in battle. The two fight for thirty days, neither able to best the other, for the hand of God deflects their spears and swords. Finally, Abū Zayd's sister discovers the truth of the matter and manages to negotiate a truce. At the end of the episode, Abū Zayd and his mother return in triumph to the Banī Hilāl and those who had falsely accused her of adultery lie dead on the battlefield. The scene we examine here, Khaḍra's request for a son, is a pivotal moment for the epic as a whole, for it is because of the wording of her request that Abū Zayd is born black and suffers the expulsion that leads to his later prowess and adventures.

At this early point in the performance the audience was still quite small: two men over fifty years old (among the staunchest devotees of the epic in the village; one of them, Shaykh Imām, attended nearly seventy performances during my ten-month stay), one highly educated young man in his twenties (a medical student), the two young men in their twenties who acted as my assistants for part of my stay (one a high school English teacher and the other a government employee), and myself (I was, at this point, in my fifth month in the village and had already recorded extensively with three other poets). It is precisely because of the limited size of this audience that so many of the comments are easily decipherable in the audio recording, yet at least one-quarter of the comments remain unclear, and most of the generalized sounds (ah, yā, hmmm, etc.) have been omitted from this transcription. Even this "expanded text" thus represents but a fraction of the average vocalized interaction:

Text 5.1 Audience Participation[1]
Shaykh Ṭāhā Abū Zayd, tape 87–101 (6/1/87)

It was Friday morning, Wish God's Blessings on the Prophet! 1
[All: *May God Bless and Preserve Him!*]
The oppressed one, My Lord [God] hears his prayers.

[Shamma] said to [Khaḍra], 2
"Let us go, you and I, down to the sea in the openlands,
Let us go calm our blood in its emptiness.[2]

"And when you gaze at the salty [sea] you shall encounter
wonders, 3
You shall encounter wonders, by the will of God."

They set out, the two of them, and the slave Saʕīda, 4
Wife of Najjāḥ, oh so beautiful.

Suddenly a white bird 5
[Voice: *Yes!*]
from the distance came to them,
A white bird, beautiful to behold.

1. Transliterated Arabic text is found in the Appendix.
2. A double entendre is created between two possible readings: *faḍā* 'openlands' and *fadāh* 'its emptiness', which are easily distinguished in speech as the first word is accented on the first syllable, the second word on the second syllable, but are rendered indistinguishable in song.

He landed and did not take flight, the bird in the wastelands, 6
All the other birds flocked round him.

Said Shamma, "O Lord, the One, the Everlasting, 7
[Voices: *Allah*!]
Glory to God, there is no god but He.

"Pray grant me a son like unto this bird, 8
And may he be handsome and the Arabs obey his [every word]."

Her request was completed, O Nobles, and the bird rose up, 9
The bird took flight, Ah!, and climbed to the heights.

Suddenly a dark bird from the distance 10
[*Laughter*]
[Voice: *This is Abū Zayd*!]
came to them,
A dark bird
[Voice: *Yes*!]
frightful to behold!
[Voice: *Heavens*!]

He beat his wings at the other birds, 11
And each one he struck with his wings did not [live to] smell his supper!
[*Laughter*]

Said Khaḍra 12
[Voice: *Yes*!]
"O how beautiful you are, O bird, and how beautiful your darkness,
[Voice: *Allah*!]
Like the palmdate when it ripens to perfection.

"O Lord, O All-Merciful, O One, O Everlasting, 13
[Voice: *God is Great*!]
[Shaykh Ṭāhā to audience member: *May God reward you*!]
Glory to God, Veiled in His Heaven!

[Audience member places cigarettes in front of Shaykh Ṭāhā]
[Shaykh Ṭāhā: *May you always have plenty!*
May you always have plenty, we wish you!]

"Pray grant me a son, like unto this bird, 14
May each one he strikes with his sword not [live to] smell his supper."
[Voice: *My goodness*!]
[Voice shouting: *Abū Zayd*!]

They made their requests, the two of them [Shamma and Khaḍra]; 15
[Then] Saʿīda said, "O Lord, pray grant me a son like my mistresses,
He fears nought, he whose fulfillment is from the Most Generous."

They went home, O Nobles, Wish God's Blessings on the Prophet! 16
[All: *May God bless and preserve Him*]
O fortunate is he who makes a request and the Most Generous [grants] its fulfillment.

Said King Sarḥān to Rizq the Hero, 17
"O cousin, listen to my words and their meanings,

"Make peace with Sharīfa, Rizq, O Kindest of the Arabs, 18
Honor her for she is of the line of Messenger of God.
[All: *May God bless and preserve Him*]

"Honor her, O Rizq, or escort her back to her people, 19
For honor is like tilled land, honor is dear,
Honor is dear and the Arabs know this."
[Voice: *Allah*!]

He made peace with her and escorted her to his pavilion, 20
And the Most Generous willed that he be rightly guided O how beautiful!

On this night the three became pregnant, 21
[Voice: *Allah*!]
O fortunate is he who makes a request and the Most Generous [grants] its fulfillment.

Her months passed, [and] Shamma the Noble gave birth to a
son, O Nobles, of rare qualities,
A boy handsome of face, O so beautiful!

★ Wish God's Blessings on the Prophet! ★

[All: *May God bless and preserve Him!*]
[Voice: *May God provide for you!*]
[Shaykh Ṭāhā: *May God reward you!*]
[Voice: *Listen . . .*]
[Shaykh Ṭāhā: *May God bless you!*]

The most basic and characteristic levels of poet/audience interaction are found in this short example. Audience responses build with the story to an emotional highpoint with the arrival of the dark bird, the omen of the hero Abū Zayd's birth, and from verses 11 to 15 nearly every phrase sung by the poet is met with a response from some member of the audience.

In the text we find an ongoing set of noninterruptive, nondemarcative exclamations similar to what researchers of conversational interaction term "backchanneling."[3] These short interjections (Allāh! my goodness! yes! hmmm, āh, etc.) do not stop the flow of the singing, but in some sense, as in conversation, signal that the listener is interested and is following the story. There are also some remarks meant to evoke a reaction from the addressee, be it audience member or poet. Each mention of the Prophet Muḥammad provokes traditional responses, and references to God or to actions attributed directly to God are often followed with the phrase "God is Great" (Allāhu akbar). In addition, many greetings and compliments in Egyptian Colloquial Arabic, as in many other Arabic dialects, also require cognate responses in a form parallel to the original remark (i.e., "May God preserve you!" "May God reward you!").[4] In example 5.1, the poet responds to compliments from audience members at line 13 and after line 23. Another typical

3. As an introduction to some of the categories and methodologies developing in the analysis of conversational interaction, see, for example, Starkey Duncan, Jr., "On the Structure of Speaker-Auditor Interaction during Speaking Turns" (1974); S. Duncan, Jr., and D. W. Fiske, *Face-to-Face Interaction: Research, Methods, and Theory* (1977); Charles Goodwin, "Restarts, Pauses, and the Achievement of a State of Mutual Gaze at Turn-Beginning" (1980); Michael Moerman, *Talking Culture: Ethnography and Conversation Analysis* (1988); G. Psathas, ed., *Everyday Language* (1979); Harvey Sacks, Emanuel Schegloff, and G. Jefferson, "A Simplest Systematics for the Organization of Turn-Taking for Conversation" (1974); and Jim Schenkein, ed., *Studies in the Organization of Conversational Interaction* (1978).

4. See Ferguson, "Root-Echo Responses."

interaction shown here is anticipation on the part of audience members (see lines 10 and 14), who often shout out the name of a character entering the story or a plot element about to occur (i.e., "He'll kill him on the third stroke!" "Here comes Abū Zayd"). Poets often acknowledge correct anticipations with a nod and a smile, and will set straight incorrect comments with a line of poetry. In midperformance poets may test the audience with quick questions: "Who's saying this?" (dā huwwa mīn biyiqūl kida?), "And who does he meet?" (hayiqābil mīn?), for example.

These interactions appear simple, yet they provide an intricate key to the pacing and mood of the performance. Poets demand a certain amount of backchanneling to verify that the audience is following the story and is still entertained. Withholding that basic feedback is the audience's primary method for communicating boredom or lack of interest. Review of performances lasting several hours almost always reveals segments where the backchanneling has died down and the poet subsequently turns to one of several techniques to reintegrate the audience by stimulating vocal participation.

References to the Prophet or to God are one such move, for they require the appropriate responses, as we saw in the madīḥ genre. Though the poets of al-Bakātūsh never speak directly of using this technique to spur audiences within the epic narrative, they do speak openly of using praise poetry of Muḥammad at the beginning of a performance to gather in the audience and to calm them down in preparation for recitation of the epic. The use of the required response mechanism to calm or focus a group has numerous parallels in daily life, where public quarrels are often tempered with religious formulas which require responses from all present, diffusing tensions and at the same time incorporating into the situation bystanders who have remained outside the dispute and who then function as arbitrators.

In a similar move, poets directly question the audience. They may ask, "Who is saying this?"—which again forces direct vocal participation.

In another, more subtle change, the poets alter the tone of the performance by inserting jokes or erotic descriptions, or switching to an auxiliary genre (particularly one such as the ḥitat baladī which draws the listeners directly into the focus of the performance). When audience members begin to react, the poet follows that lead. Every poet has a repertory of devices from dramatic hand and facial gestures, sudden shouts or changes of tempo, comic musical effects (glissandos or raps of the bow on the neck of the instrument), to swinging the instrument through the air while playing and swaying back and forth while singing.

This sense of dialogue and interactive process is apparent in the poets' own evaluations of their performances. Typically in their discussions, their initial comments always concern the *audience* of a particular performance and whether or not they were knowledgeable, lively, serious, and so forth.

Vocal participation by listeners, however, is but the simplest form of social interaction involved in a sahra performance. Sahras tend to promote another type of performance behavior apart from that of the poets; in the breaks and intermissions of the poets' performances, audience members regularly offer performances of a number of genres of verbal art such as (1) memorates (brief, first-person narratives), (2) proverbs, (3) quotations from Qurʾān, ḥadīth, songs, poetry, (4) jokes, (5) elaborated greetings and salutations, and (6) historical narratives. In short, all of the conversational genres of verbal art found in village life are likely to pop up during a sahra.

There is one major difference, however, between the fine art of daily conversation and the currents of performance within the sahra: conversational genres within the sahra tend to spring from the formal performance of the epic poet and likewise tend to develop threads of cohesion throughout an evening in interaction with the poet's performance. These linking themes and motifs initiated in less formal fashion by audience members are often later reappropriated by the poet and caused to echo within the epic. Part of the dynamic of the sahra context is the weaving of elements from the performance situation first into the performance text and then back into the sahra setting. Over and over again an evening gathering develops around an idea or a mood that is reiterated in different forms. To some extent this quality is found in any human dialogue or conversation, but the sahra context seems to invite such participation in a more formalized, more performance-oriented manner.

A simple example is found in performances in which an element of the epic is first commented upon by audience members during a tea break, which then leads to the presentation of full narratives by audience members, and then to the reincorporation of elements from their narratives into the epic. In the tale of Ḥanḍal the ʿUqaylī, for example, in a scene in which Ghānim is sent as a messenger to Ḥanḍal's pavilion with a threatening letter from the Banī Hilāl tribe, Ghānim is terrified of delivering the letter for fear Ḥanḍal will have him executed in his anger over the contents of the letter. Ghānim, who is known for both his physical cowardice and his gluttony, arrives just as a large meal is being served. In a performance by Shaykh Biyalī Abū Fahmī (2/13/87), Ghānim ate, among other things, *fatēta*. The scene was well embellished with comic touches, particularly when Ghānim tries again and again to stop eating: he was rabid (*saʿrān*), the piece of meat he was gnawing on was as big as his own leg up to his knee (*yā luqmituh qadd-I ruqbituh!*), and his stomach kept crying out "I want more, I want more" (*ana ʿāwiz kamān, ana ʿāwiz kamān!*). His eyes glistened and gleamed with tears (*tilammaʿ wi-tidammaʿ*), and his throat was bursting (*tifarqaʿ*), his hand kept shoveling, and his stomach kept crying out, "I want more, I want more."

At the next break I asked what fatēta was and learned that it is simply the local variation of a well-known dish, *fatta*, made with broth and crumbled bread. My inquiry sparked a series of short tales of good fattas and bad fattas, and soon I was quizzed about other regional specialties such as *mish* and *fasīkh*.[5] When we returned to the epic, the hero Ghānim had acquired the new epithets "father of the fatēta" (*abū l-fatēta*) and "the one of the fatēta" (*bitāʿ il-fatēta*), which stuck with him for the remaining twenty-five hours of Shaykh Biyalī's rendition of the sīra. Each iteration of the epithet provoked a round of laughter, and over a number of evenings the incident was recounted many times so that new listeners would understand. Although this instance was provoked by my own question, it proved a simple example of a process common in sahra performances, the constant movement of themes and other elements through various forms and genres during an evening gathering.

More interesting for our purposes than the creation of a simple epithet such as "father of the fatēta" are sequences of lengthy narratives which occasionally push even the epic out of the spotlight for a portion of an evening. One evening when Shaykh Ṭāhā was performing a segment from "The Wars of Tūnis" (6/24/87), audience members began to comment upon the name of the hero Diyāb (lit. wolves). The topic shifted to how times had changed, and people began listing the technological changes that they had personally lived through. The example of the shift from the *nōrāj* 'threshing floor,' which used horses or water buffalo driven round and round in a circle, to the modern gasoline-engine threshing machines was brought up. Then the discussion shifted to the subject of the hand-powered *ṭambūr* 'Archimedean water-screw' to the proliferation of livestock-driven waterwheels, to modern gasoline-powered pumps. Suddenly a young man named Muṣṭafā launched into a narrative that linked the two topics of wolves and technological change, a story of how his grandfather had spent an entire night turning a ṭambūr while fending off a wolf by tossing it scraps of his own food. Muṣṭafā added that he himself had only seen a wolf once, but that he would never

5. *Mish* is a rural cheese which is placed in earthenware jars until it has gone sour or "rotted"; it is infamous because it is often served with worms in it. *Fasīkh* is raw, salted fish served whole which one slices open and eats from the inside, peeling the pinkish flesh away from the skin with one's teeth.

forget it though it occurred when he was quite young and working as a camel driver (as he still does).

Mustafā recounted: "One night during cotton harvest, the landowner I was working for insisted I take one last load of cotton into [the town of] Qallīn, though it was nearly 2:00 A.M. I said no at first, that it was too late, and besides I couldn't go alone. But the overseer insisted. He said he would ride with me. Once we'd loaded and I was setting out, the man said he would go back and get the donkey, and then catch up with me on the way. I walked and walked and kept saying to myself, 'Any moment he'll catch up with me, any moment now.' I shouted and shouted but there was no answer—the man had lied and gone home.

I arrived in Qallīn and the people there said, 'Boy, are you crazy? It's 2:00 A.M., couldn't it wait till morning?' I told them the overseer would be along soon, so they weighed in the cotton and all. I waited and waited but the man didn't come. So I said to myself, 'I'll go home.' So I was riding the camel—perhaps 3:30 at night—to where the bridge is now—and there was the wolf. I scarcely knew it was a wolf—dog, wolf, I was young and had never seen one. But when I tried to pass, it would growl [Muṣṭafā growls], and if I tried to pass it on the side, the wolf would herd the camel back to the path. I didn't know what to do. I was afraid to get down, I couldn't get by, I thought to myself, "I could take off the camel's *kimām* [muzzle] and let it fight off the wolf—but it might turn around and bite me."

Shaykh Ṭāhā interrupted: "A fasting camel?" [*jamal ṣāyim* 'hadn't been fed'].

"Yes. And he could well turn around and bite me rather than the wolf. I thought and thought and decided: Better to be bit by the camel than eaten by the wolf! So I decided to unfasten the kimām, saying to myself, 'Don't worry about the wolf, just watch out for the camel and be ready with the stick!' So I unfastened the kimām. The wolf growled and the camel seized it in its mouth and threw it in the air higher than me. I screamed. I thought the wolf was going to land on me. When it hit the ground the camel held it, excuse me, with its feet and began to eat it [*bada yinissir fīh*—lit. 'eat and tear at it as a hawk eats its prey,' Muṣṭafā imitates the camel tossing its head from side to side]. It chewed on one piece all the way back to the village.

"I arrived at the house but I was afraid to get down in case the camel bit me—it's mind was 'changed' [*kān dimāghuh mitghayyar*]—it might do anything. So I knocked on the door and finally my father (May he rest in peace!) answered, saying, 'Where have you been?' So I told him that this and that had happened. He said that son of a bitch had come home long ago. He said, 'Stay where you are—don't get down.' And he left me on the camel. It was time for dawn prayers and every time I saw someone enter our alley I'd shout at him to go back [*rudd! rudd!*] and tell him that the camel would bite him. I thought, 'Am I going to the spend the night on this camel?' But my father appeared on the roof with a wooden ladder and a rope. He lowered the ladder on the rope and said, 'Jump and climb as fast as you can.' So I did, and he also pulled up on the rope at the same time. The camel turned to bite me but it missed. Can you imagine? That camel was tired out [*ta^cbān*] for two months."

Listeners: "Of course, of course!"

"And I was too—I kept seeing the wolf flying through the air. I'd point up in the air and shout, 'There's the wolf!' [*id-dīb ahō*]. They even had a doctor examine me—I told him too—'There's the wolf' [cringing and pointing up to the corner of the room]．

"My father said, 'I'll have my rights from that landowner.' He complained to the village headman [*^cumda*], and the headman said the man must be punished and informed the district police. My father said, 'I don't want 20 £E or 50 £E or 100 £E, I want my rights from that man.' And didn't he get a year in jail?"

The listeners nodded.

One listener: "That was during the days when ʿAbd al-Salām was village headman."

Muṣṭafà: "Yes, now that was when a headman was a headman!"

The listeners nodded.

Muṣṭafà's tale sparked a number of comments. More notably for our purposes here, however, it refocused the evening's performance on the hero Diyāb. Later discussions all dealt with Diyāb's character and his role in the epic, and when Diyāb was mentioned during the performance, Shaykh Ṭāhā lingered over the name and nodded to Muṣṭafà as did other listeners. Several times when Diyāb made an appearance in battle, audience members called out, "There's the wolf!" Conversation during each of the tea breaks that evening drifted back to the wolf story; a few similar incidents were recounted, though none was as dramatic as Muṣṭafà's tale.

During another evening's performance by Shaykh ʿAbd al-Wahhāb Ghāzī (3/16/87), the evening following his ḥiṭat baladī performance that we examined earlier, the event of a character within the epic falling asleep provoked a sequence of a half dozen tales of sleeping: tales of prodigious sleeps while home on leave from the army, tales of falling asleep while riding donkeys home at night (in one the rider supposedly fell off but continued to sleep on the ground undisturbed till morning; in the second the rider slept soundly till dawn, slumped forward on his donkey for hours after they had reached home, while the donkey patiently waited for someone to open the stable door). The last of these tales concerned a train ride back from the city of Ṭanṭa during which five friends all fell asleep, missed their stop, and awoke to find themselves in the next province. But with incredible luck, as they exited the station they spied a long-distance taxi (*serfis*) driver from a village next to al-Bakātūsh, and after recounting their story and having a good laugh, they were offered a ride home.

Clearly the effective study of such threads of cohesion, particularly on a level more sophisticated than the rough observations cited above, would necessarily be rooted in numerous recordings of entire sahras from beginning to end. I do not possess such data. Though on numerous occasions I was able to record examples of these various narrative genres, at different points in the evening I was invariably requested to turn off the tape recorder. Thus as evidence for the development of narrative themes over an evening-long performance I have only my handwritten field notes. The categories of "formal" and "informal" genres performed by the poets (listed in Chap. 4) were accepted by almost all participants as verbal art worthy of being recorded (though some listeners objected to my recording even ḥitat baladī passages). Those genres performed by poets which I have listed as "conversational" and all genres performed by audience members, however, were deemed by audience members to be outside the proper sphere of my research, primarily because many of the erotic, political, and personal matters brought up, mostly in jest, could in fact cause difficult social situations if circulated.

Such evenings of performance suggest an interesting connection to the structure of literary creations such as the *Thousand and One Nights*. It is an enduring paradox that this most famous example of Arabic literature should be best known for a narrative technique entirely untypical of Arabic literature, oral or written—the frame-tale. The historical explanation, of course, is that the work originated in Indian and Persian forms and was then translated into Arabic and stocked with further tales from Arabic oral tradition. (Still later, the collection was entirely transformed by European translators and editors, who quadrupled the number of stories by borrowing from many different sources, though they continued to purvey the product as "Arabic" to an unsuspecting Western audience.) This strategy of appropriation appears to be most directly linked to the formation of a "popular" literature as a distinct, and perhaps a distinctly written, discourse. The structure of such performance events as the sahra, in which one major genre provides the backdrop and even the instigating factor for sequences of "embedded" tales, suggests, however, a rough oral counterpart to the literary frame-tale. The rich analyses of the relationships obtaining between the frame-tale and the embedded tales and among sequences of tales, which have been developed in interpreting the *Nights* and other examples of genre, should provide valuable precedents for the examination of the dynamics inherent in the sahra when addressed as an interacting whole.[6]

Situational Interactions

Ultimately most of the aesthetic decisions made during a sahra performance are in the hands of the poet, the primary performer. In our examination of the ḥitat baladī we noted the existence and common deployment of an auxiliary genre specifically designed to incorporate audience members directly into the performance. (Poets' genealogical discussions appear to be a less formally marked genre based upon similar intent.) The ḥitat baladī is but the most formally framed space within the sahra for this process, for such incorporation occurs with some regularity throughout the performance. One mark of the virtuosity of a poet in al-Bakātūsh is his ability to to cope with developing situations in the gathering without completely breaking the frame or form of whatever genre he is performing at that moment; there are, however, many levels of such situational interactions.

The simplest form may be that of embedding extranarrative commentary within the story while maintaining the exigencies of the poetic form, though without manipulating the story itself. Toward the very end of the second night of the performance of "The Birth of Abū Zayd" by Shaykh Ṭāhā Abū Zayd mentioned earlier, the host at one point gestured to the poet that it was growing quite late. The poet, knowing that he was only minutes from the concluding scene of the episode, sang his response in verse without breaking stride (lines 6–7 below). In this scene Abū Zayd has for days unknowingly been fighting his father in battle, neither able to best the other. Returning from battle, Abū Zayd meets a maiden in his path (his sister, Shīḥa) who first tests him, then insults him, and finally mysteriously tells him to go ask his mother who his real father is. Abū Zayd confronts his mother several times before she relents and tells him the truth:

Text 5.2 Interjected Comments by Poet
Shaykh Ṭāhā Abū Zayd, tape 87–104 (6/2/87)

abūk baqā yā bnī rizq ibn^{u} nāyil, 1
illī inta Qabāluh fī maʿrak al-mīdān.

6. See Ferial Ghazoul, *The Arabian Nights: A Structural Analysis* (1980); Mia Gerhardt, *The Art of Storytelling: A Literary Study of the Thousand and One Nights* (1963); see also T. Todorov, *Grammaire du "Décameron"* (1969).

wi-dōla rijālak wi-ahlak wi-lammitak, 2
  wi-llī iḥna ʿanduh faḍl iz-ziḥlān.
ḥāmā ʿiruḍnā yā qirm bēn il-ʿarab, 3
  titQām luh ir-rayāt il-bēḍ fōq rāyiq il-bunyān.»
qāl «yā mma lēh lēh lēh lēh lammā abūyā, 4
  lē tikhbirīnī yā ḥilwit il-aʿyān.
innī baqā riḍā il-wālidēn yā niʿme walditī, 5
  inn-I riḍāhum min riḍā r-raḥmān.»

To Host: ṭawwil lī bālak 6
  yā bū bakhātī lam tikūn qalqān!
          [Laughter—voice: yā salām!]

wi-kull-I ʿām wa-ntum fī l-ʿizz-I wa-l-hane, 7
  tiʿūd layālīkum fī kull-I awān.
yithārijū l-isnēn illā wa-shīḥa aQbalat, 8
  ukht-I salāme wi-dā muQdim il-firsān . . .

"Your father, O my son, is Rizq, son of Nāyil, 1
  Whom you are facing in battle on the field.
And these are your men, your people, and your clan, 2
  And the one we are staying with is Faḍl of the Zaḥlān.
He defended our honor, O Courageous One, among the Arabs, 3
  May white banners be raised for him atop the finest of
    buildings."
He said, "O mother, why, why, why, why, of my father, 4
  Why do you inform me [only now], O Most Beautiful of the
    Nobles?
So I am the contentment of my two parents, O Bounteous Mother, 5
  May their contentment be from the contentment of the All-
    Merciful."

To Host: Lengthen your patience for me, 6
  O Abū Bakhātī, don't grow uneasy!
          [Laughter—voice: Well done!]

May all of you each year find prosperity and happiness, 7
  May your evening gatherings return time and again.
The two were arguing when suddenly Shīḥa approached, 8
  The sister of Salāma, and he was the champion of the warriors.

Textually and musically the poet remains within the frame of epic verse, though in this example he breaks with the story world of the epic to direct a comment outward to a named addressee in the audience. The two interjected verses (6–7) are not tied in any way to the narrative material that immediately proceeds and follows them.

Another common technique used by poets to maneuver through and negotiate developing situations involves maintaining the story world of the epic as well as the formal features of the genre by changing an aspect of the story so as to comment on the present situation. Small instances of this technique are relatively common in sahra performances and are particularly well applauded and are often commented upon afterward. A typical example of this process is a poet's reaction to an audience member who has, or is about to, fall asleep during a performance (which, given the long hours of agricultural labor and the late hours of the sahra performances, is understandably a common occurrence). Sometimes a poet gestures with his eyes, head, or the rabāb at the dozing listener, at the same time alerting the other audience members to some upcoming twist in the tale. Then, at the beginning of the next battle scene or scene with people arguing, for example, the poet lets out a great yell (placed in the mouth of one of the epic characters) while everyone observes, usually with great laughter and much teasing, the effect on their sleeping companion. This shout (*s̲hak̲hṭa*) is even a point of pride with several poets: after Shaykh ʿAbd al-Wahhāb Ghāzī had woken a dozing participant in precisely this manner, several listeners offered testimonies to the fact that when he was younger, Shaykh ʿAbd al-Wahhāb's s̲hak̲hṭa could startle people as far away as the village of Minyat Qallīn, two kilometers distant.

A poet may choose to manipulate the narrative even further by introducing, for example, a character with the name of the sleeping listener, who then in the story falls asleep and is awoken by one of the regular epic heroes. Or, the poet may cause one of the regular characters in the story to fall asleep, usually in comic circumstances, only to be awoken by another character with a similar shout. In the former instance the audience is made aware of the joke by the name of the newly interjected character; in the latter, audience members who know the tradition well will begin looking around at the other listeners as soon as they detect such an insertion, trying to discern who is most likely the target of the poet's wit.

This process of response to the performance situation can also, of course, lead to the suppression of materials rather than the interjection of exterior elements. Perhaps the most common example is the suppression of certain incidents, anecdotes, and jokes when female listeners are present (as in any public, outdoor performance such as a wedding) or known to be within hearing distance (as in a private home).[7] Certain scenes from the epic are structured almost entirely around erotic humor and ordinarily must be dropped out of a performance or radically censored in the presence of female listeners.

In the early period of my research in al-Bakātūsh I contracted with Shaykh Biyalī Abū Fahmī to sing the epic from beginning to end. As a result of my request, much of the flexibility inherent in this performance tradition and many of Shaykh Biyalī's skills as a performer were rendered unavailable to him. Only later, by observing his work in other contexts, did I grow to realize the dimensions of the problem. The choice of which episode to sing was taken from him, along with much of the freedom usually involved in moving back and forth through the various other genres of sahra performances; he was further constrained by the sense that these performances were "official" ones. Occasionally these competing forces within an artifically constructed context produced informative mishaps, such as the following in which Shaykh Biyalī was forced to suppress one set of images in deference to the women of the household who were listening from the next room.

Our recording project had advanced as far as the Banī Hilāl's arrival in the region of Tūnis, and this evening's performance started in quite ordinary fashion. A new element was introduced, however, when the women in the back of the house asked permission to leave the door to the men's sitting room ajar so that they might listen. They sat quietly in the portion of the room behind the door, so that they were not visible to anyone in the sitting room, and conversed only in whispers. Within half an hour, however, Shaykh Biyalī was faced with a difficult situation, for he had arrived at a very comic, highly erotic scene. The Banī Hilāl, in an attempt to free three young men of the tribe held in prison inside the city of Tūnis, had sent the maidens of the tribe to the city gate, accompanied by Abū Zayd whom they conceal in their midst. The maidens flirt with the gatekeeper (who is described as an eighty-year-old, ugly, hunchbacked, Negro slave from Africa) so that he will open the gate, supposedly so that they may sell their perfumes in the marketplace. Al-Jāzya has just avowed that she is madly in love with the

7. When I first arrived in al-Bakātūsh and asked Shaykh Biyalī Abū Fahmī to sing a version of the epic from beginning to end, he omitted the tale of Badr al-Naᶜām, which he only performed after another poet had sung it for me. The main villains of this tale are Christians, and Shaykh Biyalī did not wish to sing it for fear the anti-Christian jokes might offend me. I later discovered that the poet who first sang it for me did not know at the time that I was not Muslim. Without that slip, I might never have known about the episode's existence. As to whether there are other episodes in the al-Bakātūsh repertory whose existence I am unaware of, I believe not, but *allāhu aᶜlam* 'God only knows'!

gatekeeper; he, however, is recalcitrant and still trying to get rid of them when he proposes a singing contest:

Text 5.3: Suppression of Materials for Female Listeners[8]
Shaykh Biyalī Abū Fahmī, tape 87–029 (2/25/87)

Spoken:
She said to him: "Aren't you going to open up, Manṣūr?" [He said:] "You sing, then I'll sing after you, and if you best me in the saying [of poetry], I'll marry four of the women and you'll be at the top of the list. If I best you in the saying [of poetry], then you'll take the women and get out of here, and we'll call our love quits, and praise be to God!" Al-Jāzya said to him: "You spread out the bedding and I'll put on the cover." He said to her: "You've made a mistake—the holy law that Our Lord has established [says] that women spread out the bedding for men, for men are preferred over women, and women spread out the bedding for men, so who will 'spread the bedding' in words?" He said to her: "You 'spread out the bedding' with words! And I will 'lay the cover over you' with words." So al-Jāzya "spread out the bedding," what does she say?—he who loves the Prophet surpasses us in wishing God's blessings upon Him:

Sung:
I praise Muḥammad, the stones spoke to Him,
The stones spoke to Him
[Tunes *rabāb*]
I praise Muḥammad, the stones spoke to Him, 1
O Lord let us visit Him and rejoice in His light,
So we can rejoice in His light and achieve the visit,
and achieve the visit.

Sung in a rapid singsong manner:
The Daughter of Sarḥān, 2
Spoke in rhymes and meters,
Immediately poetry was at hand,
And in it we have matters.

"Open, O Manṣūr, 3
Open the gate of the wall,
So we can enter properly,
And go sell our perfumes.

8. Transliterated Arabic text in the Appendix.

"Open and don't be a 'fraidy, 4
If you've any spittle in you,
There is jet-dark henna
On the hands of these virgins.

"Open, O my Beloved, 5
O my musk and my scent,
I'll take you as my husband,
O strapping young gatekeeper." (2x)

The gatekeeper Manṣūr answered al-Jāzya thus. What did he say?

"I will not open my gate 6
To anyone I don't know,
And you are stingy Arabs,
To open to you is a waste."

"O Gatekeeper, open your armored gate, 7
O Gatekeeper, open your armored gate,
If they enter they will profits gain,
From the sale of their perfumes.

"Oh don't be afraid, oh don't be afraid, 8
I will show you all my features,
And then we'll play at trysting,
And then we'll play at trysting."

What did the gatekeeper Manṣūr say to her?:

"That's all well, O maiden, 9
But let's cut short the discussion,
Have you come to the gatekeeper with disaster,
To crack his head open while raidin'?

"I'll never open the door, 10
I'll never open the door,
Even to the strokes of lances
From inebriated [enraged] soldiers.

"Get along pretty one, get along pretty one, 11
You should the Khalīfa [king of Tūnis] fear,
In his hand is a sharpened spear,
Which passes with ease through stones."

"Open, O Manṣūr, 12
Open the gate of the wall,
Give us your permission.
O Face of Loss,
  Come on, Gatekeeper Manṣūr,
  Your face is the face of loss.

"Open and I will show you 13
The features of the virgins,
(*Aside*: The virgins, that is, the girls)
Open and I will show you
The features of the virgins.

"We have with us ʿAlya of the ʿUqayla, 14
And ʿAlya of the Zaḥlān,
And we have with us Lady Waṭfa of the Zaghāba,
We have with us Lady Sāra.

"Saʿdiyya and Rasmiyya, 15
Saʿdiyya and Rasmiyya,
And al-Jāzya of the Arabs,
And al-Jāzya of the Arabs,
The 'administration' all desire her,
The 'administration' all desire her."

He slammed the door and was leaving 16
The beautiful faces behind,
[But] the finest musk wafted up
From ʿAlya and from Sāra.

The gatekeeper he was moved, 17
He took his key and rose,
He took his key and rose,
And opened wide the door.

He spread out his reed matting, 18
And then took off his sandals,
And he took off his sandals
And made a rush at the virgins!

The gatekeeper spread out his reed matting 19
And he took off his sandals
And—his health!—he untied his underwear!
And he obtained disaster! yes, he obtained disaster!

Abū Zayd the Dark One 20
Came to him riding like ʿAntar,
In his hand a cutting sword,
He struck Manṣūr the rude,
He caused his "head" to roll
Like a single cucumber!

And this was the opening of the Gates of Tūnis, 21
For [the rescue of] Yaḥyā and Marʿī and Yūnis,
And this was the opening of the Gates of Tūnis,
For [the rescue of] Yaḥyā and of Yūnis,
And Yūnis was sitting in prison and heard all the commotion.

Manṣūr the gatekeeeper fell, 22
They buried him by the wall,
And they dumped upon his skull,
The eighty bushel baskets!

Wish God's Blessings on the Prophet!

Upon finishing this scene to much laughter and applause, Shaykh Biyalī turned to me and added sotto voce that this is not how the end of the scene went, but that there were women in the next room, and he would explain later. Specifically, Biyalī had changed the target of Abū Zayd's swordstroke, and it's clear even from the "expurgated" text that Manṣūr's head is probably not what bounced down the road like a cucumber (*zirr-I khiyāra* is literally a *single* cucumber): Manṣur's head was substituted at the last minute. A more typical rendering for an all male audience is that Abū Zayd came to him sword in hand and "slashed open the rude one's underwear [*fakk-I libāsuh*], and caused his cock to bounce about like a single cucumber."

As with many types of erotic humor, the act of concealment (of body parts, vocabulary, gestures, etc.) in the presence of the opposite sex often does more to reveal tensions than hide them, resulting in moments of sexually charged humor. Shaykh Biyalī's attempt to hide the "male" punch line fooled few in this audience (male or female) and generated more laughter and attention than the "male" verse ever does under normal circumstances.

The analysis of more pervasive transformations of traditional materials from performance to performance poses a more complex set of problems, involving far more subtle shifts in degrees of emphasis and focus. As an example we examine a sahra riddled with tension because of the presence of eight educated young men (ages nineteen to twenty-five), all of whom openly leaned toward modern reinterpretations of Islam (what the Western press terms "fundamentalism"). Shaykh Biyalī Abū Fahmī is usually a favorite poet of the younger crowd in al-Bakātūsh for he is a lively performer who tends toward humorous and melodramatic presentation; for these reasons he claims fewer of the older, more traditional aficionados as loyal supporters. On this particular evening, however, he found himself caught in the generational clash.

The sahra had already gotten under way when these young men arrived with a guest from town, a high school English teacher, whom they wished to introduce to me. Until their arrival, the audience had consisted entirely of older men and myself. Their presence initiated a certain amount of tension, for, more than any other social group within the village, they represented the breakdown of the old order. By dint of their university educations, in al-Bakātūsh they are accorded social status and authority far in excess of what traditional social structures would normally grant them according to their age and unmarried status. Also, the new Islamic movements have of necessity made spokespersons of young men who possess no accepted religious authority either in the institutional sense (having studied at a religious institution, for example, to become a government-appointed imām) or in the traditional sense (being a Qur'ān reciter or a confrere in a Sufi brotherhood). They are, in social terms, at the other end of nearly every social axis from the usual audiences of *Sīrat Banī Hilāl* gatherings. Their presence in the sahra was registered within the story of the epic within minutes of their arrival. As Shaykh Biyalī sang of the escalating confrontation between the Banī Hilāl tribe and Khalīfa Zanātī, the ruler of Tūnis, he began to portray the fight as one between the older and younger generations. At this point in the story several skirmishes had already taken place between the opposing forces; however, the two Hilālī heroes Abū Zayd and Ḥasan are struggling to avoid all-out war with the city of Tūnis because Diyāb, the strongest of the Hilālī warriors, has quarreled with them and absented himself from camp. Badr, son of Ghānim and brother of Diyāb, elects to ride into battle against Khalīfa, though he knows he is certain to die, for all know that the death of Khalīfa Zanātī has been foretold to be at the hand of Diyāb. Badr is killed and another young man named Badr takes his place, and so on till eighty young men, all named Badr (=Full Moon) have been killed. Finally the Qāḍī Badīr, the religious judge of the tribe, rides against Khalīfa Zanātī and is also killed. The Banī Hilāl have no choice but to declare full-scale war. They call for all four clans of the confederation to ride into battle, and a message is sent to Diyāb.

The killing of the eighty Badrs is an integral part of the traditional story line; the crystallization of the confrontation as one of generations is, however, unique to this particular performance. After the opening skirmish with the first Badr, al-Zanātī Khalīfa sings to the defeated Hilālī horsemen:

Text 5.4 Interaction with Young Men, Part 1
Shaykh Biyalī Abū Fahmī, tape 87–032 (2/26/87)

ṣarakh ʿalā ṣ-ṣaffēn: shīlū Qatīlakum 1
yā man badāluh yinzil il-mīdān

fāris li-fāris yā ʿarab la-tishāwirū 2
wallāh in nazaltū il-kull-Ī aq'bil ḥurūbikum
anā khalīfa abū saʿda murʿib ish-shugaʿān

il-hilayla gūm yiḥāribū khalīfa 3
wi-huwa fī sinn il-khamsa wi-sittīn sana;
wallāhī law gētūnī wa-nā lissa shubbān,

mā khallēt minkū wa-lā fāris, yisraḥ wa-bi-l-aghnām 4
anā khusāra gētūnī wa-nā mitQaddim fī-sinn-Ī baṭlān

wa-nā zamānī shēb 5
wallāh zamān ish-shēb lā yiʿūd li-ṣibā
mā-l-laban ir-rāyib yiʿūd ḥulbān

wi-n sābinī il-gīl la-nā mitrabbī miʿāhum 6
ṣabaḥt-I min bēn ig-gīl il-ghalbān

ḥagam badr. 7

He shouted to the two ranks, "Carry off your dead! 1
And now who will descend into battle in his stead?

"Warrior to warrior, O Arabs, indicate [an opponent], 2
By God, if you all descended together I'd meet your fighting!
I am Khalīfa, father of Saʿda, Terrifier of Valiant Men!"

The Hilālīs came to fight Khalīfa when he was in his sixty-
fifth year; 3
"By God, if you had come to me while I was still a young
man!

"I would not have left among you a single warrior to graze
your livestock; 4
What a pity you've come to me now that I am advanced in
years and worn out.

"I long ago turned gray-haired, by God, gray hair never
returns again to youth, 5
Curdled milk never again becomes fresh.

"And the generation I was raised with have all left me, 6
I have awoken midst this worthless generation!"

Badr attacked. 7

The battle lines have been clearly drawn, inside and outside the story; the aging Khalīfa Zanātī proceeds to kill the young Badr al-Majnūn (Badr the Crazy), then a second young man named Badr al-Shajīʿ (Badr the Valiant), and continues on to kill the eighty young men all by the name of Badr.[9]

At the next break in the performance, the young men presented their guest and, primarily because of their numbers and enthusiasm, soon began to dominate the discussion. Their conversation quickly drifted toward politics, and the dozen or so older men present were displeased with what they interpreted as disrespectful behavior on the part of the young men and in particular with this new turn in the conversation; they were, however, constrained by the presence of an outside, educated guest. Shaykh Biyalī tried to steer the conversation in a new direction, but one young man inadvertently cut him off. "Don't you know the meaning of the word 'Excuse me' [*lā muʾākhiza*]," the poet erupted; "Sit quietly!" The high school teacher intervened to calm Shaykh Biyalī, but the poet grew suspicious of what he took to be the teacher's ingratiating tone and his overly formal terms of respect. The young men, however, continued to converse quietly and whisper their irritation. Shaykh Biyalī picked up his rabāb and put an end to the matter by starting to play.

Suddenly Biyalī threw in a scene I had never heard before. The setting was the battle in Tūnis where the Banī Hilāl desperately needed the aid of their temperamental warrior, Diyāb, in the face of al-Zanātī's recent

9. This slaughter of the eighty Badrs evokes echoes from other sections of the epic: the capture of the eighty maidens of the Banī Hilāl by Ḥanḍal the ʿUqaylī; the slaughter of the seventy (somtimes eighty) descendants of the Prophet while they were at prayer, by this same Zanātī Khalīfa in an earlier episode of the epic. In addition, Badr 'Full Moon' is a common epithet of the Prophet Muḥammad.

slaughter of the young men of the tribe. Somehow Diyāb, usually the fiercest and most battle-loving member of the tribe, had lost his characteristic valor and was reluctant to fight. Finally, his mother and father are sent to persuade him to ride into battle "for a son should feel shame before his father" (il-walad yikhtashī min abūh). They are guided into his tent, but Ghānim fails to convince his son. Suddenly he removes the veil from Bazla, mother of Diyāb; since our hero has not seen his mother unveiled since he was a child, he is horrified to discover that she is incredibly ugly—which (as happens every few minutes with Arab epic heroes) prompts him to sing an ode:

Text 5.5 Interaction with Young Men, Part 2
Shaykh Biyalī Abū Fahmī, tape 87–032 (2/26/87)

fa-kānit umm-I diyāb wiḥsha, kān shaklahā shēn, wiḥish. kān ʿalēhā ḍabb ʿālya. in-niswān il-ḥilwīn yijībū ir-rijāl il-wiḥshīn. wi-j-jamāʿa il-wiḥshīn sāʿāt yijībū l-ḥilwīn, wi-sāʿāt ḥilw yikhallif ḥilw.

[Loud laughter]

Poet: ummāl mish binqūlak yiṭrid mi-d-dār fī wasṭ il-ʿālam?
Voice: lā yā khāl
Poet: ikhs ʿalēh
Voice: āh

[Music]

fa-ʿalā mā nismaʿ fī aQwāl il-ashʿār bi-inn-I kān Diyāb mā ʿumrūsh shāf ḥanak ummuh abadan—mā shāfsh fammahā abadan. ṭabʿan il-ʿarab bitūʿ zamān kānit il-wāḥda mindirī yibq'ā ʿalā wajhā birqaʿ yidāri wajihā. fa-l-amīr ghānim shāl il-burqaʿ min ʿalā wajh bazla, umm-I diyāb. fa-diyāb laqā ummuh shaklahā wiḥish wi-ḍ-ḍabb bitāʿhā ʿālī kibīr kida. fa-diyāb yaʿnī taʿajjib ʿalā manar ummuh, qāl yā salām, fa-diyāb baqā ghannā qaṣīda, yiqūl ēh?

Now Diyāb's mother was ugly, her face was really unattractive, ugly. She had long buckteeth. Beautiful women bear ugly men, and ugly people sometimes bear beautiful people, and sometimes a beautiful person gives birth to another beautiful person.

[Loud laughter from one of the young men which angers the poet]

Poet: Well, didn't I tell you we'd have to throw them out in front of everyone?
Voice: No, O maternal uncle.
Poet: Shame on him.
Voice: Yes.

[Music]

[The poet is persuaded to continue]

Now from what we have heard from the words of the poems, Diyāb

> had never seen his mother's "mug"—he'd never seen her mouth ever. Of course, among the Arabs of long ago, a woman was hidden, for she had a veil on her face which hid it. So Prince Ghānim lifted the veil from the face of Bazla, mother of Diyāb. And Diyāb found out that her face was ugly, and that her buckteeth were really big and long. And Diyāb, that is, he was amazed at the sight of his mother. He said, "Heavens!" And Diyāb sang an ode, what does he say?

The poem begins with words of praise for the Prophet Muḥammad; the audience responded, wishing God's blessings upon Him, and fell quiet. Then the poet gave us a sequence filled with aphorisms of how some are given great wealth by God and some are given none, how some are given good fortune and some are jinxed, how some are given polite, hardworking wives and others ugly, rude ones. It is precisely the sequence of good and bad fortune which Shaykh ʿAbd al-Wahhāb Ghāzī used in the ḥitat baladī segment we examined in Chapter 4:

Text 5.6 Interaction with Young Men, Part 3
Shaykh Biyalī Abū Fahmī, tape 87–032 (2/26/87)

awwil mā nibdā nuṣallī ʿalā n-nabī 1
nabīnā il-hudā il-ʿarabī wa-lih ḥaram masbūt
nabīnā il-hudā il-ʿarabī wa-lih ḥaram masbūt.

yiqūl il-amir diyāb ʿalā mā garā luh 2
wi-r-rizq min ʿand il-ilāh bikhūt

fīh illī yuʿṭīh rabbak jūda maʿa karam 3
wi-fīh illī yiddī luh bukhl-I lammā yimūt

wi-fīh illī yiʿṭī luh ḥawāṣil malāna 4
wi-fīh illī rabbak yiddī luh rizq-I qūt bi-qūt

We begin by wishing God's blessings on the Prophet, 1
Our Prophet of True Guidance, He has a permanent sanctuary,
Our Prophet of True Guidance, He has a permanent sanctuary.

Says Prince Diyāb from what had happened to him, 2
Sustenance from God is [good and bad] fortunes.

There is he whom Your Lord grants generosity along with honor, 3
And there is he who is given stinginess till he dies.

And there is he who is granted full harvests, 4
And there is he whom Your Lord gives sustenance bit by bit.

The subsequent verses about good sons versus bad provoked a reaction among the young men, some of whom laughed and some of whom interpreted this verse as a commentary on their own conduct and scowled. The ambiguity between humor and social commentary was made even sharper when the next verse turned on a reference to a young donkey:

Text 5.7 Interaction with Young Men, Part 4
Shaykh Biyalī Abū Fahmī, tape 87–032 (2/26/87)

wi-fīh illī yiʿṭī luh rabbak walad amīr biyinfaʿuh
wi-fīh illī yiʿṭī luh walad
bass-I yiṭlaʿ bāyiẓ wi-halfūt

fīh illī yiddī luh
wi-fīh illī yiddī luh jaḥsh-I lā muʾakhza
min suʾ bakhtuh il-ḥazīn yimūt

Spoken:
(yaʿnī mā yikūnsh ḥidda law ij-jaḥsh jē luh wi-dā ḥaẓẓuh yimūt)

And there is he whom Your Lord gives a princely son who serves him,
And there is he who is given a son,
But he turns out rotten and useless.

There is he who is given,
There is he who is given a young donkey, if you'll excuse me,
But with his bad luck the wretched thing up and dies.

Spoken:
(That is, no sooner does he get him, if he gets a young donkey, than with his luck it up and dies.)

These verses produced a clear response among the listeners, but Shaykh Biyalī shifted quickly first to humor and then on to women. As Shaykh ʿAbd al-Wahhāb did, Shaykh Biyalī enumerated the blessings of he who has a good wife and gave a comic rendition of the plight of the husband who has an ugly, domineering, miserly wife. Nearly every verse was followed by a burst of laughter. The description of the bad wife was met with guffaws: "with her legs and her neck she resembles a catfish!" (lihā riglēn wi-zōrhā tishbih il-qarmūṭ).

Shaykh Biyalī then shifted the tone of the performance drastically. Though he retained the ongoing tempo and melody, he switched to another rhyme (*-āyil*) and started the entire sequence over again from the beginning with verses of praise to the Prophet Muḥammad. Whereas the preceding verses had been met with loud laughter from the young men (they laughed partly at the comic verses and partly at the poet himself), the verses of madīḥ brought a sudden silence followed by muted responses of "May God bless and preserve Him."

Text 5.8 Interaction with Young Men, Part 5
Shaykh Biyalī Abū Fahmī, tape 87–032 (2/26/87)

nabīnā il-hudā il-ʿarabī
gā nā bi-kull ir-rasāʾil

nabīnā il-hudā il-ʿarabī
awḍaʿ linā kull ir-rasāyil

Our Arab Prophet of True Guidance,
He came to us with all the Messages (i.e., Scriptures).

Our Arab Prophet of True Guidance,
He set out for us all the Messages.

Then Diyāb was suddenly singing once again of sons, good and bad:

yaQūl allā z-zughbī diyāb ibn-I ghānim
law kān il-khāl ṭayyib ʿalā naqā
wi-l-wad wi-khāluh il-itnēn yizīnū il-qabāyil

in il-walad yaṭlaʿ li-khāluh
ka-l-khayla taṭlaʿ min duhūr is-salāyil

Says the Zughbī, Diyāb, son of Ghānim,
"If the maternal uncle is good, well-chosen,
Then the boy and his uncle both embellish the tribe.

"For the boy takes after his maternal uncle,
As the thoroughbred mare takes after generations of breeding."

Shaykh Biyalī then again returned to a sequence on maidens and how to select a good bride, and finally closed the poem with words of advice sung as an extended mawwāl:

Text 5.9 Interaction with Young Men, Part 6
Shaykh Biyalī Abū Fahmī, tape 87–032 (2/26/87)

āh li-llī yuṣbur li-l-zēn wi-sh-shēn maʿa ṣabr
il-ʿaql-I ṭamaʿ in-nifūs zayyinā
wi-dōq il-ḥarīr maʿa r-ramāyil

āh mā tuQṣud in-nadl il-bakhīl fī ḥāga
mā tuQṣud in-nadl il-bakhīl fī ḥāja
wa-lā tuQṣud ahālī il-ʿuqūl iḍ-ḍalāyil

wa-lā tuQṣud allā ahl il-karam fī buyūthum
tilāqī ʿalā wujūh in-nās iṭ-ṭayyibīn il-ʿalāyim

yā ʿamm-I wa-rjaʿ aqūlak il-jūd wi-l-karam
il-jūd wi-l-karam wi-l-ʿaTf wi-l-aṣl
lā huwa bi-kutr il-ghinī
wa-lā bi-zēnat libs il-ʿamāyim
wa-lā bi-zēnat libs il-ʿamāyim

iṣ-ṣaqr law balā rīsh ʿaḍmatuh shudād il-ʿazāyim
ṣallum ʿalā n-nabī

Ah! He who endures the beautiful and the ugly both with patience!
The mind hopes for souls such as ours,
And the touch of silk as well as sand.

Ah, don't go to the lowly miserly one for anything,
Ah, don't go to the lowly miserly one for anything,
And don't go to people with wrongdoing in their minds.

Don't go to any save people of honor in their houses,
You will find on the faces of good people signs.

O paternal uncle, I will tell you again: Generosity and Honor,
Generosity, and Honor, and Compassion, and Nobility,
These do not come from great wealth,
Nor from the wearing of beautiful turbans,
Nor from the wearing of beautiful turbans.

The eagle even were he without feathers,
His very bones possess courageous determination!
★ Wish God's Blessings on the Prophet! ★

A number of the young men and nearly all of the other listeners understood many of these verses as public criticism of the young men's behavior; at several points they had begun to squirm and whisper uneasily. When this sequence was over, Biyalī stopped abruptly for a break and put down his rabāb (though we had just taken a break and been served tea a few minutes earlier). The young men and their guest stood up precipitously and departed, with only the curtest of farewells.

The remaining listeners, all over forty-five or so, proceeded to congratulate and applaud Biyalī on his handling of the situation; then, without having drunk tea, Biyalī seized his rabāb and, in an atmosphere of high spirits, we began again. However, when we returned to the battle scene, Diyāb was no longer in his strangely timorous mood, and the comic element had been dropped entirely. The mood in fact shifted to the opposite emotional pole, for this episode was the last of the epic as it is known in al-Bakātūsh, "The Killing of al-Zanātī Khalīfa." This was also the tenth and final sahra in a series of sahrāt held over a two-week period during which Shaykh Biyalī had sung the epic beginning to end, an event that had attracted many listeners night after night. This was the end of the epic and the death of the villain—a villain, however, who had that evening been recast as the representative of a disappearing older generation, a villain struggling against his preordained demise at the hands of a younger generation whom he characterized as worthless and disappointing. I think that, after the fracas with the young men and their evident lack of respect for the sīra tradition, many of us, as we listened to the death of al-Zanātī, were reflecting upon the changing times; perhaps some even felt, as I did, that we were listening to the end of an era.

CONCLUSION

Epic Text and Context

Richard Martin, in his analysis of the act of speaking within the *Iliad*, says:

> My central conclusion is that the *Iliad* takes shape as a poetic composition in precisely the same "speaking culture" that we see foregrounded in the stylized words of the poem's heroic speakers, especially those speeches designated as *muthos*, a word I redefine as "authoritative speech-act." The poet and hero are both "performers" in a traditional medium. The genre of *muthos* composing requires that its practitioners improve on previous performances and surpass them, by artfully manipulating traditional material in new combinations. In other words, within the speeches of the poem, we see that it is traditional to be spontaneous: no hero ever merely repeats; each recomposes the traditional text he performs, be it a boast, threat, command or story, in order to project his individual personality in the most convincing manner. I suggest that the "voice" of the poet is the product of the same traditional performance technique.[1]

In the *Sīrat Banī Hilāl* epic-singing tradition, no specific term such as *muthos* guides us to such an analysis, and the specific features of muthos composing are not those of "authoritative speech-acts" within the Arabic tradition. Yet our conclusions are remarkably similar. The clues in our analysis of Arabic oral epic performances have been rather a host of parallel frames, markers, and narrative devices which constantly correlate and negotiate the relationship between poets and heroes, often through the intermediary presence of a patron. The interpretation of *Sīrat Banī Hilāl* performances which we have built up through extended description

1. Richard P. Martin, *The Language of Heroes: Speech and Performance in the "Iliad"* (1989), xiv.

of the tradition as it is found within a single village demonstrates the existence of a relationship, significantly similar to what Martin has proposed, between the speech of heroes within the epic and the speech of epic poets. Within the Hilālī tradition, however, we have the additional opportunity of observing the social reality of the *Sīrat Banī Hilāl* epic singers and thence drawing further conclusions. As we have seen, the social reality of the al-Bakātūsh poets involves a distinctly negative position for the epic singer within the greater social hierarchy; in marked contrast to the poet's marginalized status in village society, however, are the moments of centrality, power, and "voice" hc achieves in epic performance. This disjunctive persona has produced not only a fascinating process of deep self-identification with the epic tradition on the part of the poets, but has clearly, over generations, shaped and indeed constituted many aspects of the content of the epic itself—an epic tradition, as I have termed it, of heroic poets and poetic heroes.

The poets of al-Bakātūsh, however, possess an articulated counter-identity which they maintain in opposition to the negative stereotype of the Gypsy rabāb-poet held by the larger society. This subversive image of the poet as the eloquent, sharp-witted, and gracious "ur-Arab" is not, however, projected outward as a public expression of identity; it is an in-group ideal. In formulating this ideal the poets redeploy to their own ends many of the key features of the negative "Gypsy-poet" image: the suspect quality of the poet's glibness and his social criticisms in poetic performance become the most prized characteristics of the *faṣīḥ* (eloquent) "Arab"; the easy commingling of men and women in the poets' community becomes not the mark of "loose" morals but rather of ancient Arab custom and independence; the rabāb which signifies the "beggar-poets" to the larger society (it is the decisive marker of the professional poet in contrast to the nonprofessional reciter of Hilālī tales) becomes instead the respected tool of the epic-poet profession, one wielded proudly even by the famous heroes and warriors of old. The meeting point of the derogatory stereotype and this counteridentity is situated in the act of epic performance.

One distinctive narrative structure which reflects this meeting point involves the duplication of the epic performance within the epic: the creation of a complete parallel event of poet, patron, and participants. Here the poets of al-Bakātūsh habitually address issues of concern to them and to their audiences, issues at times as large as the status of poets in the world or the recent political problems in the village, at times as innocuous as the need for another round of tea or a few cigarettes for the guests. In their odes, and even more so in their prose asides to listeners, the poets deploy the ambiguity of the duplicated voice to comment upon and manipulate their own performance events.

The transition from the realm of ordinary talk to that of epic discourse is accomplished in performance through a gradated process involving not only the gradual accrual of formal markings (rhyme, musical accompaniment, measured rhythm, regular verse length, and song) but the narrative necessity of intense emotional motivation on the part of the epic character. Moreover, each movement into the world of the epic echoes the frames of the sahra performance event as a whole—instrumental introduction, madīḥ, mawwāl, spoken rhymed-prose preamble, blessings upon the Prophet, and finally, full arrival into the sīra; the performance replicates itself over and over again in miniature. As a "way of speaking," the performances of heroes and of poets are constantly equated through the use of parallel frames and markers in an ultimately self-referential system.

The epic singers of al-Bakātūsh perform in a number of different contexts, each of which entails a different relationship between the performer, the patron of the event, other participants, and the content of the performance. Economic exigencies affect style, tone, and manner of performance; the setting is also a key to what degree of flexibility the poet displays toward the criticisms and comments of other participants. Villagers display overt antagonism to performances that they label "begging" or "vagrancy"; these are, however, precisely the performances that are fully under the control of the poet, performances where no patron is present and which may be initiated by the poet himself. The issue of control over the performances, and by extension over the tradition as a whole, appears to underlie villagers' attitudes in this domain. Within the seemingly paradoxical arrangement of having a marginal social group responsible for the performance of a tradition deemed of historical relevance and value to the whole community, the issue of when and for whom the poets are to speak is a contested one.

The epic sahra, a single context among many, is a social event that involves many different types of performance by both poet and other participants. Some forms of performance are conceptualized as such and formally labeled as genres; others are perceived by participants as informal activities unworthy of notice or of being recorded; all, however, act as conduits for social interaction within the event. Different forms of verbal art engage or disengage the participants in different ways, genres with varying degrees of "openness" or "closedness." The sīra is presented as an independent story world, but one which audience members expect the poet to modulate in performance so as to comment upon the present; the ḥitat baladī on the other hand is created out of the very "stuff" of the present, using only the frame and some motifs of more independent material.

Quite often, threads of thought or sequences of associations develop out of the epic singing and the accompanying (often argumentative) evaluations of the performance: a wolf in the tale provokes the tale of a wolf, and from there we enter a discussion of wolves or other wild animals, then on to a debate about the personality of the epic character Diyāb 'Wolves'; later the poet picks up on our comments and returns them to us in narrative allusions within the epic.

Transformations, additions, and commentaries such as we examined in the last two chapters operate continually within *Sīrat Banī Hilāl* performances. Dramatic catalytic moments of interaction, however, occur less frequently—a few times an evening at most. These moments, though, are singled out by poets and audience members as particularly memorable, and they are retold and recalled far longer than any other aspect of the performance. I observed many times that once a performance had ended, listeners would discuss and comment upon many aspects of what they had just heard: the story, the characters, the poet's voice, his playing, his jokes, and so forth. Within a few hours, however, and certainly within a day or two, such commentaries had faded and participants no longer retained the aesthetic criticisms they had offered earlier. Instead, they remembered and discussed the social interaction within the performance, that is, the interplay that had taken place between the poet and the audience, or among members of the audience, especially those sparked by, or reflected in, the performed "text."[2] If they could recite any of the poetry they had heard that night, it was most often the improvised asides and jokes, not passages from the epic! A single quatrain of improvised poetry sung in the village by Sayyid Ḥawwās nearly twenty years earlier was still in circulation in café conversations during my stay; only a fraction of those who quoted the lines could remember even which episode the poet had been singing on that occasion. Any single telling of a portion of the epic melted into previous tellings; the social events of a performance stood out as the individualizing, and thus the discussable, factors.

In al-Bakātūsh one attends a performance of epic first of all to participate in and share a social experience and only secondarily to attend to the "text." In essence, the social action within the event is, in this indigenous "reading," the *text*; the epic performance is but one of many possible contexts or backgrounds for the enactment and interaction of characters and personalities from daily life in the village. The sahra is a

2. This example of aesthetic criticism fading after a brief period of time while socially based recollections remain intact should cause us to reexamine Richard Bauman's claims, using historical reconstruction of performances that had taken place *three decades* earlier, that at the La Have Island general store, aesthetic criticism of storytelling did not exist, but only a general enjoyment of the social atmosphere. Bauman, "The La Have Island General Store: Sociability and Verbal Art in a Nova Scotia Community" (1972).

stage for social interaction; though epic singing may form the focus of an evening's activities, the accompanying discussions, evaluations, arguments, and storytelling constitute, in a very real sense, the heart of the event. Here is a reading, then, in which the general terms of my research were reversed: the audience's text was my context, their context my text. In lengthy discussions, their "oral literary criticism" constantly slipped away from my own projected focus on the epic poem, to a viewpoint from which the location of the epic as the absolute center of the social "context" could no longer be maintained. As a researcher interested in the processes of performance, I could well locate my "text" within the boundaries of the epic poem, and for historical and literary purposes might continue to do so; were I, however, concerned also to understand how that "text" signifies, how it is received by its patrons and audiences as meaningful, I should also have to reverse my analysis and explore the performance of epic poetry as a "context," allowing for social meanings not "present" within the epic. The act of locating and defining "text," choosing a focus, thus becomes the crucial analytic act, yet the more we press the boundaries, the more fluid they appear to become.

In seeking reactions to and interpretations of the epic, I found again and again that I was listening to evaluations not of an individual performance or event, but of larger social patterns and of the epic as a symbolic catalyst. To a great extent, evaluations of the epic were only extensions of the speaker's position vis-à-vis the social forces he or she saw the epic as representing. Only an outsider could conceive of asking for a reaction to a performance of *Sīrat Banī Hilāl* without understanding that the response would in fact index a set of attitudes toward social values relating to folk Islamic practice, institutional Islam, and the current revisionist movements as well as to age groups, literacy, education levels, and a host of other conflicted social issues. To understand the accrual of significance of a specific episode, or of the larger tradition, to participants, would be to understand a lengthy and complex process of lamination, layer upon layer of tales retold.

Sīrat Banī Hilāl is a vast narrative tradition. It is found in many different regions of the Arab world in oral tradition and is known in its written forms even in those areas where an oral tradition does not exist or has died out. At any one site, the story of the Banī Hilāl is likely to exist simultaneously in many different forms. In the region of al-Bakātūsh itself, as I have pointed out, there are men and women who tell stories of Abū Zayd, Diyāb, and al-Zanātī Khalīfa as folktales; others in the vicinity can narrate in prose with some verse passages (recited, not sung); others read cheap "yellow-book" versions, and a handful even recite publicly from these chapbook editions; and finally, of course, there are the hereditary, professional epic-singers whom we have examined in some detail.

The epic has also become a potent symbol in modern Arabic (written) literature, yet it is deployed as a symbol for many different ideas. In Tayeb Salih's *The Light of the House*, Abū Zayd is cited as a traditional representative of manhood and virility; in Nizār al-Qabbānī's *Bread, Hashish and Moon*, he lingers in the reader's mind as the closing image of the poem, a symbol of anachronistic heroism and outdated codes of honor and chivalry; in Naguib Mahfouz's *Midaq Alley*, the rabāb poet and his epic tales are a sign of an older order displaced by modernity as he is pushed out of the café and replaced by a radio in one of the opening scenes of the novel. In Mahfouz's later work, *Children of Gebelawi*, an allegorical novel based upon the lives of the Prophets Adam, Moses, Jesus, and Muammad, the author uses the rabāb-poet as the thread of continuity and tradition who reappears in each generation.

In Sahar Khalifeh's poignant but angry novel *Wild Thorns*, about life in the Occupied West Bank of Palestine, the wounded Abu Sabir begs someone to tell him an Abū Zayd story to lift his spirits as he faces the possibility of bleeding to death, but no one present can remember one; sitting at home after having lost his fingers and his livelihood, he again asks for an Abū Zayd story, but his friends cannot remember any. Finally, when Usama, recently returned from several years abroad, refuses to listen to the West Bankers' explanations of their precarious coexistence with the Israeli state, Abu Sabir concludes that Usama cannot bear to hear the truth, and bitterly adds that Usama only wants to hear nice Abū Zayd stories.

In Gamal al-Ghitani's brooding and foreboding novel about the destructive effects of absolute power, *Al-Zeini Barakat*, the rabāb-poets are portrayed as an extension of the Internal Security's propaganda machine; the leader of the poets' guild secretly reports to the head spy for orders about which stories to sing and how to portray the heroes—the voice of authoritarianism couched as tradition.

Our path has led from a description of the village of al-Bakātūsh and of the community of poets within al-Bakātūsh to an exploration of how those social realities occasion and help constitute the epic performance tradition. The very content of the epic reflects generations of negotiations of social status, patronage, the role of poet in the world, and images of manhood, womanhood, and honor as expressed in the portrayal of heroes and heroines, villains and saints. Finally, the examining the interactive activity of performance has led us back outward to the listeners, and to the overarching social stances and views with which they approach, evaluate, patronize, and participate in the *Sīrat Banī Hilāl* tradition.

APPENDIX

Texts in Transliteration

Chapter 2. Poets Inside and Outside the Epic

Text 2.1
Shaykh Ṭāhā Abū Zayd, tape 87–115/6 (6/13/87)

laffēt bilād is-sind-I wi-l-hind-I wi-l-yaman
   ruḥt^{an} bilād^{an} tirkab il-afyāl

mā laqēt-I afras mi-z-zanātī bi-himmatuh
   wa-la jwad min zēd il-ᶜajāj-I rijāl

wa-la jwad min hazā wa-hazā illā nabīyana
   il-hāshimī li-l-muᶜgūzīn-I msāl

Text 2.2
Shaykh Biyalī Abū Fahmī, tape 87–012/12 (2/14/87)

fa-qāl luh «yā shāᶜir jamīl»
qʾāl luh «naᶜam yā bū ᶜalī»
qāl luh «durt ᶜalā nās maᶜdūda, wa-akābir ᶜarab mansūba—
   ḥaddish ᶜaṭāk il-ᶜaṭā wi-jabarak qaddī anā wi-ᶜarabī?»

ish-shāᶜir adūb. ish-shāᶜir adūb, mā kull-I shāᶜir yimsik ir-rabāba yibqʾā adūb. lēh, aṣluh yuqᶜud maᶜa nās ṭayyibīn. liʾinn-I ish-shāᶜir mā yiḥūzish-I qillit il-adab abadan. biyimshī ᶜalā r-rabāba. . . . anā mā bamgadsh-I fi sh-shuᶜara liʾnn-I anā shāᶜir! da aṣl ir-riwāyāt bitqūl kida! ish-shāᶜir adūb.

wi-lawlā adūb, mā kānsh-I yimsik ir-rabāba wi-yuqʿud wusṭ nās ṭayyibīn. iz-zayy yibqʾā shāʿir il-mulūk wi-l-ʿarab wi-yibqʾā qalīl il-adab?! yibqʾā muʾaddab. wi-l-qaʿda barḍu yismaʿ ish-shāʿir, yibqʾā barḍu fī ghāyit il-iḥtirām. fa-innī. . . .

baṣṣ-I-luh ḥasan kida wi-qāl luh, «yā shāʿir jamīl»
qāl luh «naʿam»
qāl luh «inta durt ʿalā nās maʿdūda, wa-akābir ʿarab mansūba—
    ḥaddish ʿaṭāk ʿaṭā wi-jabarak qaddī anā wi-ʿarabī?»
baṣṣ-I-luh ish-shāʿir jamīl.
iḥna qulna ish-shāʿir adūb, yaʿnī muʾaddab.
qāl luh «yā bū ʿalī, inta ka-baḥr in-nīl, wi-l-ajāwīd illī iḥna
    binliff-I ʿalēhum il-ʿarab, ka-buḥūr in-nīl. fa-l-baḥr, fīh
    miyā wa-zalāl, fa-l-baḥr mā yitfaḍḍalsh ʿan baʿḍ.
yiqaṣṣarsh wi-yiskut ḥasan baqā . . . ish-shāʿir ʿaṭāh ijāba ḥilwa
    maʿa l-ʿaql ik-kwayyis.

Text 2.3
Shaykh Biyalī Abū Fahmī, tape 87–009/1 (2/13/87)

ʿandak yā ḥanḍal tamanīn ṣabiyya 1
    wi-kull-I ṣabiyya abhar min qʾamar shaʿbān
yā raʾsahā ras il-yamāma ṣughayyara 2
    wi-sh-shaʿr sābil ʿalā l-Qumṣān
wi-l-idirāʿ zayy is-suyūf il-mifaḍḍaḍa 3
    wi-fī yad-I ʿāyid nāzil il-mīdān
wi-l-khadd ṭabaqʾ il-ward gall al-lāzī ṣanaʿ 4
    ṣanaʿit muhaymin wāḥid^{an} dayyān
khaṭarum ʿalā il-baḥr wi-zaqzaq is-samak 5
    in shāfihum ish-shēkh ṭārit wilāytuh
    in shāfhum il-ʿālim nasā l-Qurʾān
in shāfhum il-qammāsh (ʿalēhi il-ʿawaḍ!) 6
    yiḥsib iṣ-ṣūf dabalān
qʾāʿidīn fī dīwān il-ʿizz yā malik ḥanḍal 7
    allāh yiʿīnak dīwān mushayyid dīwān mushayyid
    yā ḥaḍrit il-sul[ṭān] . . . ʿidād hāyil qʾaw[ī]
fīh qʾulal bannūr ḥilwa li-l-ʿaṭshān 8
    ḥanafiyyāt fiḍḍa, ḥanafiyyāt fiḍḍa
    tinazzil nahr-I zalāl
qʾāʿidīn fī dīwānak yallāh yiṣliḥ ḥālak 9
    ḥanḍal yā sulṭān
naẓar il-malik ḥanḍal l-abū zēd wi-qʾāl luh 10
    ahlan wi-sahlan yā shāʿir il-ʿurbān
līk ʿandinā fiḍḍa līk ʿandinā dahab 11
    līk ʿandinā khēl wayya gimāl
il-arḍ arḍak yā shāʿir il-ʿarab 12
    il-arḍ arḍak wi-l-bilād dī blādak
    wi-ḥna yā sīd wi-līk ʿabīd khuddām

Spoken:
qāl abū zēd mutshakkirīn yā malik ḥanḍal 13
tiddīnī faḍḍa li-mīn aw dahab li-mīn

Sung:
ʿaṭāyā min dōl ṣabiyya awṣāfhā rawḥiyya 14
tikhdim jaddak ish-shāʿir rāgil kibīr baṭlān
radda lahu ḥanḍal l-abū zēd wi-qʾāl luh 15
khud rayya bint abū zēd yā shāʿir il-ʿarab

Spoken aside:
[qʾulnā abū zēd itjawwiz butēma ukht-I diyāb, fōq ʿalya iz-ziḥlāniyya illī kānit min qadīm khallif minhā talāta ṣubyān wa-unsa: khallif ṣabra, wi-mikhēmar, wi-ʿakrama, wi-rayya]

Sung:
itfaḍḍal rayya bint abū zēd minnī qabālak 16
wi-tiʿīsh maʿāk yā ʾamīr maḍā l-azmān
khud rayya bint abū zēd minnī qabālak 17
wi-tiʿīsh maʿāk yā ʾamīr wallāh maḍā l-azmān
yā salām lammā tākhud rayya yā shāʿir il-ʿarab 18
yirūḥ ish-shēb wi-l-kibar tirjaʿ shubbān zayy zamān
abū zēd ʿaṭā r-rimūz li-rayya itqaddimit . . . 19
ḥanḍal rāḥ masak rayya min dirāʿēhā 20
wi-qʾāl khud dī līk yā shāʿir il-ʿarab
wi-tʿīsh maʿāk yā ʿamīr bi-kull-I ʾāmān 21
wi-tʿīsh maʿāk yā ʿamīr wallāh bi-kull-I ʾamān
rayya bint abū zēd jāt sabbit il-ḥēla 22
qʾālit luh ukhraṣ yā gabān
lā kunt-I walā kān yā ḥanḍal yā khawwān
dā nā bint abū zēd shēkh il-ʿarab 23
bint-I shēkh il-ʿarab abū zēd
tiddīnī li-shāʿir bi-r-rabāba yiliff ʿa l-ʿurbān?
dā ʾanā bint abū zēd shēkh il-ʿarab 24
abū l-buṭūla min zamān
yaʿlam bi-zālik abūyā abū zēd il-hilālī 25
la-yikhallī dammak ʿa l-arḍ ṭūfān

Chapter 4. The Interplay of Genres

Text 4.12. Example of Ḥitat Baladī
Shaykh ʿAbd al-Wahhāb Ghāzī, tape 87-044 (3/15/87)

mīn maqṣuduh l-janna yiṣallī ʿalā n-nabī 1
nabī ʿarabī luh ḥaram masbūt
wi-r-rizq min ʿand illāh bikhūt wi-bikhūt

wa-fīh man yaʿṭīh   2
aywa jūda maʿa karam
wa-fīh mīn yuʿṭīh buk̲h̲l-I lammā yimūt
wa-fīh mīn yuʿṭīh janāyin muzag̲h̲rafa   3
wi-fīhā manje wi-fīhā kummitre
fīhā ʿēnab fīhā balaḥ
fīhā rummān fawākih yā k̲h̲ūyā ʿaẓīma
ir-rizq min ʿind-I rabbunā bik̲h̲ūt wi-bik̲h̲ūt
wi-fīh mīn yuʿṭīhi s̲h̲agara sanṭ-I   4
wallāh yā ʿēnī aw dakar tūt
wa-fīhi mīn yuʿṭīhi quftān wi-jūk̲h̲a   5
wa-fīh mīn yuʿṭīh k̲h̲alaq zaʿbūṭ
wa-fīhi mīn yuʿṭīh walad   6
wi-zākī muʾaddab walad mitrabbī
tīgī sīrt il-walad yirḍa abūh fī j-jalsa
yā k̲h̲ūyā raqabtuh ṭawīla ay qāʿid mabsūṭ
ādī l-walad ṭāliʿ li-k̲h̲āluh   7
k̲h̲āl il-walad rāgil min uṣūl il-buyūt
wa-fīh mīn yuʿṭīh walad wi-k̲h̲āyib wi-hāyif   8
aywa yā ʿēnī qabīḥ s̲h̲armūṭ
yigīb li-abūh il-mas̲h̲ākil wi-l-jarāyir   9
wi-d-dakākīn wi-l-qahāwī wi-l-g̲h̲ēṭān
wi-l-ōtōbīsāt wi-l-qaṭr ayy wi-kull-I buyūt
ʿalas̲h̲ān abūhu rāgil masmūʿ wi-ṭayyib   10
yirūḥū yiruddū ʿalā abūh fī filūs wi-miʿādāt
yā k̲h̲ūyā walad ṭāliʿ hāyif li-k̲h̲āluh
aṣl-I k̲h̲āluh rājil halfūt
wa-fīh mīn yuʿṭīh jawwāza ḥasīna jamīla   11
ḥilwa qawī yā k̲h̲ūyā jamīla ḥasīna
aṣīla min uṣūl il-buyūt
wi-l-wajh-I abyaḍ w-il-k̲h̲add-I yilmaʿ   12
yis̲h̲bah il-yāQūt
ʿanduh ḍūyūf māyil luh   13
kull-I iṭ-ṭalabāt tījī li-ḍ-ḍuyūf wi-zawjihā qāʿid
min dūn mā yus̲h̲ʿur walā yaʿlim
wa-lā yiqūl yā bintī hātī walā w-iddī
iṭ-ṭalabāt tījī li-ḍ-ḍuyūf
wi-zawjihā qāʿid wayyā ḍ-ḍuyūf mabsūṭ
ḥadqiyāt wa-ruzziyāt   14
waḥda aṣīla jamīla ḥilwa qawī
min uṣūl il-buyūt zawjihā qāʿid maʿa ḍ-ḍuyūf mabsūṭ
yinādī ʿa ṭ-ṭalab—naʿam wi-ḥāḍir   15
naʿam wi-ḥāḍir naʿam wi-ḥāḍir
wi-s-sinn-I yiḍḥak min wajhā abyaḍ yis̲h̲bah il-yāQūt
zawjihā in ʿās̲h̲ miʿhā tamānīn sana tisaʿīn sana   16
kammil il-miya

(wi-l-aʿmār bi-yad illāh)
hāyiʿīsh wi-yimūt fī farḥ-I baqʾā mabsūṭ
wa-fīh mīn yuʿṭīh jawwāza yā khūyā 17
rabbunā lā yikassibhā wa-lā yikassib illī gābūhā
wi-llī khallifūhā wi-llī shārū bihā
jawwāza baqā il-yōm wi-balwa musayyaḥa
ʿawīla bakhīla ʿawīla bakhīla
min aʿwal buyūt lihā l-zōr tishbih il-qarmūṭ
allāhu akbar allāhu akbar 18
ammā ḍ-ḍēf yirūḥ yam-I dārhum
tiqūm yā khūyā saḥiba n-nabbūt
anā jāyy li-ʿamm-I fulān 19
tiqūl ʿand id-daktōr yā akh
biyimūt biyimūt biyimūt biyimūt
dā-nā sāyil ʿalēh wa-nā jāyy ʿalā s-salamōniyya 20
kidā mi sh-sharq aw min ʿalā l-miqāwila min baḥrī
min sikka il-maḥaṭṭa bitāʿnā il-qaṭr
dā sana ḥilwa qawī
wi-l-quṭn-I jāwib itnāshir qinṭār is-sana
dī fī t-taʾmīnāt wa-fī l-iṣlāḥ
wi-fī l-mullāk dā bi-tisʿa wi-nuṣṣ-I aw ʿashara kidā
wi-l-ittimān wi-z-zirāʿa ḥilwa wi-saddū l-jamaʿiyya
wa-baqēt mabsūṭ
yārēt yā būyy qabl-I mā tijī bi-khamsa daqāyiq 21
il-ʿarabiyya jāʾat khaduh hāyimūt hāyimūt
sāyil ʿalēh wa-nā jāyy 22
min yam il-fazāʿiya ʿa l-gharb-I kidā
kafr is-siraḥna ʿind abū ṣubḥ ʿamm il-ḥājj muḥammad
rāgil amīr ahl il-karam il-karam mabsūṭ
sāʾil ʿalēh ʿind mad muṣṭafā rāgil ṭayyib 23
wi-l-ḥājj kāmil ayḍan
ʿammī fūlān qālū dā s-sana ḥilwa qawī
il-mara tiqūl biyimūt biyimūt
yārēt yārēt yā khūyā biyimūt
mā hiya bint-I bukhalā!
ir-rāgil qāʿid fī l-mandara
zayy bitāʿit aḥmad bakhātī
illī iḥnā ḥādritnā jālisīn fīhā
l-lēla dī li-jamʿ saʿīd
in shāʾ allāh jamʿīn khēr
bi-ṣ-ṣalā ʿalā n-nabī muḥammad
nūr in-nabī ayy milā t-tabūt
illī yikhāf ʿalā sumʿituh yiṭlaʿ mi l-bāb il-qiblī 24
min ij-jiha ish-sharqiyya illī yam il-mashrūʿ da
wi-yitlaff-I wi-yiqābil iḍ-ḍiyūf
yā marḥaba alf-I malyōnī marḥaban yā marḥaba

itfaḍḍalum taᶜālū taᶜālū
itfaḍḍalum nafaḍ ik-kanab wi-s-safīnjī wi-mukhaddāt
wi-takkāyāt wi-layyināt
il-ḥikāya il-ḥamdu li-llāh
baqat ḥilwa fī kull id-dunyā
safīnjī yāmā takāyāt yāmā wi-mabānī ḥilwa
ākhir riḍā l-ḥamdu li-llāh
qāl il-ḥamdu li-llāh
baqā aghnā in-nās illī yiᶜīsh mabsūṭ
wi-yuqᶜud yiḥayyihum 25
wi-yirushsh ᶜalēhum shwayyit sagāyir
wi-shwayyit mashrūbiyāt wi-shwayyit ḥalāwiyāt
wi-baᶜdēn lammā yiḥtād il-manhūba il-halība
bint il-maṣāyib dī tiqūl ēh:
yā dā l-ᶜadā yā dā l-ᶜadā
ᶜāwiz ēh?! luqma li-ḍ-ḍuyūf dōl yakūlum
baqā lhum sāᶜitēn qāᶜidīn ᶜandinā
anā kunt-I hāᶜīd il-kashf in-nihārda
ammā lammā shuftuhum min il-bāb ish-sharqī
anā ruḥt-I bi-surᶜa barḍu biyiʾamin ᶜalā kalāmhā
kalām il-manhūba tiqūl ēh:
anā ᶜindī ᶜiyādit ik-kashf yaᶜnī biyiʾāmin ᶜalā
kalāmhā barḍu ᶜalashān yiᶜīsh mabsūṭ
iḥnā wilādhum yā khūyā āh minnuh 26
ᶜindī ᶜiyād kashf in-nihārda
lakin lammā shūft iḍ-ḍuyūf āhum
iṣ-ṣiḥḥa baqat ḥilwa il-ḥamdu li-llāh qawī
hāt linā l-ghadā timḍīᶜ baqʾā sāᶜitēn mā adrī talāta
akl bi-l-ᶜagal tirūḥ tijīb il-akl yā khūyā
wi-twaḍḍaᶜu qudāmuh wa-tiḍrab bi-ṣōt qawī ēh
yā ddī l-khabar abyaḍ yā tijīb lihum il-murr
barḍu ᶜaqarit ᶜalēhum, hāyaklū ēh?
yisībū l-akl baqat janāza wi-illī yiᶜūzū bi-llāh . . . aṣḥābum
aṣlihā bakhīla wi-bint-I bukhala min aᶜwal buyūt
yimashshū ḍ-ḍiyūf wi-r-rāgil yā ᶜēnī 27
ᶜalā ghēr khāṭiruh
baᶜdēn māhūsh mabsūṭ
yirjaᶜ yiqūl lihā 28
lēh kidā lēh, lēh kidā lēh
ḍayyaᶜtī sumᶜitī wi-sumᶜit judūdī
inn il-karīm lā yinḍām, il-karīm lā yinḍām
wa-n-nās dōl muᶜtādīn yigū ᶜindinā
ayyām abāhātnā wi-judūdnā
wi-l-bēt dā maftūḥ min zaman qʾawī
tiqūl luh: mish shughulak uskut

yaʿnī inta fātiḥ al-baḥrī
uqʿud uqʿud sākit
wi-khēr rabbunā yāmā
wi-ḍ-ḍēf qabl-I mā yaʾtī yaʾtī bi-rizquh qudāmuh
wi-tlamm-I wi-ndāra kidā
dā-nā ṭūl in-nihār adawwar ʿalā daqīq fī d-dakākīn
ruḥt-I li-abū sulēmān wi-li-ustāz jalāl
laqēt id-daqīq ʿandihum mashḥūṭ
ṭayyib wi-hinā shwayyit ʿīsh ahom 29
uskut! mā huwa anā illī bakhabbiz
anā illī babaṭṭiṭ wi-diraʿtī yitwagaʿnī
aqʿud mish . . . ūʿā ūʿā!
wi-kilma minhā
wi-kilma min zawjihā timsik khināqa
tisharmaṭ il-zaʿbūṭ
[yaʿnī tigīb ig-galabiyya mi-l-bidāya li-n-nihāya 30
innamā iz-zaʿbūṭ ʿalashān il-Qāfiyāt]
tiqaṭṭaʿ iz-zaʿbūṭ tisharmaṭ iz-zaʿbūṭ 31
yā wiliyya fāriqīnī rūḥī dār ahlik
wallāh mā fārqak li-akūn ʿandak lammā timūt
wa-mā kān in-nīl yigīnā fī misrā, 32
ammā kān in-nīl yijīnā fī misrā
wa-lā khēr fī nīl tijīnā fī tūt
yibqʾā iz-zarʿa ʿaddā ʿumruh baqā 33
baʿd khamsa wi-talātīn yōm baqā tijī il-mayya
kull il-quṭn-I māt wi-rāḥ li-ḥāluh
wi-lammā kān in-nīl yijīnā fī misrā
lā khēr fī nīl tijīnā fī tūt
wa-mā kān il-fatta wi-l-ʿīsh 34
bi-ziyāda ʿan il-kōsa
wa-lā khēr fī zād yijī mashḥūṭ
wi-llī mā yimūt ayy minēn-I yifūt 35
wi-r-rizq min ʿand-I rabbunā ayy bikhūt wi-bikhūt
wa-fīh mīn yuʿṭih jūda wa-karam 36
wa-fīh mīn yiʿīsh fī l-bukhl ayy wa-lammā yimūt
ayy wa-fīh mīn yuʿṭīh ʿumr-I kifāyituh 37
wa-fīh mīn yuʿṭīh sana wi-yimūt
wi-r-rizq min ʿand-I il-karīm rabbunā 38
ayy bikhūt wi-bikhūt
wi-ʾafḍal-I min dā l-Qōl 39
anā wa-intum jamīʿan yā sāmiʿīn il-Qōl
ṣallum ʿalā ḥaḍrit in-nabī
nabī ʿarabī wi-luh ḥaram masbūt

Chapter 5. The Sahra as Social Interaction

Text 5.1. Audience Participation (Birth of Abū Zayd)
Shaykh Ṭāhā Abū Zayd, tape 87–101 (6/1/87)

wa-kān ṣābiḥ jimʿa ṣallum ʿalā n-nabī, 1
[All: ʿalēh iṣ-ṣalāt wi-s-salām]
wa-li-l-maẓlūm rabbī sāmiʿ li-d-duʿāh.

qālit lihā: 2
«yallāh anā wi-ntī ʿa l-baḥr-I fī l-faḍā,
yallāh nirawwaq damminā fī faḍāh.

wa-tinẓurī l-māliḥ tilāqī l-ʿajāyib, 3
tilāqī l-ʿajāyib bi-arādt illāh.»

ṭalaʿum baqā l-itnēn wa-l-ʿabd-I saʿīde, 4
zawjit najjāḥ ayā maḥlāh.
[Voice: ay]

illā wa-ṭīr 5
[Voice: aywa!]
abyaḍ min il-buʿd-I jā lahum,
dā ṭīr abyaḍ ḥilw-I fī ruʾyāh.

inḥaṭṭ-I wa-lā shāl iṭ-ṭīr fī l-khale, 6
kull iṭ-ṭiyūr aywa līh tirʿāh.

qālit shamma «yā rabb yā fard-I yā ṣamad, 7
[Voice: allāh]
illāh^{in} taʿālā lā ilāh^{a} siwāh.

tirzuqnī bi-wād anā misl-I iṭ-ṭīr hāzī, 8
wi-yakūn ḥisin tikūn il-ʿarab ṭāyiʿāh.»

tammit baqā l-ṭulbe yā-jāwīd wi-ṭ-ṭīr irtafaʿ, 9
wi-ṭ-ṭīr shāl āh wi-zād fī ʿulāh.

illā wa-ṭīr asmar min il-buʿd-I jā lahum, 10
[Laughter—Voice: Abū Zayd!]
dā ṭīr asmar

[Voice: aywa!]
bi<u>sh</u>iḥ fī ruʾyāh.
[Voice: yā salām!]

yufrud gināḥuh ʿalā ṭ-ṭiyūr,   11
kull-I man ḍarabuh bi-gināḥuh lā yi<u>sh</u>imm-I
ʿa<u>sh</u>āh . . .
        [Side Two]
kull-I man ḍarabuh bi-gināḥuh lam yi<u>sh</u>imm-I
ʿa<u>sh</u>āh

qālit-I <u>Kh</u>aḍra: 12
        [Voice: aywa]
        «yā maḥlāk-I yādī iṭ-ṭīr wi-maḥlā
samārak,
        [Voice: allāh!]
zayy il-balaḥ ammā yiṭīb bi-riḍāh.

ayā rabb-I yā raḥmān-I yā fard-I yā ṣamad,   13
        [Voice: allāh yiftaḥ ʿalēk!]
        [Shaykh Ṭāhā: allāh yikrimak!]
ilāh^{in} taʿāla muḥtajab bi-samāh.
[Shaykh Ṭāhā: yidūm ʿizzak, yidūm ʿizzak ʿalēnā!]

tirzuqnī bi-wād anā misl-I iṭ-ṭīr hāza,   14
wi-kull-I min ḍarabuh bi-sēfuh lam ya<u>sh</u>imm-I
ʿa<u>sh</u>āh.»
        [Voice: yā salām! dā abū zēd!]

ṭalabum il-isnēn: 15
qālit saʿīda «yā rabb tirzuqnī misl-I asyādī
mā-<u>khafsh</u>-I mīn kān fī l-karīm arḍāh.»

dōl rawwaḥum yā ajāwīd ṣallum ʿalā n-nabī,   16
        [All: ʿalēh iṣ-ṣalāt wi-s-salām]
ayā ba<u>kh</u>t-I min ṭalab wa-l-karīm arḍāh.

Qāl il-malik sarḥān li-rizq-I il-baṭal,   17
«yā ibn-I ʿammī smaʿ kalāmī wi-l-muʿnā.

ṣāliḥ i<u>sh</u>-<u>sh</u>arīfa rizq ayā ṭayyib il-ʿarab,   18
ikrimhā ba-innihā min silālit rasūl illāh.

yā tikrimhā yā rizq yā tiwaddīhā li-ahlihā, 19
wi-l-ᶜarḍ-I zayy iz-zirᶜ wi-l-ᶜarḍ-I ghālī,
wi-l-ᶜarḍ-I ghālī wi-l-ᶜarab ᶜarfāh.»
[Voice: allāh!]

ṣāliḥhā yā ajāwīd wi-waddīhā li-ṣīwānuh, 20
wa-arād il-karīm alā bi-l-hudā yā maḥlā.

fī hāzī l-lēla ḥamalū s-salāsa, 21
yā bakht-I min ṭalab wi-l-karīm arḍāh.

wafit shuhūrhā shamma l-aṣīla; 22
waḍaᶜit ghulām yā ajāwīd Qalīl^{an} sifātuh,
walad samīḥ il-wajh-I yā maḥlā.

* ṣallum ᶜalā n-nabī *
[All: ᶜalēhi ṣ-ṣalāt wi-s-salām]
[Shaykh Ṭāhā: allāhum yiṣallī ᶜalēh]
[Voice: yā salām . . . ismaᶜ . . .]
[Shaykh Ṭāhā: allāh yikrimak! allāh yibārik fīkum!]

Text 5.3. Suppression of Materials for Female Listeners
Shaykh Biyalī Abū Fahmī, tape 87–029 (2/25/87)

. . . qālit luh: mā-ntish fātiḥ, yā Manṣūr? qāl: intī tighannī wa-nā ghannī ᶜubālik, in zidtī ᶜannī fī l-qōl, atjawwiz arbaᶜ niswān wi-tibqī intī awwil il-qāyma, wi-in zidt-I ᶜannik fī l-qōl tākhdī in-niswān wi-timashshī min hinā wi-iḥnā baṭṭalnā il-ḥubb-I wa-l-ḥamdu li-llāh. qālit luh ij-jāzya: ifrash wa-nā aghaṭṭī. qāl lihā: intī ghalaṭṭī—ish-sharīᶜa illī rabbunā miḥallilhā bi-inn-I in-nisāʾ furrāsh ir-rijāl, liʾin ir-rijāl mitfaḍḍalīn ᶜalā n-nisāʾ, wa-n-nisāʾ furrāsh ir-rijāl, yaᶜnī illī yifrish mīn bi-l-kalām? qālhā: intī tifrishī bi-l-kalām wa-nā aghaṭṭī ᶜalēkī bi-l-kalām. fa-j-jāzya tifrish tiqūl ēh? ᶜāshiq in-nabī yazīdnā mi-ṣ-ṣalātu ᶜalēh:

Sung:
anī amdaḥ muḥammad naṭaQit luh l-ḥigāra 1
naṭaQit luh l-ḥigāra

[Tunes rabāb]

anī amdaḥ muḥammad naṭaqit luh l-ḥigāra
yā rabbī nizūruh nistamtaᶜ bi-nūruh
nistamtaᶜ bi-nūruh wa-ninūl iz-ziyāra, wa-nnūl iz-ziyāra

qālit bint-I sarḥān-ī 2
qawāfiʾ wi-awzān-ī
taww ish-shiʿr bān-ī
wi-baqā lī fīh amāra

iftaḥ yā manṣūr 3
iftāḥ bāb is-sūr
nudkhulū bi-dastūr
wi-nibīʿū l-ʿiṭāra

iftaḥ mā takhafsh-ī 4
wa-law rīQa laksh-ī
il-ḥinna l-balakhshī
fī īdēn il-ʿadārā

iftaḥ yā ḥabībī 5
yā miskan wa-ṭībī
hākhudak min nasībī
yā bawwāb naḍār, yā bawwāb naḍār

radd-I il-bawwāb manṣūr ʿā g-gāzya kida; wi-qāl ēh?

anā bābī mā ftaḥūsh-ī 6
li-llī mā baʿrafūsh-ī
wa-ntum ʿarab ṭumūsh-ī
fatḥ il-bāb līkum ʿalā khasāra

yā bawwābī iftaḥ bābak il-miṣaffaḥ 7
yā bawwābī iftaḥ bābak il-miṣaffaḥ
wi-in dakhalu biyirbaḥ
wi-biyibīʿ il-ʿiṭāra

ah mā tikūnsh-ī khāyif 8
ah mā tikūnsh-ī khāyif
awarrīk il-waṣāyif
wi-nilʿab yā wiṣāla, nilʿab yā wiṣāla

il-bawwāb manṣūr qāl lihā ēh:

mashshī yā ṣabiyy 9
balāsh manāḥiyya
tigī li-l-bawwāb raziyya
wa-lā tiduqq fōq rāsuh ghāra

abadan mi<u>sh</u> fātḥ il-bāb   10
abadan mi<u>sh</u> fātḥ il-bāb
wallāh bi-ḍarb-I ḥirāb
min ʿaskar sakāra

rūḥī yā ẓarīfa   11
rūḥī yā ẓarīfa
<u>kh</u>ūf ī min <u>kh</u>alīfa
bi-īduh ḥarba rahīfa
bitfūt min il-ḥigāra

iftaḥ yā manṣūr   12
iftaḥ bāb is-sūr
dastūrī bi-dastūr
yā wi<u>sh</u> il-<u>kh</u>usāra
ayā bawwāb manṣūr wi<u>sh</u>ak wi<u>sh</u> il-<u>kh</u>usāra

iftaḥ wa-nā awarrīk   13
awṣāf al-ʿadārā
(il-ʿadārā yaʿnī il-banāt)
iftaḥ wa-nā awarrīk
awṣāf al-ʿadārā

ʿindinā ʿālya il-ʿuqēliyya   14
wi-ʿālya iz-ziḥlāniyya
wi-ʿindinā is-sitt-I waṭfa iz-zu<u>gh</u>biyya
ʿindinā is-sitt-I sāra

saʿdiyya wi-r-rasmiyya   15
saʿdiyya wi-r-rasmiyya
wi-j-jāzya il-ʿarabiyya
il-jāzya il-ʿarabiyya
ṭamaʿān lihā l-idāra, ṭamaʿān lihā l-idāra

zaqq il-bāb wi-rāyiḥ   16
il-wujūh is-samāyiḥ
ṣaf ī il-misk fāyiḥ
min ʿālya wi-sāra

wi-l-bawwāb-I hām   17
<u>kh</u>ad il-muftāḥ wi-qām
<u>kh</u>ad il-muftāḥ wi-qām
fataḥ il-bāb jihāra

il-bawwāb firish giyāsuh 18
wi-qalaʿ madāsuh
wi-qalaʿ madāsuh
wi-hijim ʿā l-ʿadāra

il-bawwāb firish giyāsuh 19
wi-qalaʿ madāsuh
wi-salāmtuh wi-ḥall-I libāsuh
wi-nawwil ʿā l-khusāra, wi-nawwil ʿā l-khusāra

jā luh abū zēd il-asmar 20
rākib zayy-I ʿantar
fī-īduh is-sēf il-abtar
ḍarab manṣūr il-aʿgar
khallā rāsuh tidaʿwar
zayy-I zirr-I khiyāra

wi-ādī fatḥ-I bāb-I tūnis 21
li-yaḥiya wi-marʿī wi-yūnis
wi-ādī fatḥ-I bāb-I tūnis li-yaḥiya wi-yūnis
wi-yūnis qāʿid fī s-sign wi-sāmiʿ il-ʿibāra

waqaʿ il-bawwāb manṣūr 22
difinūh janb-I is-sūr
qilibū fōq dimāghuh
it-tamanīn shukāra

ṣallum ʿalā n-nabī

Works Cited

ʿAbd al-Jawwād, Muḥammad. *Fī kuttāb al-qarya* (In the village school). Cairo: Maṭbaʿat al-maʿārif, 1939.

al-Abnoudy, Abderrahman [ʿAbd al-Raḥmān al-Abnūdī]. *La geste hilalienne.* Trans. Tahar Guiga [al-Ṭāhir Qīqa]. Cairo: General Egyptian Book Organisation, 1978.

——. *al-Sīra al-hilāliyya.* 3 vols. Cairo: Maṭābiʿ al-akhbār, 1988. Vol. 1, *Khaḍra al-sharīfa*; vol. 2, *Abū zayd fī arḍ al-ʿallāmāt*; vol. 3, *Maqtal al-sulṭān sarḥān.*

Abu-Lughod, Lila. *Veiled Sentiments: Honor and Poetry in a Bedouin Society.* Berkeley: University of California Press, 1986.

Ahlwardt, Wilhelm. "Verzeichniss der arabischen Handscriften." In *Die Handscriftenverzeichnisse der königlichen Bibliotek zu Berlin.* Vol. 8, book 19. Berlin: A. Asher, 1896.

Allen, Roger. *The Arabic Novel.* Syracuse, N.Y.: Syracuse University Press, 1982.

ʿAmmar, ʿAbbās M. *The People of the Sharqiyah: Their Racial History, Serology, Physical Characteristics, Demography and Conditions of Life.* 2 vols. Cairo: Institut Français d'Archéologie Orientale, 1944.

Anastas (Father). "The Nawar or Gypsies of the East." *Journal of the Gypsy Lore Society* (n.s.), pt. 1, vol. 7, no. 4 (1913–14): 298–319; p. 2, vol. 8, no. 2 (1914–15): 140–53; part 3, vol. 8, no. 4 (1914–15): 266–80.

Asian Music 17, 1 (1985). Special issue on music and musicians in the Islamic world.

Ayoub, Abderrahman [ʿAbd al-Raḥmān Ayyūb]. "Approches de la poèsie bedouine hilalienne chez Ibn Khaldoune." In *Actes du Colloque international sur Ibn Khaldoun,* 21–26 June 1978, 321–45. Algiers: Société Nationale d'Edition et Diffusion, 1982.

——. "A propos des manuscrits de la geste des Banū Hilāl conservés à Berlin." In *Association international d'étude des civilisations méditerranéenwes: Actes du IIième congrès,* ed. M. Galley, 347–63. Algiers: Societé Nationale d'Edition et Diffusion, 1978.

——. "The Hilali Epic: Material and Memory." *Revue d'histoire maghrebine* 35–36 (1984): 189–217.

——. "Poème hilalien de Dyab le Libyen." In *Majallat kulliyat al-tarbiyya.* Tripoli, 1979.

——. "Quelques aspects évolutifs dans les versions hilaliennes de Jordanie." In *Sīrat Banī Hilāl: Aʿmāl al-nadwa al-ʿālamiyya al-ūlā ḥawla al-sīra al-hilāliyya*, Actes de la 1ère table ronde internationale sur la geste des Béni Hilāl, 26–29 June 1980, al-Ḥammāmāt, Tunisia. Ed. A. Ayoub, 59–83. Tunis: al-Dār al-tūnisiyya li-l-nashr and al-Maʿhad al-qawmī li-l-athār wa-l-funūn, 1990.

Ayoub, Abderrrahman, and M. Galley. *Images de Djāzya: À propos d'une peinture sous verre de Tunisie*. Paris: Edition du Centre National de Recherche Scientifique, 1977.

Baker, Cathryn Anita. "The Hilali Saga in the Tunisian South." Diss., Indiana University, 1978.

Basset, René. "Un épisode d'une chanson de geste arabe sur la seconde conquête de l'Afrique septentrionale par les Musulmans." *Bulletin de correspondance africaine* 4 (1885): 136–48.

Bauman, Richard. "The La Have Island General Store: Sociability and Verbal Art in a Nova Scotia Community." *Journal of American Folklore* 85 (1972): 330–43.

——. *Story, Performance, and Event: Contextual Studies of Oral Narrative*. Cambridge: Cambridge University Press, 1986.

Beissinger, Margaret. "Balkan Traditional Singers and Non-Mainstream Figures." Paper read at the American Folklore Society Meetings, 26–30 October, 1988, Boston.

Bel, Alfred. "La Djāza, chanson arabe précédée d'observations sur quelques légendes arabes et sur la geste des Benī Hilāl." *Journal asiatique* 9, 19 (1902): 289–347; 9, 20 (1902): 169–236; 10, 1 (1903): 311–66.

Bennani, Ben, ed. and trans. *Bread, Hashish and Moon: Four Modern Arab Poets*. Greensboro, N.C.: Unicorn Press, 1982.

Ben Rahhal, M. "A travers les Beni Snassen." *Bulletin de la Société de géographie d'Oran* 9 (1889): 5–50.

Berque, Jacques. "De nouveau sur les Benī Hilāl?" *Studia Islamica* 36 (1972): 99–111.

——. *Histoire sociale d'un village égyptien au XXième siècle*. Paris: Mouton, 1957.

——. "Sur la structure sociale de quelques villages égyptiens." *Annales: Économies, sociétés, civilization* 10 (Apr.–June 1955): 199–215.

Bird, Charles. "Heroic Songs of the Mande Hunters." In *African Folklore*, ed. Richard Dorson, 275–93. Bloomington: Indiana University Press, 1972.

Bloch, Jules. "Quelques formes verbales du Nuri." *Journal of the Gypsy Lore Society* (3d ser.) 11 (1932): 30–32.

Blunt, Lady Anne, trans., and put into verse by Wilfred Scawen Blunt. *The Romance of the Stealing of the Mare*. London: Reeves and Turner, 1892. Reprinted in Wilfred Scawen Blunt, *Poetical Works*, 2: 129–217. London: Macmillan, 1914.

Bohas, Georges, and Jean-Patrick Guillaume, trans. *Roman de Baibars*. Vols. 1–5. Paris: Sindbad, 1985– .

Boullata, Issa J., trans. *Modern Arab Poets, 1950–1975*. Washington, D.C.: Three Continents Press, 1976.

Breteau, Claude, Micheline Galley, and Arlette Roth. "Témoinages de la 'longue marche' hilalienne." In *Association internationale d'étude des civilisations méditerranéennes: Actes du IIième congrès*, ed. M. Galley, 329–46. Algiers: Societé Nationale d'Edition et Diffusion, 1978.

Breteau, Claude, and M. Galley. "Réflexions sur deux versions algériennes de Dyāb le Hilalien." In *Actes du 1er congrès d'études des cultures méditerranéennes d'influence arabo-berbère*, 3–6 April 1972, ed. M. Galley, 358–64. Algiers: S.N.E.D., 1973.

Burton, Richard F. *A Plain and Literal Translation of the "Arabian Nights' Entertainments," now entitled "The Book of the Thousand Nights and a Night"; with explanatory notes . . . and a Terminal Essay*. 10 vols. Benares [Stokes Newington], 1885.

Cachia, Pierre. "The Egyptian Mawwāl." *Journal of Arabic Literature* 8 (1977): 77–103.

——. "Mawwāl." *Encyclopedia of Islam*. 2d ed. Leiden, 1954; London, 1956– .

——. *Popular Narrative Ballads of Egypt*. Oxford: Clarendon Press, 1989.

Canard, Marius. "Delhemma, épopée arabe des guerres arabo-byzantines." *Byzantion* 10 (1935): 283–300.

——. "Dhū ʾl-Himma or Dhāt al-Himma." *Encyclopedia of Islam*. 2d ed. Leiden, 1954; London, 1956– .

——. "Les principaux personnages du roman de chevalrie arabe *Dhāt al-Himma wa-l-Battāl*." *Arabica* 8, 2 (1961): 158–73.

Canova, Giovanni. "Aspects de la tradition épique vivante en Egypte et Syrie." In *Sīrat Banī Hilāl: Aʿmāl al-nadwa al-ʿālamiyya al-ūlā ḥawla al-sīra al-hilāliyya*, Actes de la 1ère Table ronde internationale sur la geste des Béni Hilāl, 26–29 June 1980, al-Ḥammāmāt, Tunisia. Ed. A. Ayoub, 29–39. Tunis: al-Dār al-tūnisiyya li-l-nashr and al-Maʿhad al-qawmī li-l-athār wa-l-funūn, 1990.

——. *Egitto I: Epica*. I Suoni, Musica de Tradizione Orale, 5. Milan, 1980.

——. "Gli studi sull-epica popolare araba." *Oriente moderno* 57, 5–6 (1977): 211–26.

——. "Il poeta epico nella traditizione araba: Nota e testimonianze." *Quaderni di studi arabi* 1 (1983): 87–104.

——. "Muhammad, l'ebreo e la gazella, canto di un *maddāh* Egiziano." *Annali dell'Istituto Orientale di Napoli* 41 (1981): 195–211.

——. "Notizie sui Nawar e sugli altri gruppi Zingari presenti in Egitto." *La bisaccia dello sheikh* (Venice) (1981): 71–85. Quarterly journal of the Iranist, University of Venice Seminar.

——. "Qiṣṣat al-zīr sālim wa-aṣl al-bahlawān." In *The Arab Folk Epic*, Proceedings of the 2nd International Conference on the Arab Folk Epic, Association of Mediterranean Studies and Cairo University, 2–7 January 1985. Cairo: G.E.B.O., forthcoming.

——. "Testimonianze hilaliane nello yemen orientale." *Studi yemeniti* 1 (1985): 161–96; abstract in Arabic, 11–13.

Carbou, H. *Méthode practique pour l'étude de l'arabe parlé au Ouadai et à l'est du Tchad*. Paris: Geuthner, 1913.

Cerny, J. *Coptic Etymological Dictionary*. Cambridge: Cambridge University Press, 1976.

Charnock, R. S. "On the Gypsy Dialect called Sim." *Anthropologia* 1 (1875).

Chauvin, Victor. "Abu Zeid." *Encyclopedia of Islam*. 1st ed. Leiden, 1913–38.

Compton, Linda Fish. *Andalusian Lyrical Poetry and Old Spanish Love Songs*. New York: New York University Press, 1976.

Conder, Claude Reignier. *Heth and Moab: Explorations in Syria in 1881 and 1882*. London, 1892.

Connelly, Bridget. *Arab Folk Epic and Identity*. Berkeley: University of California Press, 1986.

Coy, Michael W. *Apprenticeship From Theory to Method and Back Again*. Albany: State University of New York Press, 1989.

Critchfield, Richard. *Shahhat, an Egyptian*. Syracuse, N.Y.: Syracuse University Press, 1978.
Cuthberson, Gilbert M. *Political Myth and Epic*. East Lansing: Michigan State Unviersity Press, 1975.
Desparmet, Joseph. "Les chansons de geste de 1830 à 1914 dans la Mitidja." *Revue africaine* 83 (1939): 192–226.
Devic, L. Marcel. *Les aventures d'Antar, fils de Cheddad*. Paris: Librairie de la Société Asiatique de l'École des Langues Orientales Vivantes, 1878.
Doughty, Charles M. *Travels in Arabia Deserta*. New York: Dover, 1979; rpt. of Jonathan Cape ed., 1936; first published 1888.
Dover, Cedric. "The Black Knight." *Phylon: The Atlantic University Review of Race and Culture* 15 (1954): 41–57, 177–89.
Duncan, Jr., Starkey. "On the Structure of Speaker-auditor Interaction during Speaking Turns." *Language in Society* 3 (1974): 161–80.
Duncan, Jr., Starkey, and D. W. Fiske. *Face-to-Face Interaction: Research, Methods, and Theory*. Hillsdale, N.J.: Erlbaum, 1977.
Erman, Adolph, and Hermann Grapow. *Wörterbuch der Aegyptischen Sprache*. Leipzig: Hinrichs, 1926–63.
Fanjul, Serafin. *El mawwāl egipcio: Expresión literaria popular*. Madrid: IHAC, 1976.
——. "The Erotic Mawwāl in Egypt." *Journal of Arabic Literature*, 8 (1977): 104–22.
——. "Le mawwal blanc." *Mélanges de l'Insitut dominicain d'études orientales du Caire* 13 (1977): 337–48.
al-Faruqi, Lois. "The Shari'ah on Music and Musicians." In *Islamic Thought and Culture*, 27–52. Herndon, Va.: International Institute of Islamic Thought, 1982.
——. "The Status of Music in Muslim Nations: Evidence from the Arab World." *Journal of the Society for Asian Music* 12, 1 (1981): 56–84.
Féraud, Laurent C. *Kitab el Adouani: Ou le Sahara de Constantine et de Tunis*. Paris: L. Arnolet, 1868.
Ferguson, Charles A. "Diglossia." *Word* 15 (1959): 325–40.
——. "Root-Echo Responses in Syrian Arabic Politeness Formulas." In *Linguistic Studies in Memory of Richard Slade Harrell*, ed. D. G. Stuart, 37–45. Washington, D.C.: Georgetown University Press, 1967.
——. "The Structure and Use of Politeness Formulas." *Language in Society* 5 (1976): 137–51.
Galland, Antoine. *Les mille et une nuits, contes arabes*. 12 books in 6 vols. Translated into French; new revised edition. Paris, 1726; 1st ed. 1704–17.
Galley, Micheline. "Femmes de la geste hilalienne." *Littérature orale arabo-berbère* 15 (1984): 31–44.
——. "Manuscrits et documents relatifs à la geste hilalienne dans les bibliothèques anglaises." *Littérature orale arabo-berbère* 12 (1981): 183–92.
——. "Manuscrits et documents sonores relatifs à la geste hilalienne." *Littérature orale arabo-berbère* 13 (1982): 53–59.
Galley, Micheline, and Abderrahman Ayoub. *Histoire des Beni Hilal et de ce qui leur advint dans leur marche vers l'ouest*. Classiques Africains, 22. Paris: Armand Colin, 1983.
Gandour, Selim. "Les ghagars." *Revue du monde égyptien* 2, 12 (Nov.–Dec. 1922): 822–31.

Gerhardt, Mia. *The Art of Storytelling: A Literary Study of the Thousand and One Nights*. Leiden: E. J. Brill, 1963.
Ghazoul, Ferial. *The Arabian Nights: A Structural Analysis*. Cairo: Cairo Institution for the Study and Presentation of Arab Cultural Values, 1980.
al-Ghitani, Gamal [Jamāl al-Ghiṭānī]. *al-Zaynī Barakāt*. 2d ed. Cairo: Maktabat Madbūlī, 1975.
——. *Al-Zayni Barakat*. Trans. Farouk Abdel Wahab. London: Viking, 1988.
Giffen, Anita. *Theory of Profane Love among the Arabs: The Development of the Genre*. New York: New York University Press, 1971.
Goodwin, Charles. "Restarts, Pauses, and the Achievement of a State of Mutual Gaze at Turn-Beginning." *Sociological Inquiry* 50, 3–4 (1980): 277–302.
Guiga, Abderrahman [ʿAbd al-Raḥmān Qīqa]. *La geste hilalienne*. Trans. by Tahar Guiga. Tunis: Maison Tunisienne de l'Edition, 1968.
——. *Min aqaṣīṣ banī hilāl*. Tunis: Dār al-tūnisiyya li-l-nashr, 1968.
Guin, M. L. *Rouba, légende arabe*. Oran, 1884.
Haddawy, Husain, trans. *The Arabian Nights*. New York: W. W. Norton, 1990.
Hall, Edward T. *Beyond Culture*. New York: Doubleday, 1976; rpt. 1989.
Hamilton, Terrick. *Antar: A Bedoueen Romance*. London: John Murray, 1819.
Ḥannā, Nabīl Ṣubḥī. *al-Binā' al-ijtimāʿī wa-l-thaqāfa fī mujtamaʿ al-ghajar*. Cairo: Dār al-maʿārif, 1983.
——. *Ghagar of Sett Guiranha: A Study of a Gypsy Community in Egypt*. Cairo Papers in Social Science. Vol. 5, monograph 1. Cairo: American University in Cairo Press, 1982.
Hanna, Sami A. "The Mawwāl in Egyptian Folklore." *Journal of American Folklore* 80 (1967): 182–90.
Hartmann, Martin. "Die Beni-Hilal-Geschichten." *Zeitschrift für afrikanische und ozeanische Studien* (Berlin) 3 (1898): 289–315.
——. "The Romance of Antar." *Encyclopedia of Islam*. 1st ed. Leiden, 1913–38.
Hatto, Arthuur T., ed. *Traditions of Heroic and Epic Poetry*. 2 vols. London: Modern Humanities Research Association, 1980.
Ḥawwās, ʿAbd al-Ḥamīd. "Madāris riwāyat al-sīra al-hilāliyya fī miṣr" (Schools of performance of *Sīrat Banī Hilāl* in Egypt). In *Sīrat Banī Hilāl: Aʿmāl al-nadwa al-ʿālamiyya al-ūlā ḥawla al-sīra al-hilāliyya*, Actes de la 1ère Table ronde internationale sur la geste des Béni Hilāl, 26–29 June 1980, al-Ḥammāmāt, Tunisia. Ed. A. Ayoub, 47–70. Tunis: al-Dār al-tūnisiyya li-l-nashr and al-Maʿhad al-qawmī li-l-athār wa-l-funūn, 1990.
Heath, Peter. "A Critical Review of Modern Scholarship on Sīrat ʿAntar ibn Shaddād and the Popular Sīra." *Journal of Arabic Literature* 15 (1984): 19–44.
——. Review of *Arab Folk Epic and Identity*, by Bridget Connelly. *Journal of the American Oriental Society* 108, 2 (1988): 315–17.
——. "The Thirsty Sword: Structure and Composition in Sīrat ʿAntar ibn Shaddād." Diss., Harvard University, 1981.
Heller, B. *Die Bedeutung des arabischen ʾAntar-romans für die vergleichende Litteraturkunde*. Leipzig: Hermann Eixhblatt, 1931.
——. "The Romance of Antar." *Encyclopedia of Islam*. 2d ed. Leiden, 1954; London, 1956– .
al-Ḥijājī, Aḥmad Shams al-Dīn. "al-Zīr sālim bayn al-sīra wa-l-masraḥ." *al-Funūn al-shaʿabiyya* 7 (Oct. 1968): 58–64.

Hinds, Martin, and El-Said Badawi. *A Dictionary of Egyptian Arabic*. Beirut: Librairie du Liban, 1986.

Hood, Mantle. *The Ethnomusicologist*. New York: McGraw Hill, 1971.

Hurreiz, Sayyid H. "Afro-Arab relations in the Sudanese Folk-tale." In *American Folklore*, ed. R. M. Dorson, 157–63. Bloomington: Indiana University Press, 1979.

——. *Ja'aliyyin Folktales: An Interplay of African, Arabian and Islamic Elements*. Indiana University Publications, African Series, 8. Bloomington: Indiana University Press, 1977.

Ḥusayn, Ṭāhā. *Mustaqbal al-thaqāfa fī miṣr* (The future of culture in Egypt). Cairo, 1938.

Hussein, Taha. *al-Ayyām*. Beirut: Dār al-kitāb al-lubnānī, 1973.

——. *The Future of Culture in Egypt*. Trans. Sidney Glazer. Washington: American Council of Learned Societies, 1954.

Hussein, Taha [Ṭāhā Ḥusayn]. *An Egyptian Childhood*. Trans. E. H. Paxton. Washington, D.C.: Three Continents Press, 1982.

Hymes, Dell. "Breakthrough into Performance." In *Folklore: Performance and Communication*, ed. Dan Ben-Amos and Kenneth S. Goldstein, 11–74. The Hague: Mouton, 1975. Reprinted in Hymes, *"In Vain I Tried to Tell You": Essays in Native American Ethnopoetics*, 79–141. Philadelphia: University of Pennsylvania Press, 1981.

——. "Breakthrough into Performance Revisited," in Hymes, *"In Vain I Tried to Tell You": Essays in Native American Ethnopoetics*, 200–259. Philadelphia: University of Pennsylvania Press, 1981.

——. "The Contribution of Folklore to Sociolinguistic Research." In Américo Paredes and Richard Bauman, eds., "Toward New Perspectives in Folklore," *Journal of American Folklore* 84 (1971): 42–50.

——. "Folklore's Nature and the Sun's Myth." *Journal of American Folklore* 88 (1975): 346–69.

——. *"In Vain I Tried to Tell You": Essays in Native American Ethnopoetics*. Philadelphia: University of Pennsylvania Press, 1981.

——. "Narrative Form as 'Grammar' of Experience: Native Americans and a Glimpse of English." *Journal of Education* 164, 2 (Spring 1982): 121–42.

Hymes, Dell, and Courtney Cazden. "Narrative Thinking and Story-Telling Rights: A Folklorist's Clue to a Critique of Education." In D. Hymes, *Language in Education: Ethnolinguistic Essays*. Washington, D.C.: Center for Applied Linguistics, 1980.

Ibn ʿAbd Rabbihi. *al-ʿIqd al-farīd*. Cairo: Lajnat al-ta'līf wa-l-tarjamah wa- l-nashr, 1968.

——. *al-ʿIqd al-farīd*. Ed. Aḥmad Amīn. Cairo, 1962.

Ibn Hishām, ʿAbd al-Malik. *The Life of Muhammad: A Translation of Ishāq's "Sīrat Rasūl Allāh."* Trans. Alfred Guillaume. London: Oxford University Press, 1955.

Ibn Khaldūn. *The Muqaddimah*. 3 vols. Trans. Franz Rosenthal. London: Routledge and Kegan Paul, 1967.

Idris, H. R. "Hilāl." *Encyclopedia of Islam*. 2d ed. Leiden, 1954; London, 1956–.

Ingham, Bruce. *Northeast Arabian Dialects* (texts 2b, 8, and 10). London: Kegan Paul International, 1982.

——. "Notes on the Dialect of the Mutair of Eastern Arabia" (text 2). *Zeitschrift für arabische Linguistik* 2 (1979): 23–35.

Johnstone, Thomas Muir. "Folk-tales and Folk-lore of Dhofar." *Journal of Oman Studies*, vol. 6, p. 1 (1980): 123–27.

——. "The Language of Poetry in Dhofar." *BSOAS* 1 (1972): 1 –17.

de Jong, F. "al-Ḳuṭb" *Encyclopedia of Islam*. 2d ed. Leiden, 1954; London, 1956–.

Kahle, Paul E. "A Gypsy Woman in Egypt in the Thirteenth Century." *Journal of the Gypsy Lore Society* (3d ser.) 29, 1–2 (Jan.–Apr. 1950): 11–15.

Kazimirski, A. de Biberstein. *Dictionnaire Arabe-Français*. Paris: Maisonneuve, 1860.

Khalifeh, Sahar [Saḥar Khalīfa]. *al-Ṣabbār* (Wild thorns). 3d ed. Damascus: Dār al-Jalīl, 1984.

——. *Wild Thorns*. Trans. Trevor LeGassick and Elizabeth Fernea. New York: Olive Branch Press, 1985.

Khouri, Mounah A., and Hamid Algar, eds. and trans. *An Anthology of Modern Arabic Poetry*. Berkeley: University of California Press, 1974.

Kinany, A. Kh. *The Development of Ġazal in Arabic Literature*. Damascus: Syrian University Printing House, 1951.

Korkut, Dede. *The Book of Dede Korkut*, trans. G. Lewis. Harmondshire, Middlesex: Penguin Books, 1974.

Kremer, A. F. von. *Aegyptèn. Forschungen über land und volk Wahrend eines Zehnjahrigen aufenthalts*. Leipzig: F. A. Brockhaus, 1863.

——. "The Gypsies in Egypt." *Anthropological Review* 2 (1864).

Lammens, H. "Ḥamza." *Encyclopedia of Islam*. 1st ed. Leiden, 1913–38.

Lane, Edward. *An Account of the Manners and Customs of the Modern Egyptians*. 1895; rpt. London: East-West Publications, 1978; Cairo: Livres de France, 1978.

——. *Arabic-English Lexicon*. Cambridge: Islamic Texts Society, 1984; rpt. of 1863 ed.

——. *"The Thousand and One Nights", commonly called in England "The Arabian Nights' Entertainments"; a new trans. from the Arabic with copious notes*. 3 vols. Ed. E. Stanley Poole. London, 1877.

Largeau, Victor. *Flore saharienne, histoires et légendes traduites de l'arabe*. Geneva: Jules Sandoz, 1879; Paris: Sandoz et Fischbacher, 1879.

de Lartigue, Raoul Julien. *Monographie de l'Aurès*. Constantine: Imprimèrie à vapeur Marle-Audrino, 1904.

Lerrick, Alison. "Taghribat Bani Hilal al-Diyaghim: Variation in the Oral Epic Poetry of Najd." Diss., Princeton University, 1984.

Levi Della Vida, G. "Sīra." *Encyclopedia of Islam*. 1st ed. Leiden, 1913–38.

Littman, Enno. "Alf laylah wa-laylah." *Encyclopedia of Islam*. 2d ed. Leiden, 1954; London, 1956–.

——. *Zigeuner-Arabisch, Wortschatz und Grammatik der arabischen Bestandteile in den morgenländischen Zigeunersprachen*. Bonn-Leipzig: Kurt Schroeder Verlag, 1920.

Lord, Albert B. *The Singer of Tales*. Cambridge: Harvard University Press, 1960.

——, trans. *Serbo-Croatian Heroic Songs Collected by Milman Parry, Vol. 3: The Wedding of Smailagić Meho*. Cambridge: Harvard University Press, 1974.

Loubignac, V. *Etude sur le dialecte des Zaïan et des Aït Sgougou*. Paris: E. Leroux, 1924–25.

Macalister, R. A. Stewart. "A Grammar and Vocabulary of the Language of the Nawar or Zutt, the Nomad Smiths of Palestine." *Journal of the Gypsy Lore Society* (n.s.), 3, 2 (Oct. 1909): 120–26; 3, 4 (Apr. 1910): 298–317.

——. "Nuri Stories." *Journal of the Gypsy Lore Society* (n.s.), 3, 4 (Apr. 1910): 127–48; 4, 1 (July 1910): 20–35; 4, 4 (Apr. 1911): 279–87; 5, 1 (1911): 54–68; 5, 3 (1912): 224–34; 6, 2 (1912): 135–41.

MacDonald, Duncan B. "A Bibliographical and Literary Study of the First Appearance of the Arabian Nights in Europe." *Library Quarterly* 2, 4 (1932): 387–420.

——. "The Romance of Baibars." *Encyclopedia of Islam*. 1st ed. Leiden, 1913–38.

MacMichael, H. A. *A History of the Arabs in the Sudan*. Cambridge: Cambridge University Press, 1922.

——. *The Tribes of Northern and Central Kordofān*. Cambridge: Cambridge University Press, 1912.

MacNaughton, Patrick R. *The Mande Blacksmith*. Bloomington: Indiana University Press, 1988.

——. "Nyamakalaw: The Mande Bards and Blacksmiths." *Word and Image*, September 1987, pp. 271–88.

Mahdi, Muhsin. *Kitāb alf laylah wa-laylah min uṣūlihi al-ʿarabiyyah al-ūlā*. Leiden: E. J. Brill, 1984.

Mahfouz, Naguib [Najīb Maḥfūẓ]. *Midaq Alley*. Trans. Trevor LeGassick. Washington, D.C.: Three Continents Press, 1981.

——. *Zuqāq al-midaqq*. Cairo: Maktabat miṣr, 1947.

Marçais, William. "La diglossie arabe." *L'enseignement public* 104, 12 (Dec. 1930): 401–9; 105, 1 (Jan. 1931): 20–39; 105, 2 (Feb. 1931): 121–33.

Martin, Richard P. *The Language of Heroes: Speech and Performance in the "Iliad."* Ithaca, N.Y.: Cornell University Press, 1989.

McPherson, Joseph W. *The Moulids of Egypt*. Cairo, 1941.

Meeker, Michael. *Literature and Violence in North Arabia*. Cambridge: Cambridge University Press, 1979.

Menocal, Maria Rosa. *The Arabic Role in Medieval Literary History*. Philadelphia: University of Pennsylvania Press, 1987.

Meredith-Owens, G. M. "Hamza b. ʿAbd al-Muttalib." *Encyclopedia of Islam*. 2d ed. Leiden, 1954; London, 1956–.

Mitchell, Timothy. "The Invention and Reinvention of the Egyptian Peasant." *International Journal of Middle East Studies* 22, 2 (May 1990): 129–50.

Moerman, Michael. *Talking Culture: Ethnography and Conversation Analysis*. Philadelphia: University of Pennsylvania Press, 1988.

Montagne, R. *La civilisation du désert: Nomades d'Orient et d'Afrique*. Paris: Hachette, 1947.

Moyle, Natalie. "The Image of the āşık in Turkish Halk Hikāyeleri." In *III. Milletlerarasi Türk Folklor Kongresi Bildirileri*, 2:269–75. Ankara: Feryal Matbaacilik, 1986.

——. *The Turkish Minstrel Tale Tradition*. New York: Garland, 1990.

Mursī, Aḥmad ʿAlī. *al-Ughniyya al-shaʿbiyya: Madkhal ilā dirāsatihā* (The folk song: An introduction to its study). Cairo: Dār al-Maʿārif, 1983.

Nelson, Kristina. *The Art of Reciting the Quran*. Austin: University of Texas Press, 1985.

Newbold, Captain F. R. S. "The Gypsies of Egypt." *Journal of the Royal Asiatic Society of Great Britain and Ireland* (London), 16 (1856): 285–312.

Nicholson, Reynold A. *A Literary History of the Arabs.* Cambridge: Cambridge University Press, 1930.
Norris, H. T. *The Adventures of Antar.* Warminster, England: Aris and Phillips, 1980.
——. *The Berbers in Arabic Literature.* Harlow/Beirut: Longman/Librairie du Liban, 1982.
——. "The Influence of the Hilaliyya on the Peoples of the Southern Maghreb and the Western Sudan." In *Sīrat Banī Hilāl: Aʿmāl al-nadwa al-ʿālamiyya al-ūlā ḥawla al-sīra al-hilāliyya,* Actes de la 1ère Table ronde internationale sur la geste des Béni Hilālm 26–29 June 1980, al-Ḥammāmāt, Tunisia. Ed. A. Ayoub, 41–57. Tunis: al-Dār al-tūnisiyya li-l-nashr and al-Maʿhad al-qawmī li-l-athār wa-l-funūn, 1990.
——. "The Rediscovery of the Ancient Sagas of the Banū Hilāl." *Bulletin of the School of Oriental and African Studies* 51, 3 (1988): 462–81.
——. *The Tuaregs: Their Islamic Legacy and Its Diffusion in the Sahel.* Warminster, England: Aris and Phillips, 1975.
——. "Western Travellers and Arab Storytellers of the Nineteenth Century: The Adventures of Abū Zayd al-Hilālī and al-Zīr Sālim as Told by Shaykh Abū Wundī of the ʿAwāzim of Jordan." *Quaderni di Studi Arabi 9 (1991): 183–92.*
Nykl, Richard. *Hispano-Arabic Poetry and Its Relations with the Old Provençal Troubadours.* 1946; rpt. Geneva: Slatkine Reprints, 1974.
Oinas, Felix, ed. *Heroic Epic and Saga.* Bloomington: Indiana University Press, 1978.
Pantuček, Svetozár. *Das Epos über den Westzug der Banü Hilāl.* Dissertationes Orientales, 27. Prague: Czechoslovakian Academy of Sciences, 1970.
Paollilo, M. *Contes et légendes de Tunisie.* Paris: Nathan, n.d.
Paret, R. "Saif b. Dhī Yazan." *Encyclopedia of Islam:* 1st ed. Leiden, 1913–38.
——. "Sīrat Baybars." *Encyclopedia of Islam.* 2d ed. Leiden, 1954; London, 1956–.
——. *Sīrat Saif ibn Dhī-Yazan: Ein arabischer Volksroman.* Hanover: H. LaFaire, 1924.
Parker, Patricia. *Literary Fat Ladies: Rhetoric, Gender, Property.* New York: Methuen, 1987.
——. "Shakespeare and Rhetoric: 'Dilation' and 'delation' in Othello." In *Shakespeare and the Question of Theory,* ed. Patricia Parker and Geoffrey Hartman, 54–74. New York: Methuen, 1985.
Parry, Milman. *The Making of Homeric Verse: The Collected Papers of Milman Parry.* Ed. Adam Parry. New York: Oxford University Press, 1971.
Patterson, J. R., trans. *Stories of Abu Zeid the Hilali in Shuwa Arabic.* London: Kegan Paul, Tranch, Trubner, 1930.
Payne, John, trans. *The Book of the Thousand Nights and One Night.* 9 vols. London, 1882–84.
Pickthall, Muhammad M. *The Meaning of the Glorious Qur'an: Text and Explanatory Translation.* Mecca: Muslim World League, 1977.
Pidal, Ramón Menéndez. *Poesía juglaresca y orígenes de las literaturas romanicas.* 6th ed. Madrid: Instituto de Estudies Políticos, 1957.
——. *Romancero hispánico (hispano-portugués, americano y sefardí).* 2 vols. Madrid: Espasa-Calpe, 1953.
Pincherle, G. "Zigeuner in Egypten." *Ethnologische Mitteilungen Aus* (Budapest) 5 (1897).
Poncet, J. "Le mythe de l'invasion hilālienne." *Annales: Économies, sociétés, civilisations* 12 (1970–71): 1099–120.

Pritchett, Frances. *Marvelous Encounters: Folk Romance in Urdu and Hindi*. New Delhi: Manohar, 1985; Riverdale, Md.: Riverdale Press, 1985.

——, trans. and ed. *The Romance Tradition in Urdu: Adventures from the Dastan of Amir Hamza*. New York: Columbia University Press, 1991.

Provotelle, Paul. *Etude sur la Tamazirt ou Zenatia de Qalaat es-Sened*. Paris: E. Leroux, 1911.

Psathas, G., ed. *Everyday Language*. New York: Irvington, 1979.

Qāsim ʿAbd al-Ḥakīm. *Ayyām al-insān al-sabʿa* (The seven days of man). Cairo: Dār al-kitāb al-ʿarabī li-l-ṭibāʿa wa-l-nashr, n.d.

Quṭb, Sayyid. *Ṭifl min al-qarya* (A child from the village). Cairo, 1945.

Rasheed, Baheega Sidky. *Egyptian Folk Songs*. New York: Oak Publications, 1964.

Reynolds, Dwight F. "Crossing and Re-Crossing the Line." In *Something Happened: Fieldwork Epiphanies*. Ed. Bruce Jackson and Sandy Ives. Champaign: University of Illinois Press, forthcoming.

——. "Feathered Brides and Bridled Fertility: Architecture, Ritual, and Change in a Northern Egyptian Village." *Muqarnas: Journal of Islamic Art and Architecture* 11 (1994): 166–178.

——. "The Interplay of Genres in Oral Epic Performance: Differentially Marked Discourse in a Northern Egyptian Tradition." In *The Ballad and Oral Literature*, ed. Joseph Harris, 292–317. Cambridge: Harvard University Press, 1991.

——. Review of *The Merchant of Art: An Egyptian Hilali Oral Epic Poet in Performance*, by Susan Slyomovics. *Oral Tradition: Special Issue on Arabic Oral Traditions* 3, 1–2 (Jan.–May 1989): pp. 267–68.

——. Review of *The Munshidin of Egypt: Their World and Their Song*, by Earle Waugh. *Parabola: The Magazine of Myth and Tradition*, 14, 3 (Fall 1989): 115–18.

——. "*Sīrat Banī Hilāl*: Introduction and Notes to an Arab Oral Epic Tradition." *Oral Tradition: Special Issue on Arabic Oral Traditions* 4, 1–2 (Jan.–May 1989): 80–100.

——. "Tradition Replacing Tradition in Egyptian Oral Epic-Singing: The Creation of a Commercial Image." *Pacific Review of Ethnomusicology* 5 (1989): 1–14.

Richmond, Diana. *ʾAntar and ʾAbla, a Bedouin Romance: Rewritten and Arranged by Diana Richmond*. London: Quartet Books, 1978.

van Ronkel, S. *De roman van Amir Hamza*. Leiden: E. J. Brill, 1895.

Rosenhouse, Judith. *The Bedouin Arabic Dialects: General Problems and a Close Analysis of North Israel Bedouin Dialects*. Wiesbaden: Otto Harrassowitz, 1984. See esp. text 4.3, pp. 192–201.

Rouger, Gustave. *Le roman d'Antar*. Paris: H. Piazza, 1923.

Saada, Lucienne. *"La geste hilalienne"; Version de Bou Thadi (Tunisie): Recueillie, établie et traduite de l'arabe par Lucienne Saada*. Paris: Gallimard, 1985.

Sacks, Harvey, Emanuel Schegloff, and G. Jefferson. "A Simplest Systematics for the Organization of Turn-Taking for Conversation." *Language* 50, 4 (1974): 696–735.

Salām, Muḥammad Zaghlūl. *al-Adab fī l-ʿaṣr al-mamlūkī* Cairo: Dār al-Maʿārif, 1971.

Ṣāliḥ, al-Ṭayyib. *Ḍawʾ al-bayt* (The light of the house). Beirut: Dār al-ʿawda, 1971.

Sampson, J. "The Ghagar of Egypt: A Chapter in the History of the Gypsy Migration." *Journal of the Gypsy Lore Society* 3d ser., 7, 1 (1928): 78–90.

Schenkein, Jim, ed. *Studies in the Organization of Conversational Interaction*. New York: Academic Press, 1978.

Schimmel, Annemarie. *And Muhammad Is His Messenger: The Veneration of the Prophet in Islamic Piety*. Chapel Hill: University of North Carolina Press, 1985.

——. *Mystical Dimensions of Islam*. Chapel Hill: University of North Carolina Press, 1975.

Schleifer, J. "The Saga of the Banū Hilāl." *Encyclopedia of Islam*. 2d ed. Leiden, 1954; London, 1956–.

Serjeant, R. J. *South Arabian Poetry I: Prose and Poetry from Hadramawt*. London: Taylor's Foreign Press, 1951.

Slyomovics, Susan. "The Death-Song of ʿAmir Khafājī: Puns in an Oral and Printed Episode of Sīrat Banī Hilāl." *Journal of Arabic Literature* 17 (1987): 62–78.

——. "Final Report on *Sīrat Banī Hilāl*: The Text of an Arab Folk Epic." *American Research Center Egypt Newsletter*, 133 (Spring 1986): 3–6.

——. *The Merchant of Art: An Egyptian Hilali Oral Epic Poet in Performance*. Berkeley: University of California Press, 1987.

Spiro, Socrates. *An Arabic-English Dictionary of the Colloquial Arabic of Egypt*. Beirut: Librairie du Liban, 1980; 1st ed. 1895.

Steinbach, Udo. *Dhat al-Himma: Kuturgeschichtliche Untersuchungen zu einem arabischen Volksroman*. Freiburger Islamstudien no. 4. Wiesbaden: Steiner Verlag, 1972.

Stumme, Hans. *Tripolitanisch-tunische Beduinenlieder*. Leipzig: J. C. Hinrichs, 1894.

al-Subkī, Taqī al-Dīn. *Muʿīd al-niʿam*. London, 1908.

Todorov, T. *Grammaire du "Décameron"*. The Hague: Mouton, 1969.

Tomiche, Nada. "Le mawwāl égyptien." In *Mélanges Marcel Cohen*, 429–38. The Hague: Mouton, 1970.

Tomiche, Nada, et al. "Documents et notules: Proverbes et *mawwāls* de la Menufeyya." *Arabica* 6 (Jan. 1959): 75–90.

Trimingham, J. Spencer. *The Sufi Orders of Islam*. Oxford: Clarendon Press, 1971.

ʿUmrān, Muḥammad. "al-K͟haṣāʾiṣ al-mūsīqiyya li-riwāyat al-sīra al-hilāliyya fī Miṣr" (Musical characteristics of *Sīrat Banī Hilāl* performance in Egypt). In *Sīrat Banī Hilāl: Aʿmāl al-nadwa al-ʿālamiyya al-ūlā ḥawla al-sīra al-hilāliyya*, Actes de la 1ère Table ronde internationale sur la geste des Béni Hilāl, 26–29 June 1980, al-Ḥammāmāt, Tunisia. Ed. A. Ayoub, 72–92. Tunis: al-Dār al-tūnisiyya li-l-nas͟hr and al-Maʿhad al-qawmī li-l-at͟hār wa-l-funūn, 1990.

Vaissière, A. "Cycle héroïque des Ouled-Hilāl." *Revue africaine* 36 (1892): 242–43.

——. "Les ouled rechaïch." *Revue africaine* 36 (1892): 312–24.

Vekerdi, Jozsef. "The Gypsy's Role in the Preservation of Non-Gypsy Folklore." *Journal of the Gypsy Lore Society* (4th ser.), 1, 2 (1976): 79–86.

Vickers, Nancy. "The Blazon of Sweet Beauty's Best: Shakespeare's Lucrece." In *Shakespeare and the Question of Theory*, ed. Patricia Parker and Geoffrey Hartman, 95–115. New York: Methuen, 1985.

——. "This Heraldry in Lucrece's Face." In *The Female Body in Western Culture: Contemporary Perspectives*, ed. Susan Suleiman, 209–22. Cambridge: Harvard University Press, 1986.

Virolleaud, C. "Le roman de l'émir Hamza, oncle de Mahomet." *Ethnographie* 53 (1958–59): 3–10.

Walker, J. "Gypsies of Modern Egypt." *Moslem World* 23 (1933): 285–88.

Wangelin, Helmut. *Das arabische Volksbuch vom König az-Zahir Baibars*. Stuttgart: W. Kohlhammer, 1936.
Ward, G. "Gypsies on the Nile in the Sixteenth Century." *Journal of the Gypsy Lore Society* (3d ser.), 13, 1 (1934): 55–56.
Wāsif, Mīlād. *Qiṣṣat al-mawwāl*. Cairo: Kutub *thaqāfiyya*, 1961.
Waugh, Earle. *The Munshidin of Egypt: Their World and Their Song*. Columbia: University of South Carolina Press, 1989.
Wensinck, A. J. "al-Khaḍir (al-Khiḍr)" *Encyclopedia of Islam*. 2d ed. Leiden, 1954; London, 1956–.
Winsteadt, E. Q. "The 'Mashaʿilliyyah' of Egypt." *Journal of the Gypsy Lore Society* n.s., 4 (1910): 76–78.
Wright, W. *A Grammar of the Arabic Language*. Cambridge: Cambridge University Press, 1979.
Yūnus, ʿAbd al-Ḥamīd. *Difāʿ ʿan al-fulklūr*. Cairo: G.E.B.O., 1973.
——. *al-Hilāliyya fī l-taʾrīkh wa-l-adab al-shaʿbī*. 2d ed. Cairo: Dār al-maʿrifa, 1968.
Zwettler, Michael. *The Oral Tradition of Classical Arabic Poetry: Its Character and Implications*. Columbus: Ohio State University Press, 1978.

Index

MYTH AND POETICS

A series edited by

GREGORY NAGY

Helen of Troy and Her Shameless Phantom
by Norman Austin

The Craft of Poetic Speech in Ancient Greece
by Claude Calame
translated by Janice Orion

Masks of Dionysus
edited by Thomas W. Carpenter and Christopher A. Faraone

The Poetics of Supplication: Homer's Iliad *and* Odyssey
by Kevin Crotty

Poet and Hero in the Persian Book of Kings
by Olga M. Davidson

The Ravenous Hyenas and the Wounded Sun: Myth and Ritual in Ancient India
by Stephanie W. Jamison

Poetry and Prophecy: The Beginnings of a Literary Tradition
edited by James Kugel

The Traffic in Praise: Pindar and the Poetics of Social Economy
by Leslie Kurke

Topographies of Hellenism: Mapping the Homeland
by Artemis Leontis

Epic Singers and Oral Tradition
by Albert Bates Lord

The Singer Resumes the Tale
by Albert Bates Lord, edited by Mary Louise Lord

The Language of Heroes: Speech and Performance in the Iliad
by Richard P. Martin

Heroic Sagas and Ballads
by Stephen A. Mitchell

Greek Mythology and Poetics
by Gregory Nagy

Myth and the Polis
edited by Dora C. Pozzi and John M. Wickersham
Knowing Words: Wisdom and Cunning in the Classical Traditions of China and Greece
by Lisa Raphals
Heroic Poets, Poetic Heroes: The Ethnography of Performance in an Arabic Oral Epic Tradition
by Dwight Fletcher Reynolds
Homer and the Sacred City
by Stephen Scully
Singers, Heroes, and Gods in the Odyssey
by Charles Segal
The Mute Immortals Speak: Pre-Islamic Poetry and the Poetics of Ritual
by Suzanne Pinckney Stetkevych
Phrasikleia: An Anthropology of Reading in Ancient Greece
by Jesper Svenbro
translated by Janet E. Lloyd
The Jewish Novel in the Ancient World
by Lawrence M. Wills